THE REFERENCE SHELF   VOLUME 38   NUMBER 5

NORTH AFRICA

EDITED BY
RONALD STEEL

THE H. W. WILSON COMPANY
NEW YORK   1967

916.103
N 864

THE REFERENCE SHELF

The books in this series contain reprints of articles, excerpts from books, and addresses on current issues and social trends in the United States and other countries. There are six separately bound numbers in each volume, all of which are generally published in the same calendar year. One number is a collection of recent speeches; each of the others is devoted to a single subject and gives background information and discussion from various points of view, concluding with a comprehensive bibliography.

Subscribers to the current volume receive the books as issued. The subscription rate is $14 in the United States and Canada ($17 foreign) for a volume of six numbers. Single numbers are $3.50 each in the United States and Canada ($4 foreign).

NORTH AFRICA

Copyright © 1967
By The H. W. Wilson Company

First Printing 1967
Second Printing 1969

Library of Congress Catalog Card No. 66-21811

PREFACE

Throughout its long and complex history, North Africa has been both unavoidable and undefinable. Unavoidable because it lies at the crossroads of two civilizations: the Western civilization of Europe, and the African civilization of the peoples who live south of the Sahara. North Africa is also undefinable, because it is neither African nor European, but a mixture of both—with a heavy dose of the Middle East thrown in for good measure. Geographically speaking, the four nations along the southern coast of the Mediterranean Sea—Morocco, Algeria, Tunisia, and Libya— are African. But if Africa means more than simply a place on the map, they are not African any more than Australia is Asian. Rather, they are something unique unto themselves: a curious fusion of peoples and civilizations.

These are societies with a long history of economic, political and social relations with the nations of southern Europe. In this relationship, the Mediterranean has not been a barrier so much as it has been a highway, linking southern Europe with northern Africa. For thousands of years ships have plied across this highway, carrying goods and ideas from one side of the Mediterranean to the other. But if the peoples of North Africa are linked to Europe by history, culture, and even by blood, they are not Europeans. Their links also go south, deep into the sun-baked wastes of the Sahara desert, and beyond to the tribes of black Africa. Many centuries ago the Negro peoples of central Africa, moving north, encountered the indigenous Berbers of northern Africa and the Arabs of the Middle East who had swept across the rim of the continent in search of a new empire. This mixture of Arab, Berber, and Negro has formed the culture of North Africa. It gives this culture its special and elusive flavor.

North Africa has always been at the crossroads of civilizations, absorbing influences from everywhere but never quite losing its

65641

own essence. Today the Arab states of North Africa, with their rich historical memories and their long centuries of repose, find themselves with a new role to play. These states, which until recently were colonies of Europe, have joined the march to independence that has swept all Africa. The colonial ties that bound them to Europe have been broken, but the social and economic ties remain strong. These are nations once again on their own after decades of foreign rule; nations in search of their own personalities. In this search they have discoverd that the glories of their past cannot be recaptured but must be forged anew in radically different circumstances. These nations have come to independence in a world which they did not make and which they do not always understand. But it is one which they must master in order to survive.

The four Arab states of North Africa represent the westernmost extension of the ancient Arab empire. They are sometimes referred to as the nations of the Maghreb, an Arabic word which sums up their location and their culture. These states have a great deal in common, and seem to form a single civilization. Yet the differences within the Arab world run deep, and the powers of nationalism are strong. Over the centuries these peoples, who on the surface seem to be so similar, have developed differences of culture, personality, and attitude. Also, we live in an age of nationalism, and nowhere is the power of nationalism stronger than in North Africa. Alike and yet perplexingly different, these nations share a common colonial past (all except Libya were until recently colonies of France) but they are all going in different directions: oil-rich Libya is a feudal welfare state; European-oriented Tunisia is avid for democratic government and economic growth; revolution-torn Algeria is still picking up the pieces after eight years of brutal warfare; and proud Morocco hovers uncertainly as a benevolent monarchy tries to apply small doses of democracy to an impatient population.

These are nations which are all being affected by forces of change which they cannot control, yet which they dare not deny. They are swept by ideas of democracy and industrialization, affluence and technology: ideas which have no place in their traditional culture, but which they cannot ignore without unleashing the disapproval of their own peoples. These are also nations in which the United States has taken a considerable interest. For a number of years there were important United States air bases in Morocco, and although the bases have now been closed down, American interest in Morocco remains strong, especially since the nation's young King, Hassan II, has sought American support to reduce his financial dependency on France. Since the fall of Ahmed Ben Bella in June 1965, the United States has been on much better terms with Algeria than before and is currently furnishing massive supplies of surplus food on which great numbers of impoverished Algerians depend for survival. Since the discovery of oil in Libya several years ago, American oil firms have been deeply involved in the Libyan economy. Thousands of American technicians now work in the Libyan oilfields, and as a result of this oil boom, the American Government has had to take a special interest in Libya. But it is in Tunisia, perhaps, that American involvement is at its greatest, for the United States has chosen this progressive North African country as a showplace of economic development. American aid per capita to Tunisia is extremely high, and the results of the aid program have been heartening beyond expectation to American officials.

The nations of North Africa are all experiencing the pangs, the dislocations, and the agonies of economic development. Their difficulties in this task are compounded by the fact that they lie between two worlds, between Europe and Africa, between ancient and modern, between the traditional and the revolutionary. Their ability to bring those two worlds together without a cataclysmic political or social upheaval will be a test of their ingenuity and their maturity. It is an endeavor in which we Americans have a great interest—not only for their sake, but for ours. If they manage to combine the world of Western technology with the world of their own traditional values—with the respect for human dignity, craftsmanship, and honor that is one of the most admirable elements in their culture—they will have done a service to all of us who live in modern industrial societies which, in their achievement of riches, may have lost some important human values along the way.

The articles in this volume are designed to introduce American readers to one of the most fascinating and most important, yet one of the most neglected, parts of Africa. The first section, a portrait of North Africa today—its political and social problems, its economic difficulties, its role in world affairs—also offers a glimpse of the physical situation which has determined its way of life and an assessment of its role in world affairs. The second section is a discussion of the Moslem religion—Islam—as a unifying force which ties the nations of North Africa to their fellow Arab nations in the Middle East—and also of the factionalism in the Arab character which separates these nations from one another. The following four sections are devoted to analyses of the individual North African countries—Morocco, Algeria, Tunisia, and Libya— and seek to put each of them into a historical perspective so that the social, economic, and political problems they now face can be more readily understood.

From this portrait of North Africa today, it is hoped that the reader will be inspired to pursue his studies of a region rich in history and deep in problems, with infinite possibilities for the future. After a long period of quiescence, the Maghreb is once again reviving and coming into its own. The process is bound to be an exciting and important one to observe.

The editor would like to thank the various authors, publishers, and organizations that have granted permission for the use of materials included in this book.

RONALD STEEL

October 1966

CONTENTS

7

IV.   Tunisia

V.   Algeria

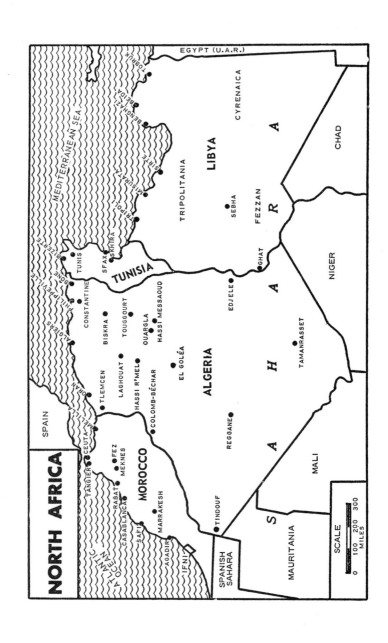

I. PORTRAIT OF THE MAGHREB

EDITOR'S INTRODUCTION

From the sands of the Egyptian desert to the breakers of the Atlantic Ocean, from the soft shores of the Mediterranean Sea to the harsh sun of the Sahara: these are the borders of Arab Africa. Within them lie the four nations of Libya, Tunisia, Algeria, and Morocco. Together they are known as the *Maghreb* (sometimes spelled Maghrib, or Magharib)—that is, the western reaches of the ancient Arab empire. These nations have a great deal in common. They have all achieved their independence only within the past decade or so. They are all basically Arab in racial stock, Islamic in religion, and underdeveloped in their economies. A traveler going from Benghazi in eastern Libya across land to Casablanca on the Atlantic coast of Morocco would be struck by the similarities of the countries he passed through. He would see women in veils and men on motor scooters. He would see ancient mosques and turbaned street vendors. But he would also see skyscrapers and traffic jams, parking meters and newsboys selling New York newspapers. These nations are studies in contrast. And the contrast is not only within each country—between the ancient and the modern —but between the different countries of the Maghreb. Although in many respects they are similar, at least on the surface, these four nations of North Africa are also profoundly different from one another. An Arab traveler might at first find all the nations of Western Europe more or less alike but would soon learn that there is a great difference between Swedes and Italians, between Dutchmen and Spaniards; by the same token, the states of North Africa are joined by a common heritage, yet separated by sharp individual differences.

This section is a portrait of the Maghreb: of the area as a whole and also of the individual states. In the first selection, Professor Halford Hoskins, a well-known expert on Arab affairs, presents some of the problems facing the states of Africa's Arab fringe. In discussing the nations of the Maghreb, he also deals with Egypt, which links the Arab West to the Arab East and whose influence on the states of North Africa is strong both in politics and in culture. Charles Gallagher, a scholar who has lived many years in the Arab world and who is with the American Universities Field Staff, provides a portrait of North Africa: its physical setting, its political and economic problems, and its social crisis.

AFRICA'S ARAB FRINGE [1]

The five states occupying the northern littoral of Africa have not been viewed as African in a continental sense until recently. Set off from the rest of Africa by the vast expanse of the Sahara desert and facing outward across the Mediterranean, an inland sea, the historical relationship of these countries with the peoples occupying the greater part of the continent has been almost nonexistent. Technological change—radio communication and facile transportation by air—and the relatively sudden upsurge of a host of newly independent states in the heart of Africa, vociferously intent on bringing their existence and their not inconsiderable problems to the notice of the world at large, have made the countries of the Mediterranean fringe conscious of their African setting.

For both geographical and historical reasons, the states of the Mediterranean littoral have had more in common with one another than with other states of the continent. All are mainly Arabic in language and Islamic in religion. All, for various periods of time, came under the control of one or another of the European powers. All have achieved independence in recent years. There, however, the principal likenesses cease. Differences in character, in geographical position, in demographic composition and in economic resources separate these states more clearly than their political boundaries do. . . .

Morocco

Morocco has contributed its own peculiar problems to the African Maghreb. Among these have been constitutional questions regarding the degree of authority to be retained by the king, and even—at times—questions concerning the continued existence of

[1] From article by Halford L. Hoskins, professor of Middle East studies, School of International Service, The American University, Washington, D.C. *Current History.* 50:136-41. Mr. '66. Reprinted by permission.

the monarchy. The political shrewdness of Hassan II, who issued an acceptable constitutional charter in June 1961 and who has chosen to identify himself with popular causes, appears to have submerged the voices of those who would have set up a republic upon the death of revered King Mohammed II in 1961.

Prominent among the nation's problems in recent years have been issues of an economic nature. The failure of foreign concessionnaires to find oil and gas in commercial quantities, after exhaustive search, denied Morocco the opportunity to pursue as independent a course of action in international affairs as presumably would have otherwise been the case. A particularly bitter disappointment was the action of France—applauded by Tunisia—in insisting on an independent role for autonomous Saharan Mauritania, to which Morocco had both historical and religious claims. Although nearly destitute of population, this dependency possesses a single mountain of high grade iron ore which may well prove to be as valuable as major oil deposits.

Other developments have brought economic hardship to Morocco. The devaluation of the French franc in 1959 resulted in the flight from Morocco of an estimated $80 million in capital. The exodus of large numbers of French *colons* after Moroccan independence in 1956 and the subsequent emigration of at least 150,000 Sephardic Jews, mainstays of Moroccan business, were depressants on the economy. Just as serious in short-term effects, although a source of satisfaction to many nationalists, was the withdrawal of United States personnel from bases acquired under the French protectorate and developed at a cost of some $400 million. While the bases themselves have been of little value to Morocco except for possible use as educational centers, the departure of freespending Americans and the consequent unemployment of thousands of Moroccans amounted to a total annual loss of not less than $60 million. Even the withdrawal in stages of French and Spanish armed forces added to a difficult financial situation.

These circumstances would have been more serious except for the availability of foreign aid. Relatively massive foreign assistance aided recovery from the destruction of Agadir by earthquake in March 1960. In that year, United States provision of more than

$73 million in budgetary support helped to bring a moderate tone to an uneasy government. In the following years, Moroccan sentiment vacillated between East and West, depending partly on the amounts and character of the assistance supplied by the Soviet Union and the United States and partly on the fortunes of the Moroccan government in the promotion of the so-called Casablanca group of North African states as a counterpoise to the Brazzaville bloc.

In the early months of 1962, France and Morocco, previously on poor terms over numerous issues, embarked on a new relationship of close cooperation including a marked increase in French economic aid. The several agreements resulting from this entente plus the action of the World Bank and its related institution, the International Finance Corporation, in promoting the development of Moroccan industry can be credited to a large extent with introducing a new measure of stability into Moroccan affairs and with establishing closer cultural relations with France—a matter of prime interest to the 160,000 French resident in Morocco. This large portion of the Maghreb thus has come to be regarded as Western-oriented and as having safely passed the nadir of its fortunes. Its growing influence in North African affairs has been marked during the last two years by the satisfactory ending of all outstanding differences with other members of the North African group and by considerably heightened prestige.

Tunisia

The approach of the French protectorate of Tunisia to independence and the nature of its internal and external problems in late years have not been wholly unlike those of Morocco. Examined in particular, the similarity disappears, for Tunisia has a distinctly individualistic record. An understanding of its behavior relates to the character of its population of three and a half million, including one fourth of a million Europeans, whose intelligentsia are the most sophisticated of any elements in the Maghreb. Moreover, the Tunisia of today to a remarkable extent is the product of one man, Habib Bourguiba. In him, France might have found a useful friend.

Bourguiba was educated at the Sorbonne, married to a French wife, and not indisposed to consider the French point of view relative to North Africa. French authorities, however, with almost unexampled obtuseness, chose to imprison and then to oppose their potential ally until, with the failure of their methods, Tunisia was accorded independence in March 1956. Replacing an anachronistic monarchy, Bourguiba has guided the nation through its years of adolescence.

Not least among the issues that confronted the Tunisian republic was its imperfect independence. In 1956, French troops still remained in Tunisia, France still held the key naval base at Bizerte, and Tunisia suffered indignities from French efforts to crush Algerian rebel forces. Under pressure, French army forces were withdrawn in 1958, but demands that the Bizerte base also be relinquished were ignored. Encouraged by delegates from thirty African countries attending the African Peoples' Congress in Tunis in January 1960, Bourguiba declaimed: "It is by liberating Tunisia from colonialism that we are participating in the real independence of Africa."

In the following month word came from the United States that the North Atlantic Treaty Organization no longer required French retention of the Bizerte base. Faced with French intransigence, Bourguiba openly aided the Algerian rebel cause and finally authorized an armed attack on the French-held base. This failed to dislodge the French, but it did bring the Bizerte issue into international prominence. The secretary-general of the Arab League said: "The entire Arab world is gathering around Tunisia." The United Arab Republic [Egypt], with which Tunisia had been on extremely poor terms, announced the sending of "total support and unreserved assistance" to its "sister" republic. Moscow granted Tunisia a ruble credit valued at $27.75 million. The Afro-Asian bloc made a formal bid at the United Nations and without a dissenting voice the General Assembly asked France to give up the Bizerte base.

Tunisia's final independence was achieved at not inconsiderable cost. The two-month shut-down of the pipeline linking Algeria's Edjele oilfield with the Tunisian port of La Skhira, closed to deny oil to France, cost the Tunisian government an estimated $3.6 million in royalties at a time when the country was suffering from the worst drought in 20 years. Tunisia's normal trade deficit doubled. Only massive doses of United States aid enabled the state to continue to function with a degree of normality. Nevertheless, in July 1962, a year after the attack on Bizerte, France began transferring to Tunisia $200 million worth of installations at the Bizerte base in anticipation of complete withdrawal. Other financial aid from the United States Agency for International Development and the International Finance Corporation of the World Bank, coupled with a strict Tunisian austerity program, carried the country through the period of crisis. In August 1963 agreements between France and Tunisia reactivated a flow of French aid that had been cut off in 1957 because of Tunisian support of the Algerian rebellion.

The Bizerte crisis was not the last of Tunisian difficulties. . . . [Since 1963] there have been difficulties with France over the nationalization of French-owned agricultural properties in Tunisia and with Egypt's President Gamal Abdel Nasser over Bourguiba's recommendation of Arab coexistence with Israel. Yet an accord was reached with Algeria for the joint use of Saharan gas and petroleum; Tunisia agreed to participate in the project for an all-African development bank; and measures were adopted at a meeting in Tunis in October 1964 looking toward unity in economic matters of the four nations of the Maghreb. Bourguiba's image as a symbol of political moderation in North Africa was scarred, but it still shines brightly in the Maghreb.

Libya

Libya, now considered to be a part of the Maghreb, is a phenomenon. When independence was thrust upon it in 1951 by the United Nations, Libya was considered to be the poorest country in the world. As recently as five years ago, it was hardly more than a political hiatus in North Africa. Of its 740,000 square miles, 95 per cent was desert. Its million inhabitants, mostly farmers and herdsmen, eked out a bare living in the coastal areas. Even the modest income received by the state from British and American bases—reminders of World War II—was applied solely to the clumsy administrative machinery devised by a patriarchal monarchy for bringing some unity into the governance of three wholly dissimilar territories—Tripolitania, Cyrenaica and Fezzan.

Then came oil. Exports, which began in 1961, now amount to more than a million barrels a day, placing Libya eighth among the oil-exporting countries. Libya may move further up the scale as discoveries continue, if oil legislation can be restricted to reasonable limits. With annual oil revenues now above the $500 million level, the untutored Libyan government is a current illustration of the adage that the appetite grows with feeding. It has yet to learn that an oil industry is not a solution to every need and that it does not necessarily obviate poverty. The problems of a people almost wholly illiterate a short span of years ago and now distracted by a view of all the trappings of modern civilized life can only be imagined. In these circumstances, some of the problems lead to somber speculation about the future.

How the oil industry, developed by Western enterprise, will fare in such an environment is uncertain. Some doubt as to the dependability of the Libyan government was created by an unexpected amendment to the law on oil agreements in 1961. A government decree issued late in 1965, apparently intended to bring Libyan regulations into line with those obtaining in the oil-producing countries of the Middle East, may restrict Libyan output materially. Adding to the apprehension of oilmen have been the machinations of Egypt's Nasser relative to Western bases. These suggest that, lacking great income from Egyptian oil resources, Nasser may be planning to acquire a dominant influence over Libyan oil once the Libyan government is no longer in the hands of aging King Idris II.

Egyptian influence pervades Libya. Having practically no teachers of its own, Libya has willingly accepted instructors from Egypt. It follows that with hundreds of Egyptian teachers and professors and dozens of Egyptian administrators in Libyan schools and with relatively many advanced students enrolled in universities at Alexandria and Cairo, pro-Nasser sentiment generally prevails. It is significant, too, that—in the absence of Libyan competition—the calculated broadcasts of Radio Cairo fill an ideological vacuum for adults. Among the results has been the growth of sentiment against the presence of bases assigned to Great Britain and the United States until the years 1973 and 1971 respectively. The willingness of both Western nations to consider the earlier surrender of their concessions, instead of enlisting public approval, only has inspired diatribes in the native press against the "imperialists."

Algeria

Algeria is the last country to have won independence in the Maghreb. There was little similarity between the Algerian struggle and the moves for independence in Morocco and Tunisia. Algeria had been under French military control after 1830 and after 1848 had been regarded as a part of metropolitan France. French colonization in Algeria had been an official, not incidental, process; thus, at the beginning of the Algerian revolt—a civil war from some points of view—the European element constituted 10 per cent of the entire population. Indeed, there might have been no rebellion but for the fact that French requirements for citizenship in the Algerian *département* discriminated against Moslems in their home country. Besides, the educated Moslem could hardly accept the fact that, after a century and a quarter of French rule and "assimilation," nearly 95 per cent of the higher administrative posts were held by persons of French extraction. The Algerian problem was political rather than economic: Algeria today could not manage well without French economic aid and income from French oil interests in the Sahara.

The war for independence, beginning late in 1954, is a most dismal story. It need be noted here only that French President Charles de Gaulle became convinced of its futility and worked out the details of Algerian independence at Évian. Only in March 1962 did the war end, with many details still pending. Beyond a few statistics, the real cost of Algerian independence cannot be indicated. The cost included some 250,000 Moslem lives. Another quarter of a million persons left the country as refugees. Not less than two and a half millions in Algeria were unemployed at the end of the war. Among the early tasks assumed by Algerian Premier Ahmed Ben Bella were the patching up of boundary difficulties with Morocco, the concluding of economic arrangements with France, and the defining of neutralism in Ben Bella's terms. This last might well have been the product of the Afro-Asian summit conference scheduled to meet in Algiers in June 1965—and touted in advance as a "second Bandung." The overthrow of left-leaning, subversive Ben Bella by his more moderate one-time associate, Colonel Houari Boumedienne, intervened decisively, however, and the conference ended before it began. Many aspects of the succeeding Algerian administration are not yet well known, but the evidence of early months suggests the presence of a stable, hardheaded and practical group, concerned more with the welfare of Algeria than with adventures elsewhere.

Egypt

Since the overthrow of the monarchy in 1954, Egyptian leadership of the states of the Arab world has grown. To a greater extent, also, since his rise to power, Gamal Abdel Nasser has been the architect of Egyptian policy. In order to maintain a position of such responsibility and prominence, he has been compelled to attempt to keep in balance the elements of his compromise personality. That is to say, he has had to adjust his not inconsiderable personal ambition to the circumstances encountered from time to time and yet to be reasonably consistent in his fundamental aims. This necessity has involved some of the most complicated situations with which leaders ever have had to deal. Almost inevitably Nasser has made mistakes, for naturally he has not always recognized or correctly estimated all of the factors in the situations he encountered. On occasion, too, he may well have overestimated his ability to obtain desired results with the means at hand. Nevertheless, he has been a principal agent in the course of developments in world affairs, even though a final assessment of the nature and worth of his accomplishments lies with the future.

Possessing no studied program for action prior to his assumption of authority, Nasser necessarily proceeded with administration on an *ad hoc* basis. There is no reason to believe, however, that his basic wishes have ever changed materially. From the outset, he has desired to improve substantially the conditions of

the masses living in the Nile Valley; to promote the unity of the
Arab peoples with Egypt at the forefront; and to exercise as much
influence as possible in the reshaping of the international environment with which Egypt and the Arab world necessarily is particularly concerned. His personal ambition has been bound up
with these aims. Among his principal shortcomings has been the
belief that a good end justified the means employed in its attain-
ment. Thus not infrequently his image has suffered from the use
of dubious means, especially when these have not succeeded.

The challenge to the Nasser regime involved in the raising of
the domestic standard of living was of no ordinary dimension.
Egypt, with a population of approximately 30 million, mostly agri-
culturists, has a population density of some 1,900 per square mile
in the habitable portion of a state embracing a total of 386,000
square miles. With an annual population increase approaching
three per cent, even the completion of the Aswan High Dam can
be only temporarily palliative. The effectiveness of a program of
birth control cannot be assured so long as peasant women visit the
countryside clinics intent on learning not how to have fewer
children but how to have more. Any improvement in the standard of living for most Egyptians must be sought principally in the
elimination of waste, including such enterprises as military operations in Yemen (reportedly requiring the participation of 40,000
troops) and in the increase of industry and trade.

Arab Socialism

Some of these problems have been approached through a program of "Arab socialism"—a non-Marxist blend of capitalism and
state socialism. This was seriously put to the test with the in-
troduction in 1960 of the second Five Year Plan, looking toward
a more systematic nationalization of big business and the development of heavy industry. Results are not yet clear. In the first
place, it has been found impossible to stop the flight abroad of
private capital. In the second place, care has had to be taken, in
the acceptance of foreign aid directly or indirectly applicable to
industry, to make sure of its proportions among available sources

in the two ideological blocs, in such manner as to enable Egypt to maintain its attitude of positive neutralism or political non-alignment essential to the success of other features of Egyptian policy. In the third place, the marketing of surplus agricultural, industrial and mineral products at worth-while prices has posed perennial problems, some of them political.

In principle, Nasser always has looked with favor on trends toward unity in the Arab world. This was apparent in his willingness to make an effort at political union with Syria in a United Arab Republic, and in his relations with Yemen and Jordan and Iraq as well as with the countries of the Maghreb. His efforts to end British control of Aden likewise can be attributed to pan-Arabism, whatever truth may attach to the charge that his eventual aim is to establish a hold on Persian Gulf oil resources.

Egyptian activity in the Maghreb beyond the confines of Libya, other than support for the rebel cause in Algeria, has been moderate. Nasser's encouragement for pan-Arabism in the Maghreb undoubtedly has been diluted somewhat by his growing interest in the newer states south of the Sahara. His participation in pan-African affairs has been augmented by the failure of some undertakings in the Arab world—notably by the breakup of the union with Syria.

Nevertheless, his African concentration has been deepened by the discovery that Israel has embarked on a systematic attempt to penetrate Africa through close economic relations with the nations rising to independence. That the Israelis, with their technical expertise and political sophistication, might win the hearts and minds of African peoples sufficiently to undo the ban on Israel's transit of the Suez Canal and to strengthen imperialistic influence in the heart of the continent was a chilling possibility to a leader intent on guiding independent Africa into a neutralist bloc. This will account, in the main, for Egypt's presence in the numerous African organizations in late years and the frequent meetings of African groups in Cairo. Under the Egyptian monarchy, Cairo was a cosmopolitan city: under Nasser, it has become an international capital.

NORTH AFRICA: PAST AND PRESENT [2]

The states of Northern Africa share three distinctive geographical features which separate the region from the rest of the continent and make it into what the first Arab conquerors called an "island on the land." These are the desert, the high mountains of the Atlas, and the inland sea which gives life to a Mediterranean countryside along a thin strip of the northern coast.

The southern and eastern approaches of the area are made up by the world's greatest desert, the Sahara, which has in historical times been much more a barrier than an avenue of communication—despite the emergence of a new Africanist school stressing the importance of trans-Saharan contacts. The Sahara is encyclopedic in its diversity; high, arid mountains range up to ten thousand feet in the lunar-looking southern reaches of Algeria and Libya, and are bounded on the north by ancient, submerged seas which have stored the petroleum products that now enrich their possessors. High steppe, rock desert, floating dunes, and incidental fertile oases coexist in a region which, with little or no rain on the whole, occasionally is subject to disastrous flash floods. To the north, the Sahara is mostly cut off from the sea by a long, continuous mountain chain—the Atlas, with many variant regional names—which stretches out like a backbone from west to east, beginning in southwestern Morocco and finally running into the Mediterranean in the Tripolitanian province of western Libya. East of that, the Jebel Akhdar of Cyrenaica forms a geographical, but not geological, extension of the chain and serves in an attenuated way the same function as the main Atlas group: to turn the coastal strip north of the mountains into a productive, Mediterranean-type enclave to the degree it is adequately protected from Saharan wind and sand by the mountain barrier. This relatively fertile region is widest where the Atlas is highest and thickest, as in Morocco where the 13,600-foot peaks of the High Atlas shelter the wide plains of northwestern Morocco, made more fruitful by abundant Atlantic rainfall. The Atlas diminishes in alti-

[2] From *A Note on Northern Africa* by Charles F. Gallagher, an AUFS Report. (v 10, no 4. Je. '64) Copyright 1964 by American Universities Field Staff, Inc. Reprinted with permission of the publisher. Dr. Gallagher, an Associate of the American Universities Field Staff, has lived for many years in the Arab world.

tude from west to east; it is little more than 7,500 feet in Algeria, the highest point in Tunisia is just over 5,000 feet, and the mountains peter out in Tripolitania as little more than hills of 2,500 feet. Accordingly, the fertile Tell of northern Algeria is a narrower, Chilean-shaped, serpentine area, more than two thirds of Tunisia lies in the arid center-south below the main Atlas dorsal, and the coastal strip which is cultivable in Libya gives out before the Gulf of Sirte where the desert finally comes down to the sea.

Everywhere the fertile land is Mediterranean in its physical makeup: the olive and cork tree flourish, oak-types and chaparral scrub brush make up a *maquis* cover not unlike that of Spain, southern France, or parts of California, and the principal crops include figs, almonds, olives, and grapes and (owing to European influence) their wine. At higher altitudes fruit trees are found, and in the desert regions the date is the staple crop.

Lest this description seem too enthusiastic, the debit side of North African geography should be stressed. The land is in good part high, uneven, and thirsty. Rainfall is irregular and often disastrous in its unpredictability. The Sahara hovering nearby keeps alive the specter of periodic climatic excesses when searing *sharqi* winds [hot sand storms] blow off the desert and parch the earth. Much of the region is a high plateau, going up to 3,000 feet, which offers disadvantages in both winter and summer; Morocco, especially, has aptly been described as a "cold country with a hot sun." Internal communications have been difficult at most times in both Morocco and Algeria because the shape of these countries is excentric and intermontane valleys are often sharply cut off one from the other. Rainfall may be abundant, as in the Rif in Morocco or Kabylia in Algeria (over sixty inches in some places) and still run off the sharp slopes wasted; on the contrary, it may be deficient as in Marrakesh (eight inches) but permit a limited oasis-type culture depending on skilled irrigation procedures, or virtually nonexistent as in southern Tunisia where less than one inch falls. Nevertheless, the southern and southeastern slopes of the Rif away from the rainfall side are semiarid and denuded, while southern Tunisia and parts of the Algerian pre-Sahara recently suffered floods which made thousands homeless. The

American reader if he wishes may establish a tenuous parallel with conditions in California. There are great similarities but at least two important differences, both derogatory to North Africa: (1) human beings and their animals have not systematically deforested and eroded California for a thousand years as has been the case in North Africa; and (2) there is as yet no technique for technological control in North Africa corresponding in degree to that available in California. . . .

The southern shore of the Mediterranean and its hinterlands in some depth have long been the realm of a complex human stock, white in skin color, and sharing a Hamitic tongue and a culture—based on stock raising, some agriculture, the use of domestic animals, and the firing of hard-core pottery—seemingly imported from the East in the late Neolithic period. These people were the "Libyans" found by the Greeks in earliest classical days, the "Afariq" (who gave their name to the entire continent), cousins of, but resistant to, the invading Phoenicians, who established the first empire in Northern Africa at Carthage around 800 B.C. Greco-Roman writers generally referred to them, as to many others, as barbarians *(barbaroi)*, and the name "Berber," carried over into Arabic when Islam appeared in Northern Africa in the seventh century, took root and is used today by both Oriental and Western intruders to designate the original inhabitants. At the bottom this culture and stock are still there; North Africa today, from the Siwa oasis of western Egypt to Agadir in Morocco and from Tamanrasset and the Tibesti to Kabylia, is still overwhelmingly Berber in blood and rural lifeways, although in thirteen centuries it has become thoroughly Arabized in language, in civilization, and, up to a point, in self-view.

In the course of history many other peoples have introduced their genes into the physical makeup of the inhabitants. Beginning in the first millennium before Christ, the area has seen the arrival of Phoenicians, Greeks, Latins, Jews, Indo-Germanic groups like the Vandals (and latter-day Europeans), and most important of all, the Arabs. The last came in two great waves, mainly in the seventh and eighth and the eleventh and twelfth centuries. Among some groups and in some places—especially in the large, traditional cities, but also in some tribal areas—they have remained an intact entity; elsewhere they have much modified the ethnic pool by blending in. . . .

Today, the four countries of Morocco, Algeria, Tunisia, and Libya contain about 30 million inhabitants, the great majority of whom are concentrated in the more fertile coastal regions already mentioned. Because vast areas are empty or sparsely populated, meaningful density is much higher than would be at first supposed, and in some regions like Kabylia and the Rif overpopulation has long been a serious problem, resolved temporarily by emigration. . . .

[In regard to population] three important facts stand out; these are the homogeneity of the population, the rural-urban balance, and the rate of growth. The peopling has become less diverse compared to a decade ago, owing to the withdrawal of much of the European element (2 million odd in 1950, perhaps 500,000 today, excluding the Spanish-held enclaves of Ceuta and Melilla which contain another 150,000) and the departure of most of the Jewish indigenous minority (only some 120,000 remain of a group which numbered half a million at the end of World War II). Thus, Moslems constitute today 98 per cent of the total resident population, citizens and noncitizens included, as against only 88 per cent fifteen years ago. Secondly, the area is still largely rural-oriented; roughly 70 per cent of the population lives on the land. Intensive and rapid urbanization is a recent phenomenon which has much changed the physiognomy of the large cities of Northern Africa in recent years, however. The populations of Casablanca and Greater Algiers have trebled in the past generation, and each holds about 1 million persons at present. Tunis has one fifth the population of the whole country, and Tripoli, because of the Libyan oil boom, is the latest addition to the ranks of mushroom towns. Massive migration to the cities in the wake of social upheaval seems to have diminished recently in Morocco and Tunisia, however, and there are signs that a temporary pause in the movement may be at hand throughout the area. Finally, the most urgent fact with respect to this question is that the population already has a low median age—more than half of all North

Africans are now under twenty—and a high growth rate. Morocco and Tunisia are increasing at nearly 3 per cent a year, to the stunned disbelief of their own statisticians who underpredicted the trend, and when statistics become available for Algeria there is likely to be a similar pattern there. The resultant ever-growing pressure on the land makes it improbable that the pause in urbanization will be more than a fleeting one.

The population problem has had and continues to have complex economic and political ramifications. In the nineteenth and during part of the twentieth century, numbers were kept down by the absence of modern medicine, and quite recently the revolution in Algeria, taken as a whole, reduced the population of that country by about 20 per cent: nearly 1 million dead or missing and an equal number of voluntary exiles. Today, disease and violence are no longer major factors, but birth control (recently inaugurated in Tunisia) and emigration (mainly to Europe) may serve as temporary safety valves. In mid-1964 there were well on to a million North Africans resident in Europe (nearly 700,000 Algerians, 100,000 Moroccans, and 25,000 Tunisians in France alone) and governmental agreements seemed likely to increase their numbers in the future. Indeed, from a long-range historical point of view, the most significant change in human geography around the shores of the western Mediterranean during the third quarter of this century will certainly have been the removal of a substantial European minority from Northern Africa and the substitution for it of a spreading North African minority in Europe. The knot remains tied but at the other end of the rope.

North Africa entered history just before the end of the second millennium B.C., with the founding of Phoenician settlements on the shores of modern Tunisia, followed by factories stretching out beyond the Strait of Gibraltar. Carthage, the successor to the Phoenician traders, exploited the region and did business with it, but there was no real colonization nor much civilizing influence except in the immediate hinterland of the city in northern Tunisia. Roman legions garrisoned all North Africa, but Roman civilization was found only at selected points in Tunisia, eastern Algeria, and coastal Libya, while most of the country was protected by a Chineselike wall of fortifications. . . . As Roman power waned in the early centuries of the Christian era, the Berbers reasserted their control in much of the area and assisted in the destruction of the Empire.

When the Arabs moved into North Africa after A.D. 650 they found both the Rum, the name given to a sedentary population of Latin culture under Byzantine rule along the coast of Tunisia, and warlike Berbers in the interior. The former capitulated quickly, but the conquest of the Berbers was protracted and difficult. No sooner was it accomplished than a revolt made North Africa again virtually independent, and for several centuries thereafter free Berber states floated on the fringe of the Arab caliphate, adopting and discarding with enthusiasm a variety of Moslem heresies.

In the middle of the eleventh century a group of veiled nomads from the Sahara, the Murabitin or Almoravids, swept into Morocco and subdued it as well as much of Spain which had been the fief of the caliphate of Córdoba. Their successors, the Muwahhidin or Almohads, were the only true North African dynasty in history, ruling the region as far east as Tripoli and holding half of Spain for a century. With the succeeding dynasty, the Merinids in Fez and their offshoots among the Hafsids in Tunis, North Africa reached the apogee of its traditional civilization and compared favorably with the merchant states of Italy and Spain of the same period. In Fez, Granada, Tlemcen, and Tunis, architecture, music, and literature flourished and remarkable writers such as Ibn Khaldun and Ibn Batuta came to prominence.

North Africa was largely untouched by the Crusades, but the area was increasingly involved in the futile defense of Moslem Spain from the *reconquista* of Spain and Portugal. From 1400 on, Iberian activity spilled over onto the North African coast, and an intermittent series of religious wars continued for centuries, with periodic European occupation of many of the coastal cities from Agadir to Tripoli. In the interior, much of the region withdrew into an isolation within which was fermented a religious reform and revival based on the appeal of local and often fundamentalist saints, as well as on the charisma of *sharifian* (descended from the Prophet) families. Also exhibiting a well-founded xenophobia, the North Africans found partial release for these sentiments by striking back at the Europeans through a satisfying and profitable piracy which continued from the sixteenth to the early nineteenth century.

European impact on North Africa ever since the Middle Ages has been heavy and unrelenting, whether negatively or positively, and in particular the "century of colonization," which began with the French arrival in Algiers in 1830, has had a seemingly permanent effect in the field of politics, economics, and cultural and social change. The historical problem of European colonization is distilled in Northern Africa, for here, as nowhere else in their empire-building, Europeans (French, Italian, and Spanish) went to settle, in their eyes permanently, in the midst of a pre-existing alien society with a complex folk culture, a high traditional civilization, and a world religion close in spirit to Christianity but . . . [in other ways] deeply opposed to it.

In retrospect, the closeness of the relationship between Europe and North Africa dictated that there be either total assimilation or a violent resistance. In fact, both were attempted and both coexisted for some time. The French made a determined effort at assimilation, especially in Algeria, and in the period between the two World Wars it was a foresighted or a brave pundit who would have predicted a breakaway of their North African provinces in any near future. Italy under fascism made Libya the "fourth shore" of its Mediterranean dream, and Spain looked on possession of the two shores surrounding the Pillars of Hercules as its natural and eternal right. On the other hand, the history of the region after 1830 could be read as that of an area never fully conquered. In Algeria resistance continued for a generation and flared bitterly in Kabylia in 1857 and in 1870-71 before subsiding for two generations. Tunisia pursued the more moderate path of political opposition but took it early and persistently; political activity began in earnest soon after the turn of the century, and from the 1911 Tunis riots on, an unbroken continuity of resistance confronted the protector, culminating in the 1934-38 period which saw the formation and outlawing of the Neo-

Destour (the New Constitution Party). The Senusi brotherhood of Cyrenaica put up a violent struggle against Italian domination in the 1920's and were crushed or harried into exile only for the short decade preceding World War II. Morocco provides the best example of all: it took more than twenty years to "pacify" the country (1912-1934), immediately after which the armed struggle in the countryside gave way to a new, ideologically based urban opposition which eventually completed the task of restoring national independence.

The year 1930 may fairly be considered the turning point almost everywhere. A nascent nationalism in the modern sense was stirred in its Islamic roots by a French decree attempting to alienate Moroccan Berbers from orthodox Moslem jurisprudence. That decade saw the growth of the Neo-Destour in Tunisia, the precursors of the Istiqlal and other minor parties in Morocco, and a marked stepping up of political activity, which had begun after World War I among the Algerians in France, by Ferhat Abbas and the religious leaders in Algeria itself. The Popular Front (1936-38) in France encouraged, but ultimately disappointed, nationalist hopes; these, however, were revived by World War II, and rightly so. Paradoxically, Libya benefited first through having had the good fortune to belong to a loser; the United Nations trusteeship in that country relinquished power to a sovereign state at the end of 1951. Tunisia won internal autonomy in 1955 following a pledge made the preceding year, largely under the pressure of events in the then French states of Indochina, and formal independence for the country came early in 1956. At almost exactly the same time, Morocco became sovereign once again, after forty-four years of protectorate status, during the last three of which an armed resistance movement in the cities, protesting the exiling of the Sultan (later King) Mohammed V, threatened to make the country untenable for France. Already two years before, in November 1954, the Algerian revolution had broken out. It lasted eight years, reduced much of rural Algeria to desolation, permanently changed the nature of Algerian society, brought down the Fourth Republic and its parliamentary government system in France in 1958, and pushed the homeland to the brink of civil war on two occasions. In terms of a general overturn of the whole of a society, as well as with respect to lives lost, it was without question the most violent anticolonial revolution of this generation. In the eyes of much of the Afro-Asian world, the accession of Algeria to independence in July 1962 placed that country for the moment in the vanguard of the anticolonial liberation struggle, as well as in a strategic position between the Afro-Asian bloc as a whole, the positive neutralists, and the Communist bloc as it then existed. If today . . . Algeria continues to occupy that position, moving skillfully among the power blocs and the Arab and African worlds toward its self-proclaimed goal of a specifically Algerian socialism, its maneuvers recall the historic constant of North Africa, shifting in ebb and flow over thousands of years in alternating response to the European and Asiatic tugs on its African-based soul.

The four independent countries of Northern Africa show a wide range in their degree of political development and awareness, as well as in the kinds of national political organizations they have formed. Morocco and Libya are among the world's few remaining monarchies. Algeria and Tunisia are republics stressing special brands of that most elusive formula, socialism. Yet both the kingdoms and the republics have, in many respects, as little in common between themselves as they do with each other. Morocco is a long-established land, secure in its own traditions and historically attached to a national dynasty which has ruled for three hundred years. Libya is a country put together by the accidents of international politics and the labor of foreign advisers; unlike Morocco, its sense of national being is rudimentary, its traditions nebulous, and its personality still unformed. Tunisia, like Morocco, has long been a center of Moslem civilization in the area. For most of recorded history the Tunis region has been the cultural heartland of the North African littoral. The existence of a solid middle class and a bulwarking village hinterland of quality, plus Tunisia's position at the crossroads of the Mediterranean, combine to give a unique flavor to this country which has been and remains comparatively homogeneous, tranquil, and open to fruitful outside influences. Algeria, on the other hand, was long a kind of alleyway between Morocco and Tunisia, and what there was of nascent national consciousness was ruthlessly stamped out during 132 years of direct rule as a province of France. With many fewer pillars of cultural tradition to lean against than its neighbors have, Algeria is in the difficult position today of having had to create its own institutions and personality out of the void of a revolution and a frantic will to defy authority and history.

All these considerations are mirrored in the realities of the political organization in each state. Although Morocco became a constitutional monarchy in 1962, with a directly elected lower house and an indirectly named upper chamber, effective power is still wielded by the king. A modern, activist, European-trained politician-statesman in part, Hassan II is also in great measure a traditional autocrat who firmly believes he has the right solutions, even if these must in the 1960's be secured through maneuvering a multiparty parliamentary system, most of whose leading figures are either under his sway or unable to oppose the prestige he draws from his position and the power he holds through intelligence and drive.

In Libya, although the lines of power are drawn on the surface in the same way between an authoritarian royal family and a weak, unstable parliament, the underlying causes are quite different. The great Libyan problem is to build a nation out of very dissimilar, noncomplementary regions flung out over a vast space (Tripolitania, Cyrenaica, and the sparsely inhabited desert-oasis region of the Fezzan), the first two of which have long felt much mutual antagonism. The king, chosen from the Senusi brotherhood, symbolizes the unyielding Cyrenaican resistance to foreign domination, which the more numerous and urbane Tripolitanians did not participate in. For a generation Tripolitania has suffered pangs of guilt which it has assuaged by contesting the preeminence of Cyrenaicans whom it has considered unfit to rule a more advanced area. The transformation of Libya . . . [a few years ago] from a clumsy, three-headed federal state to a unitary one is the overriding political event in the country's political history as an independent state, and it may indicate that with the passing of bitterness and recrimination stemming from the Italian occupation of 1911-1943 the cornerstone of a true nation has been laid.

The Tunisian political system exists as the result of the high degree of national integration and sophistication that country has attained. Alone of the countries of Northern Africa, indeed of all the Arab states, Tunisia has possessed for thirty years a fully functioning, mass-supported political party operating throughout the country in both urban and rural areas and helping to efface class and regional differences. The Neo-Destour, founded in 1934, has been the means by which so many Tunisians (more than half the total population) have been brought into an active participation in nation-building. Its founder, Habib Bourguiba, now President of the Republic (1959-1965) has been the chief architect of the political and social transformation of Tunisia, as well as the leader of the long battle for independence.

The Neo-Destour operates in Tunisia through a widespread system of local cells, regional federations, and committees responsible to the central party organization. It maintains a host of affiliated organizations relating to labor, education, women's affairs, commerce and industry, agriculture, *et al.* Working through a national front system, it has secured an overwhelmingly dominant representation in parliament, to the extent that in Tunisia there is no practical difference between the state and the party for operational purposes. Most ministers are active party members who spend their free time in junketing to the countryside for campaigns of "explanation" and indoctrination. The triumph of the Neo-Destour is that of a new class in both Tunisia and the Arab World, an "indeterminate dominant" group drawing on a wide spectrum of professional persons, lawyers, journalists, the younger urban middle and upper classes, intellectuals, some merchants and tradesmen, labor, youth, and, above all, women (who have been more fully emancipated in Tunisia than anywhere else in the Arab world). The party's dethronement of the traditional *bourgeoisie* in the bloodless revolution begun in the 1930's and ending only in 1955 was the crucial turning point in recent Tunisian political history. This event was made possible by the pre-existence of an embryonic national social integration whose causes are deeply rooted in history, but it was given shape and direction by the party and by Bourguiba. An authoritarian but not totalitarian instrument—the average Tunisian has a considerable degree of freedom in most areas—dedicated to secular modernization and a "humanistic, Destourian" socialism, the Neo-Destour is probably the outstanding single political institution developed in any Arab country.

Algeria officially describes itself as a "popular and democratic republic." Despite this Communist-sounding terminology, its official doctrine is that of a "specifically Algerian socialism.". . . As in Tunisia, but more fully and formally, the National Liberation Front Party (FLN) is indistinguishable from the state. . . . The FLN describes itself as the "motor of the country" and plans to reconstruct itself as an elitist, avant-garde group rather than as a mass organization. The scales of power in Algeria, however, swing toward the proletariat and not toward a broad "new class" as in Tunisia. Moreover, the military have a role to play there beyond that allotted them in other states of the area. The Algerian revolution was undertaken in desperation by peasants who turned themselves into a guerrilla army. City workers, intellectuals, and professional political figures who later joined the movement have never had full influence or control; that is shared by army leaders from the "external forces," guerrilla chiefs who fought inside the country, and men like Ahmed Ben Bella who were prominent in the pre-revolution underground and who, in his particular case, achieved martyrdom through chance imprisonment. Technically, Algeria is a parliamentary republic with a strong executive; in practice little debate has taken place and most government action has been taken by surprise decree or by inspiration on the spur of the moment. As might be expected in the aftermath of the revolution, Algeria suffers greatly today from a lack of trained cadres and civil servants. Some of the most pressing problems of the first . . . years of independence have been technical, administrative, and fiscal ones. . . .

Throughout most of their history the countries of Northern Africa have shared similar economies. These are based on Mediterranean-type agriculture, extensive stock-raising in the drier regions and the steppes, and some subsidiary oasis cultivation in the southern extremities. Emphasis on one or another of these may have varied both in time and by region, depending on climatic changes and irregularities of water, vegetation cover, and the like, but generally the resemblances have outweighed the dissimilarities.

From the days of Roman Africa to the modern farms of Morocco, and from the Libyan shores to the sheltered valley of the Sus around Agadir, the principal subsistence crops have been the hard cereals, durum wheat and barley, plus figs and olives. More recently, the main cash crops for export have consisted of citrus fruit, olives and their oil, specialty vegetables, and wine. Beginning in this century the extractive industries have played an important role; phosphates have for some time been the principal earner in Morocco, and iron ore, lead, cobalt, zinc, and antimony are found in the area. In the twenty years since World War II, a complex of secondary and processing industries has been developed. Fish and vegetable canning, fruit juice processing, tanning, cement, glass, and paper industries, shoemaking and leatherware, plus a growing textile industry, form the core of this growth. In many fields here, as with the newer industrial endeavors, similarity in the economic structure leads to outright rivalry; several of the countries have under construction or in planning their own steel mills, oil refineries, and chemical complexes.

The long and intricate relationship with colonialist Europe has further shaped the North African economies along roughly parallel lines. All have been distorted by the so-called "dual economy" pattern, in which a modern, European-type agriculture, industrial circuit, processing and shipping facilities, and export market economies were superimposed on and alongside local cultivation methods and traditional ways in commerce and artisanry. Today the European farmer is physically gone in all the countries except Morocco, and the state has in most cases assumed the responsibility for agricultural progress and reform. In industry the situation is more fluid, but it can be said that much direct European control, and more influence, persists in Morocco and

Libya, while in Algeria and Tunisia the legacy, although more abstract, is certainly not absent.

Today, however, in economic choice as in political decision, the various countries are coming to crossroads where there can be seen divergences which could shape their future development along more and more separate lines unless there is a fairly rapid reharmonization of final goals. For one thing, Algeria and Tunisia are in the midst of a thorough revamping of archaic rural structures through the establishment of differing kinds of self-managed cooperative or collective units. Morocco and Libya have not yet undertaken any real rural reform, and Libya may be too deeply involved in other aspects of its economy to begin one now. For another, the growth of the oil industry in Libya and Algeria is tending to create special problems for those countries and to reduce chances for over-all integrated regional development, at least in the short run. North African oil—with forward estimates of one quarter the proved reserves of the Middle East, one eighth of the world total, and an amount equal to that of continental North America—has become a prime factor in international political economy. . . .

That the countries of North Africa have been going through a crisis of identity since independence is beyond question. The passion is multifold: the nurturing of their youthful selves is subject to the acceptance or rejection of the heritage of the Middle East and modern Europe, as well as tempered by a new and perhaps fortuitous, but nonetheless deeply felt, sense of belonging to Africa as a whole. The problem of assembling all the borrowed and bequeathed items is not just geographical and cultural, moreover. It is equally political, and being political touches the inner citadel of religious faith and thought. . . .

Much of the meaning of North Africa appears, as I see it, to lie in precisely the uncertainties and ambiguities in which it has cloaked itself. It is not one of those areas, or countries, which in itself fascinates us by the quality of its thought and literature, the nobility of its monuments, or the admirability of its technical achievements. Wholly unlike its tutors, Middle Eastern or European, it has never been a creative, idea-fermenting society. It has been, however, a remarkably assimilative one, subtly receptive in the midst of inner indifference at almost all periods of its history. Thus today, if the substratum of Algeria has a strong African folk feeling to it, the ethical framework of the country is Islamic, the masses identify with a neo-heroic ethic of Arabism, the intellectual component is Gallic in tools and flavor, and political thinking attempts to distill an ideology out of the teachings of Mohammed, Jaurès, Lenin, and Castro. The *succès d'estime* of North Africa has been to maintain its integrity while being most profoundly connected with and supported by its neighbor civilizations. . . .

As a study in cultural interaction and its weaknesses, as a laboratory of the kind of change and interchange which is clearly slated for the world in coming decades, North Africa is outstanding and in many ways unique. The violence of the Algerian revolution yesterday, the profundity of the social modernization of Tunisia today, the massiveness of the shadow of North African emigration to Europe tomorrow, these show how fluid the situation is but suggest, too, that this fluidity is the opportunity of a society which has not yet set itself. Many other areas of the world might well envy this one for the choices still open to it.

II. ISLAM AND A UNITED MAGHREB

EDITOR'S INTRODUCTION

North Africa is not just a geographical expression; it is also a state of mind. This is because the North African nations, however different they may be in many respects, are united by only one powerful force: they are all Islamic. They all adhere to the Moslem faith. Moreover, as Arabs, they all are inspired by historic memories of the Arab empire that once stretched from the gates of India to the plains of Castile. Not all Moslems are Arabs (Indonesia, Turkey, and Iran are Moslem, for example, and not Arab), but nearly all Arabs are Moslems. And as Moslems they have certain dreams, fears, and ambitions in common. One of these dreams is that the Arab world—torn into feuding segments for centuries—should one day be reunited. It is a dream that Arab leaders publicly proclaim in their speeches every day. Yet it is a dream which seems very far from being put into practice. This is partly because of the factionalism that is so strong in the Arab character, and partly because of the national pride of the Arab states. If there is to be a single Arab nation, who shall govern it? Where shall its capital be? What will become of the individual member states? Arabs speak of unity, but they also fear it, because they do not want to put themselves under the rule of foreigners—even though they might be Arabs. This is why President Nasser's speeches have met with so much applause but so little action. Arabs admire Nasser, but Arab leaders also fear him. Cairo has become, once again as in ancient times, a kind of new Mecca. But it is one that Arab leaders approach hesitantly, for fear they may be engulfed by the outspread arms of the wiliest of all Arab leaders: Gamal Abdel Nasser.

The articles in this section deal with the Arabs as a people, with Islam as a religion and a cultural force, and with the prognosis for eventual Arab unity. In the first article, Michael Adams assesses Arab history from the perspective of the Arab character. Professor P. J. Vatikiotis, of the University of London, views Islam as a world force and as a political ideal. In the third article,

Professor I. William Zartman considers the prospects for uniting the states of the Maghreb. The fourth article assesses the state of Pan-Arabism and the efforts of Egypt's Nasser to lead an Arab revolution.

WHO ARE THE ARABS? [1]

The Arabs once ruled over a great empire, to whose passing they have never become wholly reconciled. Nor was that empire —which in its heyday was more extensive than its Roman predecessor—dependent merely on Arab courage or armed might. It was at first the physical expression of a great religious idea; and when that began to fade, the arts of secular civilization made of Baghdad and Damascus, of Cairo and Córdoba, the intellectual capitals of the early medieval world.

When we dismiss as bombast the claim that there is one Arab world from the Atlantic to the Euphrates, we should remember that this indeed was once the scope of the Arab empire. With motives as mixed as those of most imperialists, the followers of Mohammed burst out from their Arabian homeland, within a century after the Prophet's death, to extend their rule and promote their faith throughout Mesopotamia, Syria, Palestine, Egypt, and the whole of the North African shore, as well as Spain and Sicily. And in all of these lands save Spain and Sicily and a bitterly contested part of Palestine, the culture and language and religion of the Arabs still holds the field.

The Arab empire disintegrated for reasons which have always influenced Arab development and which continue to affect it today. The Arabs have always been individualists, reluctant to accept authority except in moments of crisis and prone to rebel against it as soon as the crisis has passed. . . . Their loyalties tend to be close and exclusive, and the pattern of their social organization continues to be conditioned by the concepts of the family and the tribe. Nationalism has for them a romantic and universal significance which is seldom appropriate to, and indeed often conflicts with, the facts of their modern political existence.

[1] From article by Michael Adams, *Guardian* correspondent. *The Guardian* (London). Mr. 14, '66. Reprinted by permission.

The Western mind associates the Arabs with the desert, and while most Arabs today are townsmen this earlier association is right and revealing. It was the desert that bred them and conditioned their original attitudes. It was in the desert that they formulated their view of life, a view which gave them the strength and character to undertake their amazing conquests. In the desert they were never conquered, and Arabia itself remains the unviolated heartland of their dreams. But beyond the confines of a world they understood and with whose harsh certainties they were at home, the Arabs lost their clear sense of purpose; nor in the renaissance which they have experienced in the past hundred years, have they yet succeeded in finding a new one or refashioning the old to suit their modern needs.

The old enmity between the Desert and the Town, between the traditional, tribal outlook and that of the modernists, is still a factor in the development of the Arabs. . . . The Arab is torn always between his desire to play an influential role on the modern scene and his awareness that his past triumphs were won against a very different background. He feels that history and the achievements of his ancestors entitle him to an esteem which somehow escapes him; and he is aware at the same time that his handling of his present environment is essentially inadequate. The result is an unsettling and sometimes dangerous schizophrenia. The Arab feels that if only things could be as they once were, he would be seen to be superior to his fellows, but he acknowledges, somewhat scornfully, that as things are the important prizes in life go to others more skillful than himself in the arts of political manipulation.

How then are the Arabs to reassert their greatness, or at least to escape from the limitations imposed on them by an unkind fate? This is their problem, and their ambition, in the modern world. The instrument on which they rely is Arab unity, the collaboration at all levels of the component parts of that ancient empire in a drive for social and political regeneration. And at first sight fate, which for so long has been unkind to them, seems to have smiled on the enterprise. Their physical environment, which until very recently condemned them to poverty and discomfort, now offers to the Arabs, in the form of oil, miraculous wealth: and wealth in modern terms should spell power. And yet, paradoxically, the power eludes them and even much of the wealth slips through their fingers.

Worst of all, instead of helping them to unite and to use their resources in support of a common plan, the oil and its revenues have actually hindered the unification of the Arabs, giving significance to frontiers between them which before were merely lines on a map, encouraging jealousy and rancor between the very leaders who so loudly proclaim their unity of purpose. For nature, whimsical or still (but more subtly) cruel, has been generous to Iraq, but not to neighboring Jordan; to Saudi Arabia, but not to Egypt; to Libya and Algeria, but not to little Tunisia sandwiched between them.

Perhaps the failures and the disappointments are too often allowed to hide the palpable achievements. Some of the oil revenues have been well spent and—more significantly—even without oil the rulers of modern Egypt have given a lead to the whole Arab world in the creation of a social structure which corresponds to the needs of the twentieth century. The change within a generation has been tremendous and can only be appreciated by contrasting the present atmosphere throughout the Arab lands with the stagnation which prevailed forty years ago, when dawn was breaking after the long dark age of Turkish rule. In education, in industrialization and technology, in communications, perhaps most of all in its awareness of its own social problems and responsibilities, the Arab world is on the move. The progress is halting, forever disturbed by the irrelevancies of a nationalist fervor whose objectives are outdated—but it is tangible, and in view of the political history of the postwar period it is even remarkable.

What the Arabs most need, it would seem, is to frame for themselves a realistic ambition (and realism has never been their strong point); to turn their backs on the vision of past glories restored, and come to terms with the modern world, accepting its shortcomings, and their own.

ISLAM AS A WORLD FORCE [2]

A tradition attributed to the Prophet Mohammed says that unbelief is one nation. This, at one and the same time, emphasizes, at least theoretically, the solidarity of all Moslems, and establishes the division between them and unbelievers. Those who confess the faith "there is no god but Allah, and Mohammed is His Prophet" are united as brothers in a community of believers. In classical times, they were further united in the belief that Islam was the one true, universal, and final religion. During times of military and political ascendancy Moslems further believed that they were supreme and that their state, encompassed in a universal Islamic empire, was invincible. Their dominion was "the house of Islam." Other parts of the known world, which they had not yet conquered and whose inhabitants they had not yet subjugated, constituted "the house of war." Between these two houses, or worlds, there was theoretically a perpetual state of war which could only end when "the house of war" was subjugated. To achieve this, the faith proclaimed the waging of holy war (*jihad*) as a collective obligation of the Moslem community and as a foremost responsibility of the sovereign caliph.

This division between the Moslem realm and the rest of the world was effectively sustained for no more than one hundred years after the rise of Islam. The great Arab conquests of the seventh and eighth centuries culminated in the establishment of a vast empire extending from North Africa in the west to the borders of China and India in the east. Within the vast confines of this empire, Moslem jurists hammered out a legal system for the regulation of the believers' conduct and the relations between them. It derived from the word of God, revealed to the Prophet as the Holy Koran, as well as from the *sunna* and tradition of the Prophet. It was therefore a revealed law which recognized one sovereign source: God. All believers—both rulers and ruled—were subject to its provisions.

[2] From article by P. J. Vatikiotis, professor of politics, Department of Economic and Political Studies, School of Oriental and African Studies, University of London. *New Society* (London). p 10-12. S. 23, '65. Reprinted by permission.

The Sacred Law

Two things, besides the confession of faith, gave the Moslems at this early stage of their history a strong sense of identity and solidarity. One was the Sacred Law, the only law regulating the lives of Moslems everywhere. The other was Arabic, the language in which the Sacred Law was revealed to the Prophet. But over time, much of the strong faith was lost, and life in an evolving modern state was no longer regulated by the Sacred Law. Yet, until as recently as the nineteenth century, the sensation of Islamic identity and solidarity was a reality for many Moslems. Why?

Partly, because for some twelve hundred years the Moslem community maintained its identity through the Sacred Law. Partly, because in the first six centuries of its existence, Islam managed to transform the simple religion of the Arab Prophet from the Arabian desert into a high civilization. A religious and cultural unity among Moslems everywhere was maintained. And for a long time, this unity was symbolized by the sovereign caliph, leader of the community of believers.

So much for the religious and communal identity and solidarity of Moslems. But what about their political solidarity and unity? This did not obtain for more than a century. Even in the first thirty years after the death of the Prophet there was dissension and conflict within the community between legitimists and others. Immediately after the extension of the empire westwards and eastwards, its territorial and administrative unity was eroded by ambitious local governors, satraps, and rival caliphs. Rival Moslem empires to the orthodox caliphate in Baghdad arose in North Africa and Egypt as early as the ninth and tenth centuries. Conflict and warfare between Moslems struggling for power became common. Only briefly in the confrontation with the infidel Crusades and later against the Mongol and Tartar invaders was Moslem solidarity mobilized by powerful military leaders.

For almost five centuries the Ottoman empire (founded by a caste of Turkish warriors) sustained, by a combination of military ability and administrative flexibility, the last great Islamic empire. Basic loyalty within it was to Islam and the Sultan-caliph. Moslems defined their identity and loyalty in terms of their membership in the community of believers.

It was not until the middle of the nineteenth century that this Islamic solidarity and sense of communal unity were eroded by outside influences and forces. The encroachments of Europe, which weakened the center of power that had sustained this unity in diversity, also eroded the empire's foundations among the diverse members of the community. Notions of secular nationalism and liberal conceptions of government and of social and economic progress had a disruptive effect upon the traditional bases of Islamic society. For a while, Pan-Islamic movements arose to strengthen the Islamic community against the threat from Christian Europe. Rulers, like the Ottoman Sultan, briefly adopted such movements as the basis of a policy that might galvanize their subjects against their infidel enemies. Religious reformers proposed Pan-Islamism as the answer to the European intellectual and political menace. In the final analysis, the lack of military power to sustain these attempts at strengthening Moslem solidarity, and the weight and momentum of the European encroachment, rendered the Pan-Islamic idea ineffectual.

Sentimental Deference

The sentimental solidarity of Moslems with their Sultan in Istanbul was inadequate to counter the more positive desire for national independence rationalized from such elements as language, territory, and common heritage. The Arabs, for example, raised a revolt against the Moslem sovereign in 1916-17 with the help of the infidel British. In Egypt, a preoccupation with independence from Britain sustained briefly at the turn of the century a sentimental, though superficial, deference for the Sultan in Istanbul. Yet the nationalists who had based their program upon ideas they had borrowed from the liberal West discovered an Egyptian nation for which they desired an independent state. The fragmentation of the Moslem empire, one might say, was in full swing. Admittedly it was precipitated by the defeat of its supreme sovereign, the Ottoman Sultan. Yet, the fragmentation was there from the beginning.

As early as the ninth and tenth centuries competing Moslem rulers allied themselves with infidels in fighting against one another. In modern times, a puritan Wahabi Ibn Saud fought against a Hashimite Husein in the Hejaz and ousted him from his kingdom. In the Palestine Arab-Israeli war, Moslem heads of states could not agree upon concerted policy and action to prevent the establishment of an Israeli state. Predominantly Moslem states have been at diplomatic loggerheads for some time now: Egypt versus Turkey, Iraq versus Egypt, Egyptian supported republicans versus Saudi supported Zaydi tribal monarchists in the Yemen. These are only a few examples.

Another traditional crack in Islamic solidarity has been the traditional though muted enmity between orthodox (*sunni*) Islam and heterodox (*shii*) Islam. The latter, a minority in many Moslem states, finds its adherents often at a political disadvantage even in such modern states as Iraq. Ethnic divisions have added to this fragmentation, rendering internal solidarity in some Moslem states dangerously problematic. Such divisions have led to armed clashes between coreligionists who happen to belong to different ethnic and linguistic groups. Thus, the Kurds in Iraq, and the Kabyles in Algeria.

Nationalist Impact

The impact of the Western notion of the territorial nation-state upon Islamic solidarity has been shattering. Having divided the world into "the house of peace" and "the house of war," the Moslem created an ideological dichotomy which was rigidly unrealistic and dangerous. It was unrealistic because Islam did not succeed in converting the rest of the world. It was dangerous because Islam has not been able to assert itself as a sovereign religious entity. By making such extensive claims to loyalty and obedience, the Islamic community eventually became vulnerable to the inroads made by the idea of the nation-state. The claim of Islam to a universal religious truth that was to be ultimately embodied in a political reality (a universal house of peace) was far too ambitious for the power and resources of its adherents to realize.

Islam, like Christianity before it, therefore has had to succumb to the advantages and utility of secular authority (not that it was always totally free from it). The nation-state, based as it is on a secular conception of power, and whose authority is territorially confined, eroded further the concept of Islamic solidarity. With nation-statehood came national interest, not always compatible with the interest of the more nebulous Moslem community at large. The sense of Islamic community became more instrumental in providing the most common denominator upon which to base *national* solidarity. Its value emerged as an integrating force in building a homogeneous nation and polity with allegiance to a secular territorial nation-state. It was also a useful instrument in the more radical political and economic programs of the revolutionary nationalism of the 1950's and 1960's. It has been preempted as an instrument of state policy.

Ally of Revolution

This symbolic integrating value can be observed in the efforts of radical regimes to build modern, industrialized, powerful states. In Egypt, for example, extreme religious militancy has been forcefully eradicated by the regime. At the same time, the leaders of religious teaching and tradition have been mobilized by the state in the service of its revolution. Moreover, a religious-political campaign to extend the influence of Egypt in Africa was begun in 1958. Interpretations of what is the "true" Islam, motivated by the requirements of national policy, have been used in inter-Islamic conflicts to advance the national interest of one state over that of another. In short, whereas Islam at the turn of the century was associated with political reaction and backwardness, it is being presented today as the creditable ally of radical revolution, reform and progress. As such, it divides the Moslem community of nations into those that favor radical reform and whose citizens are consequently "good" Moslems, and those who do not and whose followers are therefore "sinners."

The sense of Islamic solidarity and identity has also expressed itself in the struggle against European domination and colonialism. At one point in the Algerian struggle of independence, the response of Algerians to the French slogan of *Algérie française* was not *Algérie algérienne* but *Algérie musulmane.* Similarly much of the momentum of the opposition to European control in many Moslem lands of the Middle East nourished itself from this Islamic base. While its leaders may have subscribed to basically European conceptions of nationalism and independence, the mass of the public understood their antipathy and opposition to foreign rulers in the simple emotional terms of the unity of the Islamic community.

There is, then, a sentiment for Islamic solidarity and unity today. What does not exist is effective Islamic solidarity in economic and political terms. Nation-statehood has undermined this possibility, if not totally precluded it. Predominantly Moslem Arab states, for example, base their inter-Arab policy upon national interest. Wars of words and actual combat have occurred between them. For the moment, at least, leaders of Arab states meeting in Casablanca have signed a "solidarity pact" which enjoins them to refrain from making propaganda against one another. Yet, intrigues, attempted coups to undermine one regime or another, continue. Egypt's religious propaganda in the Moslem parts of independent Africa, for example, has not been an unqualified success. Moslem Africans may feel a sense of religious solidarity with Egyptians and Arab Moslems generally, but not with their particular brand of Arab nationalism or their desire for leadership.

So long as the Moslem community is divided into secularly conceived, territorial nation-states which occupy an area that is no longer directly controlled by big powers but simply exposed to their influence and competition, the struggle for power and leadership among these states is possible, and is not restrained by the basically religious and spiritual sense of Islamic solidarity. Moreover, the adherence of leaders of Moslem states to different ideas, and their adoption of opposing policies renders this struggle even more certain. Political and economic radicalism has undermined Islamic solidarity. . . .

It is conceivable that a strong Moslem leader who can successfully unite under his hegemony a large number of Moslems in a vast geographical area may some day be able to revive and activate the old feeling of Islamic solidarity and make it into a reality and a potent force in the world. But this does not seem a likely possibility in the near future.

UNITING THE ARAB MAGHREB [3]

The idea of North African unity is an old dream. The implications of its simple title, *al-Maghreb al-Arab* ("The Arab West"), is one of natural, preexisting unity based on the culture and the geography of the region. Since it shares a common Mediterranean coast, climate, and cultivation, and occupies the entire northern shore of the Sahara, the Maghreb is easily conceived of as a geographic unit. Its culture, too, is unified on the basis of Arabic and Islam, and differences in dialect or in religious practice (within the framework of the Malikite Rite which is common to North Africa) are no greater than in any other area of the same . . . size. The inhabitants of Casablanca and Algiers and Tunis, or Fez and Tlemcen and Qairwan, or the Atlas and the Aures mountains and the Tunisian Tell are frequently closer to each other in their ways of life than they are to their fellow countrymen.

There is even a precedent for Maghreb unity. In the latter half of the twelfth century, Abdulmumin established the Almohad dynasty—whose name, from *al-Muwahiddin,* the unitarians, referred to its religion and not to its politics—and enlarged the kingdom of Spain and Morocco to include Algeria and Tunisia as well. In 1162 he called himself *khalifa,* independent from the Moslem Middle East. However, by the beginning of the next century the Maghreb was again divided into three parts. The only other examples of North African unity were under foreign

[3] From *Sahara—Bridge or Barrier?*, by I. William Zartman, assistant professor, Institute of International Studies, University of South Carolina. *International Conciliation.* 541:34-41. Ja. '63. Published by the Carnegie Endowment for International Peace. Reprinted by permission.

domination, first by the Romans and much later by the French. Each colonial power, however, administered its North African territory as three provinces. The existence of three states, therefore, has an older historical basis than does Maghreb unity. The fact is that an Algerian is not a Moroccan or a Tunisian (or a Libyan) any more than a Dane is a Norwegian or a Swede (or a Finn), and unity is at least as far from the Maghreb as it is from Scandinavia.

However, there are Maghreb leaders who are convinced of the importance of cooperation which could lead eventually to closer forms of unity. One reason is the hope of gaining bargaining power in international councils. Another is the desire to avoid competition among highly similar economies. Another is the desire to benefit from the natural resources of the other members, strongest in Tunisia, which has only its own phosphates, and weakest in Algeria, which is plentifully supplied. Another is the possibility, based on cultural similarity, of economical pooling of resources in the creation of a common Arabized education system. It should be noted, however, that all these reasons are aspects of a broad attempt to gain strength through union against the pressure—be it political, economic, or cultural—of a uniting Europe to the north. Pan-Maghrebism is therefore both an attempt to solve the real problems of its members and an attempt to formalize an existing sense of identification.

Modern Pan-Maghrebism owes much to the influence of the father of Pan-Arabism, Shekib Arslan. In 1927, young Maghreb nationalists in contact with him created in Paris the Association of Moslem Students of North Africa. . . . The Association numbered among its founding members many of the present rulers of Morocco . . . and Tunisia, and some of the older Algerian nationalists. . . . After World War II, Maghreb nationalists joined the rising Arab nationalism in the Middle East. The Front for the Defense of the Maghreb participated in a conference on North African problems organized in Cairo in 1945, and Habib Bourguiba (now president of Tunisia) at the end of the year asked the newly formed Arab League to admit North African observers, although by country, not by region. In February 1947 another Cairo conference on North Africa resolved to create a Bureau of the Arab Maghreb to lead the propaganda war for North African independence. Bourguiba was soon joined in Cairo by other North African nationalist exiles, including Abdel Krim Khattabi, the Riffi warrior who in 1948 set up a Liberation Committee of the Arab Maghreb. Abdel Krim was life president and Bourguiba, secretary-general. At the same time, in Paris, during the National Assembly debate on the Algerian statute, Algerian Moslem deputies presented several bills that included suggestions for a "North African Federation within the framework of the French Union."

However, since France rejected any such federalism and North Africa to an increasing extent rejected French professions of assimilation, independence became a precondition to the creation of an Arab Maghreb. The existence of separate regimes in the three countries meant that the political aspect of the struggle for independence had to be carried out separately. Yet as violent pressure grew, coordination in the military field increased. The Moroccan Army of Liberation (ALM) was created to begin its activity on 1 November 1954, in coordination with the first attack by the Algerian National Liberation Front (FLN). It found itself unprepared when the date arrived, but began, instead, eleven months later. The "head" of the ALM, Abdel Krim Khatib, was an Algerian chosen by the Moroccan resistance leaders for liaison rather than leadership functions. In March 1957 the FLN concluded agreements with the Tunisian government which provided for bases and training camps on Tunisian territory. These bases eventually contained some 25,000 men with a general headquarters at Ghardimaou. Similar installations for some ten thousand men were arranged on Moroccan territory. When independence came to Morocco the ALM alone of all Moroccan nationalist organizations refused for some months to lay down its arms and recognize the king until the liberation of all North Africa was achieved.

The independence of Morocco and Tunisia in March 1956 had its effects on the Pan-Maghreb movement. On the one hand, it meant the end of the struggle for most of the people and leaders of the two countries; Algeria was of great sentimental but less practical interest to them. The enjoyment of independence or, more seriously, national reconstruction, were primordial occupations. On the other hand, independence allowed diplomatic freedom both to aid the FLN and to pursue the objectives of an Arab Maghreb, as the state leaders might wish. Often both goals could be covered at the same time.

The first official move came soon after independence in the form of a meeting in Paris between Moroccan Foreign Minister Balafrej and Tunisian Vice Premier Bahi Ladgham, leaders of the Istiqlal and the Neo-Destour parties, respectively, to discuss a "unified North African policy." At the end of October 1956 a meeting with Mohammed V and the FLN leaders, including Ahmed Ben Bella, was organized by Bourguiba in Tunis. The conference turned into an indignant protest meeting after the French kidnapped and imprisoned the Algerian delegates on their way to Tunis. The following June, Bourguiba reiterated a proposal he had made earlier for a Franco-North African community in which France would recognize the independence of all the Maghreb in exchange for cooperation. Meanwhile, in October 1956 and November 1957, Morocco and Tunisia proposed their good offices in the Algerian revolution. Later, in October 1959, Morocco tried alone, and the following year Tunisia was instrumental in starting the talks that finally led to Algerian independence. . . .

With Algerian independence, the initiative has shifted to that nation, with its predominance in size, resources, and dynamism. But it is unlikely that Algeria "feels" Pan-Maghrebism as deeply as do some Tunisians or Moroccans. By waiting for Algerian independence to create the Maghreb, North African leaders gave Algerian nationalism time to grow strong and, at the same time, removed the unifying anti-French impetus of Pan-Maghrebism. None of the present Algerian leaders has ever spoken of the Arab Maghreb with the fervor of an Allal al-Fassi or the insistence of a Bourguiba or the logic of an Abderrahim Bouabid.

Bouabid, former Moroccan Economics Minister and Vice Premier and a leader of the activist opposition, National Union of Popular Forces (UNFP), and his supporters are now the most articulate spokesmen for the Arab Maghreb. In their view the basic idea is neither cultural, as it is for al-Fassi, nor political, as it is for Bourguiba, but economic. To them, North Africa, confronted with the European Economic Community (Common Market) will be forced to "specialize in underdevelopment" by the growing agricultural self-sufficiency of Europe. Alone, none of the countries can overcome this danger. Together, they can take rational and self-supporting measures of economic defense. Bouabid suggests reconversion of agricultural production to reduce imports, reorientation of trade away from dominance by Europe, nationalization of foreign commerce, and creation of a common tariff for the whole of the Maghreb. He also proposes an exchange of resources between an agricultural Morocco and an Algeria endowed with sources of energy; this proposition has evoked a favorable echo in some Algerian circles. The resulting economic union would then gradually become tighter through the successive steps of confederation and federation until a single nation would be created. Bouabid and the UNFP have the advantage of coherence. They have the disadvantage of impotence, for although they are the second largest party in Morocco their influence as the opposition party under the monarchy is relatively small.

There are other problems to be met before an Arab Maghreb can be created. Is it in fact true that a state of thirty million inhabitants has a better chance and greater means of pulling itself more rapidly out of underdevelopment than a country of four (or eleven or twelve) million locked up in its political and economic frontiers? What forces would create an Arab Maghreb? The UNFP is close in temperament to some forces in Algeria, but the two are frequently at serious odds with both Hassan II and Bourguiba. How would the Arab Maghreb be created? Bourguiba continues to speak of a union of governments and the UNFP of action by the masses, but Bourguiba's proposal has met with a deaf ear from the other governments. In November

1962 Ahmed Tlili of the General Union of Tunisian Workers announced the imminent revival of plans for a Maghreb Labor Confederation, but the existing Maghreb labor union secretariat does not function. Could the Arab Maghreb be formed as long as Morocco has a king? How would the monarchy fit into a republican Maghreb? None of these problems is insurmountable, and all are of a newer nature than those faced by the architects of the Common Market. But the fact is that an Arab Maghreb must be *created*. It will not spring into being from the heritage of history, or the logic of economics, or the pressure of the masses. To date, the strongest feeling in the Maghreb is the feeling of Tunisian, Algerian, and Moroccan nationalism.

PAN-ARABISM [4]

What is "Arabism"? A nationality? An ideology? A culture? Many experts have thrown up their hands in attempts to define it. Some simply state that Arabism today is a "state of mind." One is an Arab, in other words, more by conscious choice than by racial, religious, cultural or linguistic affiliation, although these factors (the last three in particular) may be said to represent significant common denominators. . . .

This revival has focused world attention once again on the character of a people who for centuries past have lived in the shadow of darkness and neglect. Any traveler in the Middle East is immediately struck by the more famous Arab characteristics—hospitality and generosity, the studied formality governing social conduct, Arab pride and sensitivity to criticism, and the ingratiating manner that appears to permeate Arab society.

Such generally recognized features of the modern Arab personality are the product of history and circumstance—the pressing hardships of life in the desert, for example, which are said to have given rise to the stress upon hospitality, or the values of Islam or the long history of Arab subordination to foreign rule. Some experts, focusing upon the political make-up of the

[4] From *Great Decisions 1964*. (3, Egypt and the Middle East: What Prospects for Stability?) Foreign Policy Association. 345 E. 46th St. New York 10017. '64. p 32-6. Reprinted by permission.

Arabs, have linked the volatile nature of Arab politics to the more volatile aspects of the Arab character—the fierce rivalry instilled from youth, the strong feelings of family or tribal loyalty, the suspicious and secretive attitudes which invest politics and political institutions with a strong flavor of intrigue. . . .

"Arab life," one authority has noted, "is filled with interpersonal rivalry—tribal feuds in the desert, family and village feuds in the settled areas, and intergroup hostility (more controlled, however) in the towns. Arab political writers never tire of stressing not only Arab brotherhood but also Arab contentiousness which they blame, together with imperialism, for the Arab failure to achieve total unity."

In the light of past history, as well as current Arab psychology, the stormy nature of current inter-Arab relations should come as no surprise. The history of the Arabian peninsula reveals a long record of dynastic rivalry and factional squabbling. Arab pride and particularism have worked to inhibit compromise and the subordination of one group to any of the others. The colonial powers, moreover, employed the principle of "divide and conquer" as a way of achieving their own ends. And Soviet Russia, since World War II, has pursued a policy designed to encourage the claims to autonomy of the Kurd minority in Iraq.

Oddly enough, Egypt, the leading Arab state today, was first set upon its course of Pan-Arab nationalism (i.e., the unity of all Arab-speaking peoples) by the reactionary King Farouk, who dreamed of a restored Arab caliphate—the office of "successor" to Mohammed—with himself as caliph. Colonel Nasser has willingly taken up the unity banner. "There is no doubt that the Arab circle is the most important and the most closely connected with us," he wrote in 1953. "Its history merges with ours. We have suffered the same hardships, lived the same crises and when we fell prostrate under the spikes of the horses of conquerors they [the Arabs] lay with us."

Time and time again Nasser has seemed on the verge of making real progress toward his goal of unification, only to be set back by, it would seem, elements of the very "Arabism" that is his cause. Radio Cairo, the self-proclaimed "Voice of the Arabs," has trumpeted a steady blast of unity propaganda throughout the Arab world. Such has been Nasser's hold on the aspirations of Arab nationalists that, as one author recounts, "The ubiquitous rioters in Amman [Jordan], during the disturbances of 1957, were said to keep one ear cocked to the café radios blaring the Voice of the Arabs program from Cairo. When the Voice reported that the Arab patriots were attacking the British Bank of the Middle East, for example, the faithful listeners would rush to do just that, picking up stones from piles foresightedly placed in advance in strategic spots."

With considerable fanfare in 1958 Nasser's followers in Syria propelled themselves headlong into union with Egypt under the UAR. For a brief period the ideal of Arab unity appeared to be heading toward fulfillment. But almost from the start practical difficulties abounded. The "united" armies of the two countries squabbled incessantly. Syria's economy lagged; her businessmen feared they would be taken over by "Arab socialism." Syrian politicians who had engineered the unity move soon regretted the abolition of parties and the loss of their political freedom. They complained that Syrian problems were neglected in Cairo. And indeed, burdened by Egypt's many difficulties, Nasser and his advisers soon found that they had neither the time nor the personnel for properly governing the Northern Region.

When the break came in 1961 both sides appeared almost relieved. The Syrians blamed Egyptian pride and greed. Nasser blamed "reactionary, imperialist" forces. Both reaffirmed their devotion to the cause of Arab unity.

That cause received a serious—perhaps mortal—setback with the breakup of the UAR. Many Arabs, probably the great majority, felt real sorrow at this blow to their ideal. Some even began speaking of a loose federation of independent Arab states, with solidarity of international purpose, as the most that could be hoped for. But Nasser has never for a moment abandoned his primary ambition, though he has shown greater caution recently in pressing toward its realization. His dream remains the unity of all Arabs "from the Atlantic to the Indian Ocean" under Egyptian aegis. . . .

As Nasser looked to the Arab West—to North Africa—developments were less than promising. As he looked to the Arab East —to Syria and Iraq—they were plainly disheartening. The Baathists stood firm in their determination to preserve their political survival even at the cost of Arab unity—a long-sought Baathist goal. Baath leaders—notably their chief theoretician Michel Aflak—regard themselves as the ideological fathers of modern Arab unity. They are in turn regarded by Nasserites as "armchair nationalists" who have "theorized" while Nasser has acted. They are a politically potent group now, however, not only in Syria and Iraq, which they control, but in Jordan, Libya and Saudi Arabia. . . .

Like Arab nationalism, Arab unity has been fostered by more or less negative influences, by what Arabs are against rather than what they are for. The "four devils" of modern Arab nationalism are Zionism, colonialism, economic imperialism and alliance with reactionary traditionalism. As the Number One Arab nationalist, never ceasing to harangue against these four devils, Nasser also represents in his person a powerful force for Arab unity. There is no doubt that should unity be achieved, the domestic and international position of the Arabs would be radically altered. Commanding both oil wealth and the strategic Suez Canal, Nasser and Pan-Arabism would become a major force on the world scene.

On the plus side, such a development might at last insure the stability so long absent from the turbulent Middle East, erecting at the same time a firm barrier against Soviet penetration. On the minus side, Arab unity could unleash the bloody conflict with Israel which today, because of Arab weakness, seems somewhat remote. Even so, some Israelis are said to feel that Arab unity might eliminate the need for rival Arab governments to surpass each other in anti-Israeli propaganda, and thus lessen the chance of war. . . .

Gamal Abdel Nasser, the Arab nationalism he symbolizes and the Arab unity he seeks are far from settling influences in the crisis-prone Middle East. Many of the area's political storms are traceable to this man and his cause. Yet there are those, including many Americans, who believe that Nasser's aspirations both within Egypt and without are legitimate and that his towering figure offers the best prospects for eventual stability. Nasser, they say, is neither so fanatical nor so unreasonable as some Arab nationalists of the past—leaders of the Moslem Brotherhood, for example. And though he has "done business" with the Soviets, his actions prove him a staunch and vigilant anti-Communist at home. Moreover, even without Nasser, these analysts feel, Arab nationalism would constitute an unsettling revolutionary force.

The Egyptian president himself has taken a similar view with regard to his role and that of Arab nationalism. In *The Philosophy of the Revolution* he speaks of Arab leadership as a "role wandering aimlessly about [the Middle East] seeking an actor to play it." He concludes that destiny has tapped Egypt for the part: "I do not know why this role, tired of roaming about in this vast region which extends to every place around us, should at last settle down, weary and worn out, on our frontiers beckoning us to move, to dress up for it and to perform it since there is nobody else who can do so."

Having donned the role for Egypt, has Nasser played it with finesse? Has he won anything more substantial than applause? His performance at home awaits the success—or the failure—of Arab socialism. His performance abroad, however, has already been marked by considerable acclaim. In little more than a decade Nasser has become one of the most prominent personalities among world statesmen—not a trifling achievement for the leader of a comparatively small and impoverished nation.

Nasser's bold and pragmatic foreign policy has brought him gains in virtually every area except that which is closest to his heart: Arab unity. Probably his most striking achievements have been to win Egypt full independence in internal and external affairs and to make himself a major force in world affairs.

In his relations with the great powers he can claim an impressive string of victories. In 1954 he negotiated the withdrawal of British troops from Egypt after seventy-four years of occupation, having indicated he might consider a defensive alliance with the West when complete independence was achieved. Once Britain had gone, however, he declined any such commitment and railed furiously against creation of the Western-sponsored Baghdad pact in 1955, because this "Northern Tier" alliance against Russia included Arab Iraq. In his passion for Arab independence and nonalignment, he openly pressured other Arab states, such as Lebanon and Jordan, against entering into military compacts with the Western powers. And he has looked on with satisfaction as the West acquiesced to these pressures.

When he was unable to obtain arms in the West, Nasser turned to the Communists for massive purchases in 1955 and successfully resisted Western retaliatory pressures. One such pressure—United States withdrawal of offers to help build the Aswan High Dam—he boldly countered by seizing the Suez Canal, retaining it despite ensuing Anglo-French-Israeli intervention. He has bargained considerable aid from the Soviets as a counter to Western influence and, since 1958, vice versa. He has seen the Algerian rebels, to whom he gave refuge and assistance, overcome French colonialism, and has helped reduce by one the number of Western-supported monarchs ruling in the Arabian peninsula. . . .

In the Afro-Asian world of newly independent states, Nasser has established himself as a spokesman for the nonaligned. Under his rule, Cairo has become a diplomatic center of Afro-Asian activities, providing refuge to nationalist leaders of colonial Africa, training for Arab revolutionaries and opportunities for study to students from the nonaligned world.

Most successful in his dealings with the great powers, Nasser has come off less well in his many tangles with the smaller countries that surround him. The state of Arab disunity testifies to that. The Arab League, a once obedient instrument of Egyptian policy, has lately degenerated into a faction-ridden conglomeration of thirteen states devoted to the airing of inter-Arab squabbles. . . .

Similar difficulties confront Egypt in her relations to the south and east on the African continent. As early as 1953 Nasser had affirmed that next to the "Arab circle," the "African circle," with its struggling independence movements against "imperialism," was most important to Egypt's future. In 1959 he launched a vigorous African policy designed to support anticolonialist movements, bring Egypt into closer relations with such African states as Mali, Ghana and Guinea, and block an Israeli trade bid that was meeting with considerable success.

For the most part, however, Nasser's bid for leadership in Africa has been rebuffed, as in the Arab world. The so-called "Casablanca group" (Egypt, Algeria, Morocco, Ghana, Guinea and Mali), which Nasser tried to use as a vehicle for Egypt's African policy, is now virtually defunct. And while Nasser can count generally on African support for his "anti-imperialist" stands, he has been for the most part unable to gather African allies for his battles with Israel or his Arab neighbors. Ghana's relations with Israel, for example, remain every bit as cordial as with Egypt.

Some critics have speculated that Nasser alternately shifts the focus of his policy from the Arab world to Africa depending upon in which of the two regions he feels himself stronger. Though in years past he has enjoyed considerable influence in both areas, there are some indications that his personal prestige, if not his popularity, is beginning to wane outside Egypt. For one thing, Nasser is no longer the unique figure of Africa and the Middle East that he once was. Africa has produced a crop of new leaders . . . who are every bit as ambitious and strong-willed as the Egyptian strong man. And in the Middle East the Baath is openly challenging Nasser's proprietary claim on Arab nationalism and socialism, and has even charged Egypt's foreign policy with being "soft on Zionism."

III. MOROCCO

EDITOR'S INTRODUCTION

Morocco is a fitting country with which to begin a study of Arab Africa, for it is, in many respects, the most Arab of all the North African states. It is in Morocco that the Moslem religion is observed most strictly. It is in Moroccan cities such as Fez and Meknes that the traveler feels himself not in Africa at all, but rather in the Middle East. Morocco, while taking great steps toward modernization, has also resisted much of the Europeanization that is so pronounced in Algeria and Tunisia. This resistance is largely due to Morocco's history, to the fact that she was never a European colony, but only a protectorate of France. The protectorate did not begin until 1912, and the country was not pacified until twenty years later. Moroccans are a proud people, with proud memories of the Arab kingdoms which once ruled most of Spain and which spread to southwestern France. Once again independent, and under the leadership of a young king who carries on a dynasty more than three hundred years old, Morocco is struggling to find her place between the world of her glorious imperial past and the new world of technology and rationality which is foreign to her traditions but which she cannot ignore. A study in contrasts, the passionate, beautiful and disturbed land of Morocco offers a glimpse of the tensions which are shaking North Africa today.

In the first article, the editors of the *British Survey* present a view of Morocco from the struggle for independence until the present time. The following two articles view some of the problems of Morocco's struggle to modernize her economy. The next three articles deal with Morocco's young monarch, King Hassan II. C. L. Sulzberger sees Hassan following a middle-of-the-road path in foreign policy; the present writer assesses Hassan's efforts to bring his country democracy and economic development within a traditional framework; and Claire Sterling considers the problems facing Hassan as Morocco is swept by forces of change. Peter Braestrup recounts the strange kidnapping and disappearance of the Moroccan left-wing leader Mehdi Ben Barka—an event which had widespread political repercussions within Morocco and even in France. In the next article C. L. Sulzberger relates the history of the United States air bases in Morocco. In the final selection, the London *Economist* describes the vast but little-known expanse of desert along Morocco's southern border known as the Spanish Sahara—an area which Moroccans claim is rightfully theirs.

MOROCCO TODAY [1]

Morocco has been independent . . . [since 1956], after forty years of being divided into Spanish and French protectorates. At the beginning of this century it was an underdeveloped country, isolated from the rest of the world by ignorance and fanaticism. It is now a modern sovereign state, playing its part in world politics. The former Spanish and French protectorates, imposed in 1912, as well as the International Zone of Tangier, have been unified. Morocco still has many difficulties to overcome. But with financial and technical help from both Western and Eastern countries, a determined effort is being made to improve the people's standard of living, and to secure the foundations of political progress.

Moroccan dissatisfaction with foreign rule led to the formation of political organizations fairly soon after the 1914-18 war. The most important of these were the Moroccan League, formed by Ahmed Balafrej in 1926, and various student unions. Demonstrations and unrest led to the suppression of Moroccan political parties by the French, but developments during the 1939-45 war weakened French control and introduced influences favorable to the rise of nationalism. In particular, the Sultan of Morocco, for long regarded more or less as a French puppet, was brought to lead the movement for national independence. His views were certainly influenced by his war-time contacts with President Roosevelt.

The Allies, under General Eisenhower, landed in Morocco in 1942, thus terminating the control exercised by the French au-

[1] From *British Survey* (London). Popular Series 222:1-16. F. '63. Published by the British Society for International Understanding. 36 Craven St. London W.C. 2. Reprinted by permission.

thorities in the name of Marshal Pétain's Vichy Government.
Subsequently Morocco was reoccupied by General de Gaulle's Free
French forces. Politically, the crucial moment was in January
1943, when President Roosevelt, Mr. Churchill and Generals de
Gaulle and Giraud met in Casablanca to discuss military operations in North Africa. On that occasion, the United States President saw the Sultan, Mohammed Ben Youssef, and no doubt
impressed him with the American view that the end of colonial
rule would be one of the inevitable consequences of the war.
From then onwards the Sultan increasingly opposed the French
administration of Morocco, refusing to countersign laws and rejecting all French compromise offers, holding out for unqualified
independence and the abolition of the Protectorate. In this
struggle he was supported by the Istiqlal (Independence Party)
which had been formed in 1943.

Because the Sultan openly sided with the nationalists, he was
arrested by the French Resident-General, General Guillaume, on
August 20, 1953. He and some of the royal family were flown to
exile in Madagascar. An old relative, Moulay Ben Arafa, was
placed on the throne in his place.

Fighting and terrorism flared up throughout the French Protectorate. There was less trouble in the Spanish Protectorate,
where the Kalifa continued openly to represent the exiled Sultan.
Spain did not recognize the deposition of Mohammed Ben Youssef.
Tangier remained quiet. The situation was complicated by the
powerful Pasha of Marrakesh, El Glaoui, who openly declared
himself on the side of the French. At Rabat, the aged Sultan Ben
Arafa, despite repeated attempts to assassinate him, refused to
abdicate, although Paris was beginning to realize that the situation would not improve until the exiled ruler had been brought
back.

Finally, the French reluctantly agreed to terminate their Protectorate. The old Sultan was at last persuaded to abdicate and
retire to exile in France.

On November 18, 1955, Sultan Mohammed Ben Youssef returned from exile amid scenes of great rejoicing. In March 1956,

France agreed to Morocco's independence. Shortly afterwards, Spain did the same. The nations administering Tangier also agreed to its integration into the Kingdom of Morocco.

But, although Morocco was independent, it still had to rely for financial and technical help on France, and to a lesser degree on Spain. For some time Europeans continued to occupy their previous jobs in the civil service and other positions in public and private enterprise, because so few Moroccans had been trained to take over. However, young Moroccans were immediately sent to Europe for training and now many Europeans have been replaced.

After his return the Sultan changed his title to King Mohammed V. His country, instead of being the Sherifian Empire, was to be called the Kingdom of Morocco. The king promised to rule democratically and give his people a constitution. Although ruler of a Moslem land, he promised religious freedom and he guaranteed the safety of foreigners and their possessions.

Mohammed V was a loved and venerated king. For one thing the Sultan had always been Chief Imam, that is the religious head of Islam in the country. Mohammed V had also led his country's struggle for independence, and thus was considered a national hero. He was also a wise statesman. An Assembly was established in November 1956. Its members were chosen from the different political parties which began to emerge. The king's eldest son, Moulay Hassan, was proclaimed Crown Prince. This was a break with tradition. A new ruler had always been chosen, after a Sultan's death, by the Ulemas—or religious leaders—from among members of the reigning family; he did not have to be one of the Sultan's sons.

In 1960, because of difficulties between the king and the left-wing government, led by Mr. Abdallah Ibrahim, the king dissolved it. In a broadcast, he announced that he would, for a time, head his own government. Mohammed V also promised that a constitution would be prepared, and in November 1960 a special council was set up to draft it. However, the king was not to see the end of its labors, for he died unexpectedly after an operation in February 1961. Crown Prince Moulay Hassan ascended the throne as Hassan II.

The sudden removal of the popular and powerful personality of King Mohammed caused some doubts whether the new ruler would be able to exercise the same degree of strong authority. It was feared that left-wing politicians might try to proclaim a republic. But the young king firmly took control and declared his intention of carrying on his father's policy. His popularity has continued to increase since his accession. He married a young Moroccan lady, whose family is related to his, shortly after he came to the throne. In August 1962 a daughter, Lalla Mariam, was born.

Like his father, Hassan II is head of his own government. He is always busy traveling round Morocco on tours of inspection, laying the foundation stones of new factories and opening new roads, housing estates and trade fairs. On Fridays, dressed in traditional robes, he rides in state to the mosque surrounded by his Black Guard. Usually, however, he wears modern dress, as do most of his ministers.

Hassan II has fulfilled his father's promise of a democratic constitution. A draft was presented to the nation, and received overwhelming approval in a plebiscite, held in December 1962. It . . . [provided] for the establishment of a constitutional monarchy, and a parliament . . . to be elected before the end of 1963.

Morocco thus seems to have embarked on the road of internal political development with some prospects of success. In the early stages after independence, there was some difficulty in persuading the members of the "Liberation Army," who had fought the French, to return to normal conditions or to join the regular forces. Some of them allowed their resentment to carry them into attempts at revolt (notably in February 1960) and clandestine hoarding of arms, and in August 1961 a trial of thirty-one persons accused of plotting against the state took place. Since then, however, things have quietened down, and, no doubt, this has encouraged King Hassan II to proceed with the plans for a constitution.

The main political parties are the Istiqlal, and the left-wing National Union of Popular Forces, which broke away from the former in 1959. There are two other significant parties—the

Constitutional Democratic party and the Popular Movement. King Hassan's government includes representatives of the Istiqlal, the Constitutional Democrats and the Popular Movement. The Communist party is small, and has been banned for some years. . . .

Land and People

Morocco covers some 173,000 square miles. It lies between the Atlantic and the Mediterranean, at Africa's northwestern corner. Its neighbors are Algeria and the Spanish Sahara (Rio de Oro).

There are two important mountain ranges—the Rif in the north and the Atlas in the south. Toubkal, the highest peak, rises to about 14,000 feet. The Atlas Mountains separate the fertile coastal plains from the Sahara Desert. Although mostly barren, Morocco's mountains have some fine cedar, oak and cork oak forests where wild boars, jackals, lynxes and Barbary apes live in their natural state. These apes are the same as those on Gibraltar, which is separated from Morocco by the strait of that name.

Most Moroccan rivers flow into the Atlantic. The largest are the Sebou, Bou Regreg, Oum er Rbia, Sous and Dra. Smaller rivers, called *oued,* are generally dry during the hot months—from June till October—but often flood after the winter rains.

The climate varies from the dry heat and desert conditions of the south to the Mediterranean type of climate in the north. In winter the mountains are covered with snow and there are several winter sports resorts. In summer people throng the beaches lining the 500 miles of Atlantic coast.

Rabat (population approximately 200,000) is Morocco's capital, but Casablanca (population just under 1 million) is its largest city and commercial center. It is also one of Africa's large ports. Fez, Marrakesh, Meknes, Tetuan, Tangier, Essaouira (previously called Mogador), Oujda, El Jadida, Safi and Kenitra (formerly Port-Lyautey) are other big towns.

This is chiefly an agricultural country; 72 per cent of the people earn their living on the land. Morocco also has mines and a large fishing industry. It is the world's second-largest producer of phosphates. Its most important exports are citrus fruit, tomatoes, wheat, hides, wine, cork, tinned sardines and phosphates. France buys nearly half Morocco's exports, but trade with many other countries is growing.

Morocco imports wheat, manufactured goods, petrol, sugar and certain foodstuffs, France being the main supplier.

Today there are nearly 12 million Moroccans. They are divided into three main groups. About one third are Berbers. These descendants of the original inhabitants still live in the mountains and outlying districts. Although they come from different tribes, they all belong to three distinct groupings: the Riffis in the north, the Brabers of the center, and the Chleuhs of the south. They speak various dialects quite different from Arabic. Many of them are nomads, living in black goat-hair tents, moving from place to place with their flocks and herds. In the mountains they live in *ksar*, flat-roofed, mud-walled villages. Their chiefs, the *caids*, lived in casbahs. Today most of these fortresses, which were built of yellow or red clay, are empty, and the *caids* now live in modern houses.

The great majority of Moroccans are of Arab descent. They inhabit the towns and villages on the plains. Their language is a modified form of Arabic. Most of the officials, scholars, businessmen, farmers and factory workers are of Arab origin.

There are also some 200,000 Jews still living in the country, who have Moroccan nationality. Until the protectorates they were forced to live in certain quarters of the towns called *mellah*. They were quite often ill-treated. Since independence they are supposed to enjoy the same rights and privileges as other Moroccans, but there is still some discrimination against them. Many have managed to emigrate to Israel.

Although many thousands of Europeans have left, there are still about 160,000 French in Morocco today. This is only half the number there used to be. Although nearly all French civil servants and other officials have now departed, Morocco has had to ask France for more teachers.

Most of the people still live on the land, but in the towns the trade union movement has spread since 1956. Now every trade has its union, which is affiliated to either the Union Marocaine du Travail or the Union Général des Travailleurs Marocains. Wages and working hours have been fixed by law. Only the peasants continue to work in the fields from sunrise till dusk. Naturally, progress and an improved standard of living have affected town-dwellers the most. Peasants still live in mud huts in villages surrounded by prickly pear hedges, and dress in the traditional way. Even their agricultural methods have scarcely altered in many places.

Since independence, Moroccan women have become increasingly emancipated. This is most obvious in the towns. Except for poor families, the bride never saw her husband until she was taken, hidden in a box on the back of a mule, to his house for the wedding. After that she rarely went out, and was never seen unveiled. A husband could divorce his wife by merely repeating three times before witnesses: "I repudiate you."

Today this has changed. Although polygamy is not forbidden, it is frowned on. Divorces have to go through special courts. And young people generally mix freely. In fact, boys in jeans and girls in short skirts are seen about together. In summer they go swimming. Only the older generation still clings to the veil.

On Fridays, the Moslem sabbath, families now go out together. But in the country, peasants on their way to and from the weekly *souk* (market) still go in separate groups. Girls now attend school in increasing numbers and many young women are getting jobs or training for careers.

Progress Since Independence

One of the most urgent things which had to be done after independence was to organize education. At the time over 90 per cent of the people were illiterate. During the protectorates there were enough schools and teachers for European children, but few Moroccans learned to read and write. The only education most children got was at the *kittab,* small schools, where boys were taught to read and recite the Koran.

A few later went to the *medrasa.* These colleges were attached to some big mosques. But the education they offered was mostly religious and traditional. Today all the *kittab* have been closed and new schools have been built, many by volunteers, throughout the country. Many of the European schools have also been taken over, but, as there are still not enough Moroccan teachers, over eight thousand French teachers have stayed on. . . . All lessons are given in Arabic, but along modern lines. French is taught as a compulsory foreign language.

All Moroccans are keen to learn and many evening classes have been organized for adults. Although the Koranic universities still remain (including the one-thousand-year-old Kairouine at Fez which is famous throughout the Arab world), a new modern university is being organized in Rabat.

The government's plans do not only concentrate on the modernization of agriculture and the improvement of educational facilities. Morocco has iron ore, lead, cobalt and other mines. It is the world's main exporter of phosphates. An industrialization program is taking place to make use of the raw materials found in Morocco and thus reduce the imports which are a strain on the economy.

To carry out this program the B.E.P.I.—Bureau d'Études et de Participations Industrielles—was instituted at the beginning of 1958. Through it the development of new industries is planned with the help of foreign and local investments. Since 1958 a cotton mill has been built at Fez and an oil refinery near Casablanca. New projects are a large chemical complex at Safi, a sugar refinery, and an iron and steel mill in the north.

Foreign Policy

Although Morocco continues to conduct most of its foreign trade with France, it is trying to extend trade with other countries. Germany, Italy and the United States as well as Great Britain are investing in the new industries. The United States of America has also helped with large loans. There is also a growing trade with Russia and other Communist countries, including China. Foreign technicians are coming to Morocco to help set up the new industries and train their personnel.

Morocco's foreign relations are somewhat disturbed by a variety of territorial claims. In the south, Morocco claims Mauritania, now independent. This claim is based on the fact that the area belonged to the Moroccan Empire in the eleventh century. In the north, the Spanish enclaves of Ceuta and Melilla still rankle, although the Spaniards have held them since 1581 and 1496 respectively. There have been incidents involving Spanish fishing boats fishing in Morocco's recently extended territorial waters. The Moroccans also claim the Ifni enclave, where armed clashes have taken place. . . .

Now that Algeria is independent, there have been incidents at the outpost of Tindouf, which is on the ill-defined Saharan frontier between Morocco and Algeria. The exact definition of this frontier now that oil has been found under the sand may give rise to difficulties.

In January 1961 a meeting of African leaders from states concerned with the Congo crisis took place in Casablanca. The group of states, consisting of Morocco, Ghana, Guinea, Mali and the United Arab Republic, which emerged from this first conference, has taken up a militantly "anticolonial" policy.

MOROCCO BETWEEN TWO WORLDS [2]

Morocco is . . . a young country—50 per cent of the population is under twenty-one—trying to make a success of the independence achieved, or rather regained, eight years ago; and the men who rule her are . . . likely to be found wearing suits of French cut and driving large cars in the Europeanized towns of Rabat and Casablanca. Their wives and daughters, too, are more likely to be preceding than following them, for the upper-class women of Morocco, following the example set by their royal family, are achieving emancipation apace. At a European party in Fez the twenty-four-year-old daughter of a leading citizen, who had arrived unescorted, spoke to me freely of her welfare committees and political ambitions; and in all towns unveiled daughters in European dress walking with veiled mothers in caftans exemplify a generation which claims the full social freedom—including the

[2] From "Morocco's Struggle Towards Modernity," by a special correspondent. *The Times* (London). Ag. 1, '64. Reprinted by permission.

right to choose their own husbands—which their poorer Berber sisters have always enjoyed.

Modernsm, in fact, is in the air. In so far as it breeds conscientiousness and promotes social reform, it can be beneficial; . . . charitable workers in outdistricts report gratifying keenness and interest in social welfare in the remotest provincial officials. Its application to administration, however, holds two dangers: an over-abrupt swing from traditionalism which may dislocate the social structure of a deeply traditional society; or a blind nationalism which may injure its precarious economy.

Both dangers are real. The policy of detribalization, which has been deliberately adopted with a view to converting Morocco into a homogeneous democratic state, has inevitably aroused the ire of the Berber chieftains, who still wield paramount influence in the mountains, and a number of them recently forcibly demonstrated their determination to have their views more adequately represented in the counsels of the government. Failing satisfaction, they could well create a security problem. Alternatively, the younger educated townsfolk are mostly admirers of President Nasser's "Arab Socialism" . . . and could form a serious dissident element should circumstances combine to weaken the authority of the regime.

Such circumstances could well be economic, and it is here that the second danger seems likeliest. Morocco is not a rich country, for the natural phosphates, manganese, and iron ore which, with tourist receipts and agricultural produce, make up the bulk of her external income are a poor substitute for the oil which is bringing wealth to her neighbors. She has, moreover, been overspending. . . .

Unemployment is rife, especially in Tangier, where a flight of foreign capital and firms when its special regime came to an end in 1960 coincided with an influx of tribesmen from the poverty stricken Rif mountains, who came in search of nonexistent work and stayed to swell the ranks of the beggars round the cafés. The economies which austerity can effect must be limited, especially in face of imperative demands from every ministry for expansion to meet the needs of an emergent state; and one of the measures announced, a suspension of administrative recruitment, sounds impracticable, since its application could only drive numbers of graduates to despair and subversion.

Clearly exports must be maintained at all costs. In 1962, however, a third of these consisted of agricultural produce, the greater part of it from French-owned properties; and as both Algeria and Tunisia have now nationalized all foreign-owned agricultural land, [there is] political pressure in favor of similar action. . . .

To judge by what has happened in Algeria, any attempt by the state to evict the *colons* and run their farms in their stead would lead to a further and catastrophic fall in production, with a corresponding reduction of exportable surpluses and of the income they earn. Moreover the French government, with whom Morocco has so far maintained good relations and who have responded with lavish budgetary and technical aid, might well react as they did in Tunisia and thus deprive Morocco of assistance on which she is at present dependent.

A heavy responsibility lies on the head of state, and here Morocco is undoubtedly fortunate. King Hassan II . . . on his accession in 1961 changed almost overnight from a pleasure-loving young man to a responsible ruler and a shrewd statesman. . . .

In a country with so long an independent history—the forty-five years of the French and Spanish protectorates was the only interruption of an independence which had lasted since the Arab conquest in the seventh century—the prestige of the monarchy must be very great, and in the difficult days to come the people of Morocco may well be thankful that their King's experienced hand is on the helm.

ON THE MOROCCAN FARM [3]

Nine years of independence with as many governments have done little to solve Morocco's agricultural problems. The one undisputed fact is that while the population is increasing by 3.2 per cent each year, farm output is declining. Yet agriculturally, the difficulties are not insurmountable. Morocco is blessed by a rela-

[3] From "Morocco: Back to Autocracy; Down to Earth." *The Economist* (London). 215:1266+. Je. 12, '65. Reprinted by permission.

tively abundant rainfall and with a rich alluvial soil along its wide Atlantic belt. It is here on this coastal plain that the modern farms, mostly European, have been growing their citrus fruit and vegetables for export. Cereals and livestock, on the other hand, come mainly from the traditional sector—those vast stretches of upland, dominated by a ridge of high mountains running through the heart of the country. And here the yields are so wretchedly low that Morocco has to import not only meat, dairy products, sugar and vegetable oils, but cereals too (from the United States).

All parties are agreed that this traditional sector must be modernized. A beginning had tentatively been made by the outgoing government. The trouble is that a policy of forceful state intervention has little chance of succeeding without the concerted support of the political parties. And the parties did not agree on the overriding question of how this kind of modernization should be imposed on a country where the ownership of land is not a relatively simple affair of landlords and tenants, owner-occupiers and farm-workers. In Morocco it is infinitely complicated by archaic and feudal chains binding man to man, or man to the soil, by a complexity of law, custom and debt.

Each of the parties has its own policy for agrarian reforms but only the left-wing National Union of Popular Forces (UNFP) and the powerful trade union organization, the UMT, want to sweep away the whole complicated spiderweb by the wholesale distribution of land to the peasants. They argue that only by giving the actual workers on the land full responsibility and a true stake in the development of their property can the necessary schemes for cooperative assistance, planned development and production by quotas work out. Moreover, so the left-wing argument continues, only by nationalizing the marketing of farm produce can the country as a whole reap full benefit.

But all this spells out social and political revolution. The growing Moroccan middle class, though determinedly town-dwelling, draws much of its economic and political power from the land it owns. It is not at all prepared to forgo the life of power and splendor that it saw coming to it with independence.

The only seizure of land to which all parties can agree is another raid on the country's colonial past: the confiscation of European holdings, the flourishing modern concerns that still produce 40 per cent of Morocco's exports. Most Moroccans are prepared to jeopardize the efficiency of this sector rather than to continue seeing the export trade being used, as the French have been using it, as an escape for capital.

But the expropriation of French-held land is above all a nationalistic decision and, as such, is one that the king has in principle to accept. Were it only a question of assuring that Morocco gets its dues from the foreign estates, the problem might be better, and more quickly, dealt with by working out a fiscal solution.

HASSAN'S MIDDLE ROAD [4]

Hassan II, Morocco's young king, is one of Africa's few chiefs of state who is not bemused by slogans. He sees no contradiction between monarchy and socialism, between territorial claims and good external relations, or between industrialization and improved living standards for farmers.

A small, trim sportsman, Hassan sniffs at various brands of "socialism" proclaimed by other Arab capitals such as Algiers and Cairo. "They want to impoverish the rich," he comments acidly. "We prefer to enrich the poor."

This is evidently directed at President Ben Bella of Algeria, which started a border war with Morocco . . . and was badly trounced. Ben Bella proclaims an "Arab socialism" akin to Nasser's. Hassan observes: "I am a Socialist also; but I want to be constructive."

He sees no reason why the monarchic system cannot successfully lead an underdeveloped state in Africa where, he says:

There are many monarchies without kings—autocrats with more power than kings. Africa requires peace and stability. The last way to achieve this is for one form of regime to try and overthrow others. . . .

[4] From "Middle-of-the-Road in Africa," by C. L. Sulzberger, foreign affairs columnist. New York *Times*. p 40. Ap. 29, '64. © 1964 by The New York Times Company. Reprinted by permission.

When the Algerians attacked us they were clearly attempting to change our form of government and impose their own. Some of their friends [an oblique reference to Nasser and Castro] told them our monarchy was feeble and would easily crumple. Colonel Boumedienne of the Algerian Army said their revolution, like Nasser's, must spread in order to survive. . . .

As a nonaligned country we were in a delicate position. We had no allies; Algeria was helped by Cairo and Havana. Well, the affair is over now. Everything is calm. And Morocco is not seeking to alter its position of nonalignment. . . .

King Hassan does not consider Morocco has yet attained its natural boundaries. Yet he is neither recalcitrant nor impatient. This country hopes eventually to gain control of the Spanish Sahara and Spanish enclaves, but, rather than press the matter, it is confident this will ultimately be settled by "the process of African liberation."

. . . In Madrid, Hassan reminded Franco that Morocco's "rights to the south are solid." But both leaders agreed a good atmosphere was a necessary prerequisite to border changes. Hassan acknowledges: "Franco is right to think mutual problems must be regulated in a proper ambience."

Morocco is at present more concerned with arranging a proper "ambience" with other North African states. It has ousted Egyptian teachers and technicians who had stirred up left-wing opposition. It is now improving irritated relations with Tunisia. The king hopes careful diplomacy may eventually arrange economic cooperation within the so-called Maghreb . . . so they can present a joint front in seeking association with the European Common Market.

He is determined that ideological slogans shall not confuse sensible economic development. He wants Morocco to expand its industries—"but not for any prestige purpose that is essentially unsound. We want to raise our standard of living by improving our agriculture. We can never forget we are essentially agricultural. Our factory proletariat and farm proletariat must work together. We must improve agricultural living standards to create an internal market for industrial production."

This moderate approach does not appeal to extremists of either left or right but Hassan intends to persevere on his chosen middle course. Since the Algerian attack was smashed—and with it most of Morocco's Ben Bellist and Nasserist apologists—his position has grown stronger.

The king intends to capitalize on this ascendancy. He says: "The years of our independence struggle showed me the value of perseverance. Even if one has difficult moments, one must follow the correct road." As a slogan in turbulent Africa this may not be flamboyant; but it is refreshingly sane.

MOROCCO'S RELUCTANT AUTOCRAT [5]

"The country cries out for a strong, stable government," King Hassan II declared in June [1965] as he shuttered up the Moroccan parliament, dismissed the fumbling government of Ahmed Bahnini, and named himself premier. Thus the curtain rang down, temporarily at least, on a two-year experiment in parliamentary government that gave Moroccans a degree of political liberty unique in Africa. Unfortunately, it also gave them a legislature split into twelve feuding parties which managed to pass only four major bills (one of them an attempt to ban the foreign-language press) since it came into existence in 1963.

In the dazzling diversity of its parties and in its incapacity to deal with the grave problems facing the nation, the Moroccan parliament resembled nothing so much as the French National Assembly during the last days of the Fourth Republic. And like General de Gaulle, whom he admires and emulates, young Hassan apparently decided that the nation can no longer afford the luxury of a party system mired in paralysis. . . .

If Hassan has become an autocrat, following an old tradition in the Arab world, he has every reason for being a reluctant one, for he takes on a set of headaches that have eluded solution ever since Morocco gained its independence from France in 1956. A nation of infinite possibilities and unlimited problems, Morocco is struggling with the classic dilemmas of underdevelopment, plus a few special ones of her own: an exploding population cutting

[5] Article by Ronald Steel, author of books and articles on foreign affairs. *New Leader.* 48:9-11. Ag. 30, '65. Reprinted by permission.

ever-smaller slices out of the same insufficient pie, economic stagnation resulting from inadequate investment and flights of capital
into foreign bank accounts, a restless urban proletariat which refuses to accept unemployment and misery as its natural lot, land-
hungry peasants demanding a share of the earth they till, a
privileged elite which has no intention of sharing its riches, a
politically powerful bourgeoisie resistant to any serious reforms,
discontented intellectuals preaching a "Cuban solution" for
Morocco's problems, an army which is constantly prodding the
king to take over dictatorial powers, and an economy plagued by
rampant inflation, mounting imports, and lagging exports to pay
for them. In short, the typical case of a nation living beyond its
means, trying desperately to keep pace with its own catapulting
population, inheritor of a glorious past fallen on sorrowful times,
and trapped by the cruel laws of economics in a terrible choice
between the political freedoms it seeks to preserve and the social
revolution which it may not be able to prevent.

Architect of a liberal constitution which may be more suited
to republican France than to monarchist Morocco, Hassan has
tried to provide a modern framework for a traditionalist society.
He has given women the right to vote and he set up a model
parliament; yet outside a few major cities on the coast, women
are rarely seen in public without the veil, and the model parliament has so far not functioned effectively. He has pushed industrialization, and this summer proudly inaugurated the impressive chemical complex at Safi; yet the agricultural sector,
which is Morocco's lifeblood, is stagnant and hobbled by inefficiency.

The rich coastal lands, which have been mostly in French
hands, produce the vegetables and citrus fruits that account for 40
per cent of the nation's exports, while the interior lands are
farmed so badly that Morocco must import meat, dairy products
and sugar, and even cereals from the United States. The land is
potentially rich, but cries out for modernization and for irrigation
projects. This would increase yields, boost exports, and furnish an
important source of foreign exchange. The land-owning
bourgeoisie, however, bitterly opposes any changes in the tenure

system, and irrigation costs money for which there are a thousand other demands.

A monarch in the modern mold, Hassan has shown an uncommon awareness of Morocco's problems, but is still unwilling to make the painful choices that modernization demands. Instead of pushing through agrarian reform, he has taken the politically easier path of nationalizing foreign-owned land—thereby speeding a mass exodus of French capital. While the Left applauds, the economy suffers, and the peasants are no better off. Stepping up the pace of nationalization since becoming premier, Hassan has now put some 60 per cent of all exports under government control, including phosphates, which are a major source of foreign revenue.

But this socialization has failed to appease the Left, which will be satisfied with nothing less than a social revolution on the Algerian model, even if it drives the country to economic ruin. Meanwhile socialization has scared the business community into holding back on investments and resisting reforms that might reduce the privileges it has long enjoyed.

Hassan has tried to straddle two worlds: to preserve the status of the bourgeoisie while alleviating the lot of the poor, and to nationalize key areas of the economy without frightening private investors. But if socialization scares off investors, a refusal to socialize invites a mass uprising. Damned if he does and damned if he doesn't, he is engaged in a constant balancing act. Morocco cannot have it both ways: It cannot obtain massive foreign investment to finance a welfare state. Without the oil riches of Libya or Algeria to pay for its development program, and without a serious "Communist problem" that might stimulate support from Washington, Morocco must finance reforms out of the limited resources of its economy, and whatever small help it can pick up from abroad.

If the situation at home is stormy, there are few current troubles abroad, now that the Algerian border dispute of 1963 has been at least temporarily put to rest, and a running feud with Mauritania is in the deep freeze. Remarkably adroit in his foreign policy, Hassan has avoided the excesses of Arab nationalism, maintaining a guarded truce with a hostile Nasser, restoring ties with Algiers after Ben Bella's attempt to push him off the throne, and playing a leading role in African third-world-manship. Combining cold war neutralism with an evident sympathy for the West, he has managed the not inconsiderable feat of simultaneous friendship with Washington, Havana, Paris, Moscow and Peking.

If Hassan can manage to keep at peace with his neighbors and on good terms with the financiers (bureaucratic or capitalistic, as the case may be) in France, Russia and America, he will have the breathing space he needs to get the Moroccan economy on its feet. This is no easy task, for it means pushing through a severe austerity program, stabilizing prices, attacking the roots of unemployment, redistributing land, controlling the flight of capital, and attracting foreign investment.

The potential is there; it simply has to be realized. If the farms were modernized and irrigated, Morocco's rich soil could feed her growing population and bring in much-needed foreign revenue, particularly if the long-stalled accord with the Common Market is resolved and Morocco's superb fruits and vegetables can flow freely into Europe. Rich in phosphates, the nation's soil harbors other minerals which have barely been tapped. Particularly promising is the nascent, but fast-growing, tourist industry which this year is expected to introduce 500,000 visitors to the sunshine and the unspoiled beauty of the Moroccan landscape. And above all, there are the Moroccans themselves, a hard-working, imaginative people whose exuberance is one of the country's great unexploited resources.

Rich in potential, rich in problems, Morocco faces a poignant dilemma: trying to reconcile the values of a traditional society with the demands of an industrial age, seeking change without destruction and reform without revolution. It is a dilemma with no easy solution and no sure answers. Crowded by extremists on both sides, Hassan struggles to steer a middle way that will test not only the statesmanship of this reluctant autocrat, but the viability of Morocco's hard-won democratic institutions.

TROUBLED YOUNG KING [6]

As an ancient kingdom on a continent of raw young republics, Morocco is set apart from its neighbors, a hopeless anachronism to some, an enviable bastion of tradition to others. The throne may have swayed a bit under the blasting wind of change: Hassan is said to be a direct descendant of the Prophet Mohammed, and he is of course the spiritual ruler of his people; but, since he wrote a parliamentary constitution with his own hand, he does not have the full temporal authority exercised by his forefathers since the seventeenth century. But in practice he is still an absolute monarch, one of the last of his kind in the world and, fortunately for the Alouite dynasty in these Jacobin times, a clever one.

Although Morocco is a very old nation, it is a youthful country. Three quarters of Hassan's subjects were younger than he was when he ascended the throne . . . [in 1961] at the age of thirty-one. They were already getting restive during his father's reign. The late Mohammed V had kept their loyalty not by clinging to despotic ancestral ways, but by winning independence from France before a lot of other Africans had even begun to ask for it. His son has shown something of the same intuitive political flair.

To a traveler coming from the nervous new police states dotting the continent, the atmosphere of freedom in Morocco is refreshing. If the king's person is "inviolable and sacred," neither his government nor parliament is exempt from a running popular criticism in which Hassan himself occasionally joins. ("Our members of parliament seem to spend their time putting banana peels under each other's feet," he remarked on the radio not long ago.) The press says what it pleases, though it may not please to attack the monarchy as such. The five political parties wrangle to their hearts' content. Conversation is relaxed, with no precautionary backward glances. The right to strike is written into the constitution, . . . and the Moroccan Labor Federation (UMT),

[6] From "Morocco's Troubled Young King," by Claire Sterling, *Reporter* correspondent. *The Reporter*. 32:21-5. Je. 17, '65. Copyright 1965 by The Reporter Magazine Company. Reprinted by permission.

with 600,000 members, is the largest and most aggressively in-dependent in Africa.

There is, of course, another Moroccan world utterly remote from this easy egalitarianism. During my visit here I spent an evening in it as guest of an aristocratic family. As there were men in our party, the lady of the house remained secluded in her wing of the sumptuous Moorish palace; and our host did not sit down with us to the elaborate ten-course dinner served by the family slaves. But his patriarchal presence was strong in the vast carpeted room, and it was not until he went out to pace in the garden that his daughters, elegantly gowned in caftans of gold-threaded *mousseline de soie,* fished a bottle of forbidden whisky from behind the divan cushions and poured it surreptitiously into the crystal goblets of orange juice he had thoughtfully pro-vided. Theirs is the world Hassan was born to and grew up in, centuries away from the French university where he got his law degree or the kind of society he is attempting, with evident sin-cerity, to create. Try as he may to be a good democrat, he is al-ways the princely offspring of a sultan, surrounded by tradition-conscious nobles who rarely permit him or his subjects to forget it.

At the back of their minds, Moroccans know that their demo-cratic privileges exist on the king's sufferance, and that what he has given he may presumably take away. Mohammed V kept them waiting five years for a constitution after the French with-drew, and died before getting around to it. Hassan repaired the breach two years later, but only with a draft designed, as he said himself, "to bring forth a parliament that will walk with me"— which it does, insofar as it moves at all. Still, the parliament has been elected by a suffrage free enough to give the king's own party, the Front for the Defense of Constitutional Institutions (FDIC) no more than a 52 per cent majority. Weak as it is, furthermore, it has rescued the Moroccans from what many of them would consider a much worse fate: the dreary one-party dictatorship so common among Africa's newly liberated republics.

A short-sighted monarch might have been tempted to try that. The only party in existence for some time after independence, the Istiqlal, was seemingly ideal for the purpose. Formed during the resistance to French rule, and drawing its strength from the safer classes—businessmen, older intellectuals, artisans, small-town notables—the Istiqlal is an intensely traditionalist Islamic movement whose leaders would like nothing better than to rule Morocco in the king's name, pretty much as the sultans of yore used to rule it. But nothing could have appealed less to Hassan, or his father before him, than the idea of entrusting crown and country to a party of such strait-laced and autocratic inclinations.

It was primarily to circumvent the Istiqlal that Hassan devised a multiparty system, and it has obviously been worth the trouble. Admittedly, he has his hands full with a spate of parties. But except for a small group in exile, not one of them would deliberately try to sink the monarchy lest they themselves be sunk by whatever might replace it. That holds even for the party furthest to the Left, the National Union of Popular Forces (UNFP). Having split away from the Istiqlal in search of a more invigorating future, UNFP leaders are particularly indebted to Hassan. If the king doesn't often take their advice, he lets them argue their case with the voters. They could not expect as much indulgence from their former Istiqlal colleagues.

The trouble is that with all this freedom, Morocco doesn't seem to be getting anywhere. In fact, it is appreciably worse off than it was under the French protectorate.

In 1955, the last year of French control, the economy was booming and by rights should have kept on booming. The country could scarcely have been called undeveloped. The Moroccans came into their own with excellent roads, railroads, and harbors, an abundant water and power supply, a prosperous modern agricultural sector, a promising industrial base, big cities, and plenty of money in the bank. They were blessed also with exceptional natural advantages: a fine climate, good soil, huge phosphate deposits, rich mines of lead, manganese, and iron ore, and accessibility to the whole European market. With careful management and a helping hand from France, they should have had nothing to worry about.

Yet they have been losing ground inch by inch over the last nine years. The decline was not noticeable at first because, after an early flutter of apprehension, the 350,000 French *colons* here found they could do business more or less as usual in an independent Morocco, and stayed on. Until 1963, a succession of royal cabinets apparently thought it wiser to profit from the continuing French presence rather than yield to nagging nationalist pressure for the Moroccanization of employment and seizure of French-held lands (750,000 of the country's 5 million arable hectares). The only faintly threatening move was made by Premier Abdallah Ibrahim of the UNFP, who confiscated 40,000 hectares of homestead lands in 1959—and eventually was fired for his pains by Mohammed V, who thereupon took over the premiership himself.

Since the first national parliamentary elections in 1963, however, a fresh succession of cabinets has been obliged to take the electorate into greater account. The *colons* have now lost 250,000 hectares of their land and are supposed to lose the rest in the course of a three-year plan just announced. That in itself would have been enough to frighten them away. But the government has increased its control over banking, worked out a plan to Moroccanize the labor force, and imposed restrictions to stop an alarming drain of foreign currency, caused at least partly by the *colons'* determination to get their capital out of the country. Their last doubts gone, the *colons* themselves are going by the thousands . . . and with their departure has come a dismal day of reckoning.

So long as the French were living, working, and investing here, the Moroccans did not feel the accumulating effects of their government's negligence and mismanagement. Now that the long period of grace is up, they have suddenly realized how much time and money have been squandered. With about $75 million a year from France and another $30 million annually from the United States, they should have been able to encourage local investment, develop new industries, and go at least part of the way towards modernizing agriculture. Somehow, the funds have been swallowed up instead by a yawning budget and trade deficit. Any number of development projects have been proposed: an American team of experts has suggested at least twenty-five—including a $4 million sugar mill to save some of the $45 million spent in foreign currency for sugar imports (from Cuba, at that). But these proposals have bogged down one after another, in baffling succession. The United States has been partly responsible, by insisting on a precision in specifications that would be preposterous in any but a highly advanced industrial society: at least two important projects—a Pan American Airways hotel and a McKesson & Robbins pharmaceutical plant—have petered out because Moroccan civil servants simply could not cope with the paper work. On the whole, however, the problem of trained personnel has been a minor handicap compared to those generated by indecision, ministerial politicking, and graft.

Since 1955, the Moroccan population has grown from 9 to 13 million, and will probably reach 18 million by 1975. Meanwhile, agricultural production has not only failed to keep pace but actually dropped by 5 per cent, industry and commerce are stagnant, and unemployment is spreading like a blight through the cities and outlying *bled*. One in every three *fellaheen* can find work only at harvest time, one in three urban workers has no job at all, and out of Casablanca's 1.2 million people at least 400,000 Moroccans are either unemployed or underemployed. (Entire families live on the earnings of a single shoe-shine boy.)

It is no wonder then that Casablanca went up in an emotional blaze late last March [1965] like a dry forest at the touch of a match. The rioting started as a demonstration by schoolchildren, some of them third- or fourth-graders, against a government edict limiting the age for passing final high-school examinations to seventeen. The measure was reasonable, considering the state's limited resources and the enormous number of young Moroccans pressing for an education. But it meant that slower students would have no place to go after seventeen, except, that is, into the streets.

No sooner had the students marched out in protest than they were joined by the youth who were on the streets already, to be followed shortly afterward by what looked very nearly like the whole population of Casablanca. Burning cars, overturning buses, breaking windows, heaving cobblestones, the mobs stampeded through the city, completely beyond police control. By the next afternoon, the rioting had spread to Marrakesh, Meknes, Rabat, and Fez, and barricades had been flung up in Casablanca's old city, the Medina. The king sent in his army and the troops opened fire, killing four hundred men, women, and children and wounding a thousand others.

It was not quite a revolutionary situation, though it might have been. The UMT did call a general strike after the shooting started, but carefully limited the walkout to one afternoon. "We could have stayed out a week or more, the way our people were feeling," the UMT's general secretary, Mahjoub Ben Seddik, told me later. "But where would that have led?" As he knew, it might easily have led to a full-blown institutional crisis that he was neither prepared for nor wanted.

Nevertheless, at least some of the rioters had called the monarchy into question for the first time in living memory. Brushing aside Premier Ahmed Bahnini's lame assertion that they were foreign *provocateurs*, Hassan took to the radio for a remarkable talk with his subjects. Speaking in the broadest Arab vernacular and using the intimate "thou," he conceded at once that the rioting had reflected a popular discontent both justified and understandable. But the manner of expressing it, he added, was unworthy of the Moroccans' history and genius.

I cannot permit the law of the jungle to prevail in our civilized country [he went on]. I have personally put at your disposal all the legal means to express your needs: freedom of speech, press, and assembly, a plurality of parties and trade unions, a constitution and parliament. It is unthinkable that children should have been pushed into vandalism and pillage. Is that the way you want to educate your sons? I warn you that once taught to profane the dignity of others, they will not respect you either. As for you professors, intellectuals, do you lack the courage to speak for yourselves instead of hiding behind your pupils? Why did you close the schools and send them into the streets, instead of going out yourselves? Where is your bravery and commonsense? These are not the acts of a thinking intellectual . . . you would be better off illiterate.

Education, unemployment, and hunger were grave problems, Hassan continued, and he would make no lying promises about a brilliant future. The "bitter reality" would require hard work from everybody, particularly those chosen by the people to represent them in parliament.

To you, members of parliament [he concluded] I say: enough of your hollow speeches and vain words. Stop saying things you don't believe yourselves. Stop brandishing slogans about this or that reform, for most of you are totally ignorant of what you're talking about. The essential for each of you has been flattery, not a concern for the general welfare. I myself believe firmly in democracy, but I doubt your faith in it. For if you were conscientious democrats you would not have wasted time in your banalities but would rather have given us laws. In the third year of our constitutional experiment, the Official Bulletin has published only three laws. Who is responsible? The author of the constitution? Those who adopted it by referendum? No, and no again. It is those who apply it.

The issue could hardly have been put more succinctly, if not for one important omission. While Hassan's dilatory parliament can certainly be blamed for this depressing state of affairs, the parliament could have been prodded into action by cabinet ministers whom he is free to appoint and dismiss at will. In the end, responsibility for the Moroccans' suffering lies squarely with the king himself.

Actually, the king is none too free either. Heavy demands are made upon him from all sides: the army, on which the security of the throne depends; the Istiqlal, whose long arm reaches into the court and state bureaucracy at every level; the wealthy pashas with daughters to be married off properly, sons to be placed in suitable positions, and vast estates to protect (the heirs of El Glaoui, the late Pasha of Marrakesh, own 35,000 acres); and the ubiquitous royal family of brothers, sisters, uncles, cousins who, especially when it comes to financial matters, will not yield a finger's breadth of their royal prerogatives.

If Hassan is blocked at every turn, it is often by members of his household. There is scarcely an enterprise worth mentioning here where some relative of his does not hold either a director's seat or a large block of shares. Even the state-owned phosphate mines, whose exports run to $91 million a year—a quarter of Morocco's total—are subcontracted to a private company in which a brother of Hassan's is a major stockholder. With such illustrious examples before them, few cabinet ministers can resist any chance to feather their own nests. While the *fellaheen,* for instance, are still waiting for the government to distribute the 250,000 hectares of land confiscated from the *colons,* at least two cabinet ministers are known to have bought up several thousand hectares of this land privately, with credit from state banks. Dozens of *fellaheen* who used to own that land are still alive to see it pass from the hands of the French, who took it away from them twenty or thirty years ago.

Whether or not Hassan knows of all this (and his courtiers don't always tell him), he cannot afford to let it go on much longer. Popular as he is, he does not personally inspire the almost mystical reverence his father did, and his people have grown more demanding. The Casablanca riots have given him shocking proof of urban unrest, and even the *fellaheen,* the most loyal and least volatile of his subjects, are showing an unexpected flash of spirit. Not only have 100,000 of them joined the UMT's agrarian union, but they staged an unprecedented strike for higher wages during the last harvest—and won it, what's more. Unless he is prepared to fall back on the army, adding another police-state to the long African list, he will have to come up very soon with a more effective and representative government.

The army itself would much prefer the first solution. It began to think in these terms in 1963, shortly after the voters had gone to the polls for the first time and directly after the discovery of a plot by an extremist group in the UNFP to assassinate the king. For either or both reasons, high army officers evidently felt that the monarchy was over-exposed in its novel constitutional setting. . . . Deeply worried by the licentious popular mood . . . [the army] has insisted on an ever-greater role in the administration: seven of the sixteen provincial governors are now regular army officers, three more are reservists, and three hundred junior officers are detailed to the ministry of interior for service in the provincial governments. They would be more than willing to enlarge on these services if Hassan should choose to call on them.

Committed as he is to his democratic experiment, the king would surely regard this as an ignoble defeat. Rather than accept it, he has been trying since March to correct an obvious and possibly fatal flaw in the experiment: his own reluctance, after giving his people all the equipment for a democratic government, to let them use it. His qualms have been justified. None of the existing parties, from the noisy and narrow-minded Istiqlal to the court-ridden FDIC and its minor satellites to the erratic left-wing UNFP, could inspire his full confidence; and few premiers since 1955 have shown an aptitude for energetic and honest leadership. The only one of modest promise was the UNFP's Abdallah Ibrahim, who stepped on so many palace (and French) toes that Mohammed V turned him out in less than two years. The question is whether Hassan can find the fortitude to recall him—or somebody like him.

He has already made some overtures, first by pardoning several UNFP members imprisoned since the 1963 conspiracy, then by opening discreet negotiations with the UNFP for a government of "national union." But the going has not been easy. The party's present leaders, representing a quarter of the electorate . . . would welcome a chance to influence government policy. But Ibrahim refuses to join a cabinet without a clear understanding that the king will merely reign, while an independent government governs. "Anything short of that," he told me, "would simply mean doing things as they've been done for nine years— not better and faster than the French, as we'd hoped, but worse and incredibly slower."

Ibrahim is fully supported in this by his trade-union friends in the UMT, the only organization with deep popular roots in the country. "We cannot go on with a king and premier all in one," says Ben Seddik. "His majesty has held back from making the decisive change for fear of breaking too many eggs. But now that so many heads have been broken, he must not hesitate any longer. If he fails, the future is written in heaven." . . .

Mohammed V, profoundly affected by the Algerian war, had turned sharply leftward in 1960, pulling the most extreme of Africa's nationalist states—the UAR [United Arab Republic], Mali, Guinea, Ghana, and Algerian FLN [National Liberation Front]—into what was known as the Casablanca Group. The group is defunct now, since Hassan has been moving in just the opposite direction. . . . Moroccan foreign policy has been sensible and restrained. Despite an occasional wistful glance at Mauritania, which the Istiqlal insists should be part of a Greater Morocco, Hassan and his foreign minister refrain meticulously from interfering in the affairs of other African states; and in the Organization for African Unity, they strongly oppose interference from other quarters. Their position is moderate in the Arab League, where they recently refused to follow Nasser in breaking with West Germany over Israel. . . . They have sided respectively with East and West in the UN according to the point at issue; and while their relations with the Communist states are cordial, the Russian and Red Chinese embassies in Rabat are expected to remain within the bounds of diplomatic protocol, and they do. The example they set may be mocked in . . . Cairo, but it is levelheaded enough to win growing respect in most other African capitals.

It is also rare enough to merit warm American interest in the future of Hassan and his monarchy. The French are interested too, of course, particularly since they have $3 billion invested here (whereas our own private investments are negligible). But the *colons* are leaving now, and with the future so uncertain when they have gone, Hassan is particularly anxious to avoid overdependence on France. More and more lately, he has been turning to the United States for money, advice, and comprehension. He certainly needs it all, if only because of what might happen to Morocco if he fails.

A MOROCCAN KIDNAPPING [7]

"Is my brother living? Is he dead? Let those who claim to know speak out."

Thus did Mehdi Ben Barka's brother, Abdelkader, wearily appeal on French television . . . for news of the central figure in a trans-Mediterranean scandal that . . . rocked Paris and

[7] From "Ben Barka Case: Why the Abduction?" by Peter Braestrup, correspondent. New York *Times.* p 16. Ja. 23, '66. © 1966 by The New York Times Company. Reprinted by permission.

threatened a break between President de Gaulle and King Hassan II of Morocco.

Mr. Ben Barka, a forty-five-year-old left-wing political exile who had wandered abroad since mid-1963, was kidnapped at noon . . . [in Paris on October 29, 1965].

He was taken by a car from the sidewalk outside a new American-style "drug store" on the Boulevard Saint-Germain-des-Prés on the Left Bank. Involved in the plot against him were French secret agents, French underworld figures and, allegedly, three Moroccan officials headed by the Interior Minister, General Mohammed Oufkir.

Why was Mr. Ben Barka kidnapped?

Was this little, intense, bushy-browed founder of Morocco's left-wing opposition regarded as a political threat to the king? Or was General Oufkir, as Abdelkader Ben Barka charges, trying to cut short a reconciliation between the king and his long-time foe?

The answer lies perhaps in the cruel intricacies of Moroccan politics, a special Arab blend of personal feuds and shifting alliances, of sudden "fraternity" and sudden denunciation.

A Grocer's Son

Mehdi Ben Barka, the son of a grocer, had been an articulate tempestuous fighter in this Byzantine climate much of his life.

He was still a teen-age student of mathematics at a secondary school in his native Rabat when he joined the semiclandestine movement for Moroccan independence from France. . . .

Not long afterward, at the University of Algiers, he became first a member, then president of the Association of North African Students, grouping young nationalist firebrands from Tunisia, Morocco and Algeria.

During this period, he was arrested several times by the French police and was released quickly each time. . . .

When Mr. Ben Barka returned to Rabat in 1943, his fellow Moroccan intellectuals were seething with nationalist fervor, stimulated by allied promises of self-determination and France's wartime defeats.

Moslem high school students refused to attend classes in protest against French rule. Mr. Ben Barka himself took part in street clashes with French riot policemen in Fez and Casablanca.

At the age of twenty-four, ostensibly only a high school teacher of mathematics at Rabat, he became one of the most active leaders of the nationalist Istiqlal (Independence) party.

The Sultan of Morocco, who later became independent Morocco's first king as Mohammed V, chose Mr. Ben Barka as one of the tutors for his young son, Prince Hassan. The prince was to succeed to the throne in 1961.

No lasting bond was created between the bright but fun-loving prince and his austere tutor who was later to attack bitterly the luxurious living habits of independent Morocco's ruling classes.

"Ben Barka's an ambitious man," the prince was reported to have told the radical's friends. "He wants to do too much, and so he won't accomplish anything in the end."

In the fight for independence, Mr. Ben Barka spent more than three years between 1951 and 1954 under house arrest in the Moroccan Sahara, helped reorganize the Istiqlal party and participated in the negotiations in 1955 that led to the end of the French protectorate.

After independence in 1956 he was elected president of the National Consultative Assembly, which became his personal forum if little more.

Although Mr. Ben Barka pledged fidelity to Mohammed V, the king tired of the Assembly's polemics and dissolved it.

Meanwhile Mr. Ben Barka had broken with the conservative wing of Istiqlal, made off with the left wing and founded the National Union of Popular Forces in 1959.

With strong Socialist leanings, vaguely echoing the slogans of the French left, the new party had the support of big-city labor leaders and Morocco's politically active students.

Police Abuses Denounced

While his fellow leftists gained ministerial posts in periodic cabinet shuffles, Mr. Ben Barka fiercely attacked police abuses in fiery Arabic, called for the seizure of French-owned farmland and "the mobilization of Morocco's human resources."

It was Mr. Ben Barka's heyday. He was hailed by left-wing Paris intellectuals and by Moroccan street crowds.

Of the Istiqlal old guard, his former companions and political elders, he would say:

"They talk of a revolution in Morocco. But they only talk. In fact, all they have done is take over power from the French."

Mr. Ben Barka drew the enmity of Rabat conservatives, the army, the Moslem landowners and jealous left-wingers as well.

From 1960 to 1962, he lived in Paris as a kind of semi-exile, studying "econometrics," traveling to Peking, Havana, Cairo and other "revolutionary" capitals. He was deeply impressed by the austere Chinese Communist approach.

"That's the only way an underdeveloped country like ours can grow," he told a friend later.

But in Morocco, where even leaders of the officially banned Communist party build backyard swimming pools, the Peking approach found little but verbal sympathy.

Mr. Ben Barka won election from Rabat to Morocco's short-lived National Assembly in 1963.

Soon afterward, in July, the government unveiled a left-wing "plot" against the king. Mr. Ben Barka happened to be traveling abroad and escaped arrest.

He was sentenced to death twice in absentia—once for allegedly having been involved in the July "plot," and again for publicly having sided in Cairo with Algeria in the brief Algerian-Moroccan border war later in 1963. . . .

Installing his wife, whom he had married in 1949, and four children in Cairo at the Nasser regime's expense, he roamed the "revolutionary" world again.

He became a member of the Communist-backed African-Asian Solidarity Commission in Cairo.

He appeared in Algiers but got little attention from the Algerians despite his sympathy for the then President Ahmed Ben Bella's brand of Arab socialism.

. . . [In 1965] he was put in charge of preparing the tricontinental conference of revolutionists held . . . [in January 1966] in Havana. But it was Moscow and Peking that called the shots, not Mr. Ben Barka.

Back home, as time went on, former Deputy Premier Abderrahim Bouabid and his allies took over as real leaders of the left-wing party that Mr. Ben Barka had founded.

In recent months, they began the traditional undercover dickering with King Hassan II for posts in a new cabinet. Mr. Ben Barka's name dropped out from political gossip.

Meanwhile, shuttling back and forth from Paris to Geneva to his family in Cairo, Mr. Ben Barka also began some undercover reconciliation talks with representatives of the king.

In 1964, he worried aloud to friends about being followed, kidnapped or assassinated by General Oufkir's agents and foreign accomplices. Later, he seemed more optimistic, discussing compromises, "new options," even a possible modus vivendi with the King's regime.

But if his political power had waned, Mr. Ben Barka still had enemies, notably General Oufkir. What is more, after his kidnapping, his old party associates did not raise much public fuss. The royal palace was silent.

As for the urban poor who once cheered Mr. Ben Barka's calls for "social justice" and "the installation of a concrete democracy," they seemed to have all but forgotten him. Only a handful of Moroccan students demonstrated in his name.

AMERICAN BASES IN MOROCCO [8]

In terms of cost-efficiency the great network of abandoned air bases in Morocco would seem an incredible boondoggle. The installations at Nouasseur, Sidi Slimane, Boulhaut and Ben Guerir were operational for little more than a decade and cost a half billion dollars to construct. They have now been handed over to a Moroccan government which has about as much use for them as for a fleet of icebreakers.

[8] From "The Price of Peace Runs High," by C. L. Sulzberger, foreign affairs columnist. New York *Times.* p 30. Ap. 27, '64. © 1964 by The New York Times Company. Reprinted by permission.

From their conception in 1950 to their death last December [1963] the story of the bases is a mixture of crisis construction and crash diplomacy. It produced charges of inefficiency, wastage, congressional inquiries and misunderstandings between the United States, France and Morocco. When the bases teemed with nuclear bombers, General Norstad invited the late Sultan to visit them. He politely declined; despite their enormous size, Morocco didn't even officially acknowledge their existence.

American bomber bases in Moroccco developed suddenly out of the Korean war. Washington feared the Far Eastern battle might lead to world conflict and, in those early days of NATO, we had extremely limited possibilities of delivering atomic weapons to targets in the U.S.S.R. Morocco was still under French suzerainty, so an accord was negotiated between the Truman Administration and the government of France, signed in December 1950. Building contracts were let on a cost-plus, fixed-fee basis.

In 1950 this country was a French protectorate and its sovereign was never consulted in negotiations by either Washington or Paris. As a result, when Morocco gained full independence in 1956, the United States of America had no written understanding with its government acknowledging our presence.

And, as elsewhere in Africa, emotional clamor began for the removal of foreign bases. The United States was in an awkward position because of its lack of tenancy rights. Legally speaking, we had paid the French $500 million for properties which they had no valid right to sell.

Fortunately, changes in strategic techniques coincided with these changes in political reality. NATO's strength had burgeoned; possibilities opened for other bases in Spain; new weapons systems appeared in substance or on drawing boards. History courteously rendered the Moroccan bases unnecessary just as their tenure became embarrassing. In 1959 President Eisenhower promised King Mohammed V we would quit them by this year.

The long runways are now idle, a waste space of almost 50,000 acres sown with cracking concrete beside hangars and repair shops tenanted by bats and pigeons. The $15 million that was fed each year into the Moroccan economy through salaries and disbursements has dried up. Vestigial United States facilities at Kenitra, where Americans linger on to instruct Moroccans or handle communications with our Mediterranean fleet, are under Morocco's flag.

There is talk of turning the principal field at Nouasseur into an international airport but this seems absurd. Existing facilities are adequate for any foreseeable commercial traffic Morocco can expect. Today the famous bases appear only a massive monument to the cold war of the fifties—a latter-day set of pyramids, grand and useless.

Nevertheless, when viewing this barren prospect one cannot forget how recently it served a vital use. No one can say what might have happened in the nervous world of Korea and fledgling NATO had there been no strategic bases in Morocco.

SPANISH SAHARA [9]

One of the older African colonial remnants is Rio de Oro, which in 1958 became the province of Spanish Sahara. By the time the French had finished nibbling at the once extensive Spanish occupation of North Africa, Rio de Oro had shrunk to a desert enclave the size of Britain, with a frontier that was carefully arranged to leave all the mineral wealth and natural harbors in French hands. The loss of Port Étienne and the iron ore east of there was so humiliating that the president of the Spanish commission that ceded them to France in 1900 committed suicide on the way home. In *L'Express* recently a French correspondent suggested that Spain might be willing to sell Rio de Oro in exchange for guarantees for Tetuan and Ceuta and Spain's other footholds in Morocco. If this were actually the case then recent Spanish policy in the Saharan province would be even more inexplicable than it already is.

General Franco has invested an enormous amount of money, nearly . . . [$140 million], in building a capital city, called El Aaiun, in the north of the province. Into this most curious city everything from telegraph poles to doorknobs has been carried

[9] From "Spanish Sahara; Windmills in the Desert." *The Economist* (London). 213:253-4. O. 17, '64. Reprinted by permission.

ashore in amphibious vehicles. The only thing El Aaiun ever had to offer was water, and it was this that persuaded the Spanish government to choose it as the capital of Provincia del Sahara. It used to be a garrison settlement but has now grown to the size of a considerable city. It lies about twenty miles from the sea in a dry river bed and from a distance looks like a long low sprawl of traditional Saharan domed buildings. Once inside El Aaiun, however, one might almost be in Spain. There are policemen on point duty, babies in prams, a casino, more than thirty bars, a local newspaper, a variety of shops, a supermarket—and a huge Roman Catholic church. The main difference is that all the Spaniards there are paid two and a half times what they would get in Spain and are usually on two-year contracts.

Most cities are where they are for some observable reason. El Aaiun has no apparent reason to exist except that the Spanish government willed it into being. The area is so barren that even the soil has to be imported; there is no agriculture, mineral exploitation or industry. The only other town in Provincia del Sahara of any size is Villa Cisneros, and this does not produce anything either. The existence and continuing expansion of El Aaiun is baffling. Perhaps it is necessary as a sort of psychological infrastructure to the future development of the province. Spaniards who are lured into this barren land will certainly need a faithful replica of a Spanish city to restore them at the weekends.

The Spanish began entrenching their position in the Saharan province during the mid-1950's when it was already clear that most other colonial powers in Africa were on the way out. Why Spain chose to do this is unclear. At this time the mineral wealth of Rio de Oro was negligible, so far as anyone knew, and the prospects for establishing any other economic foundation were equally remote. The motive the Spaniards themselves give is not one that it is popular to ascribe to General Franco. According to the governor general of the Sahara the work being done in the province is altruistic, without expectation of material gain: Spain's task, he says, is to develop and raise the standard of living of the Saharan people to match that of the Spaniards at home.

This high-minded declaration is coupled with the promise that whatever wealth the land produces will stay there. Don Quixote is the favorite image used by the Spanish themselves to describe their government's behavior. The Spaniards say they are there with the assent of the local population who certainly seem peaceful and well treated. The nomadic Moors are encouraged to move from place to place at their own wish, provided with free medical services and with a continuous roundelay of the thirty local songs on Radio Sahara. The children are educated along with Spanish children at numerous, new and admirable schools. If they have not got proper clothes or shoes, they get these free as well. The nomads do not get this kind of attention in Mauritania or Morocco, so Spain is understandably popular.

Whether the Spanish taxpayer will ever see anything for his money is a moot point. The oil companies came and went, leaving the impression that there was no oil to be found. The results of the surveys were confidential and an uncomfortable question mark hangs over the deserted oil rigs in the northeast. What has been found in the last year, though, is one of the world's richest deposits of phosphate, with proven reserves estimated at . . . [1 billion] tons. When a new town, railway and new port have been built to exploit this mineral, the Saharan province might begin to repay the stubborn and determined investment the Spaniards are making. Otherwise, however dedicated and unselfish the motive, it is difficult to see how a complex city like El Aaiun can continue in being.

IV. TUNISIA

EDITOR'S INTRODUCTION

Tunisia is, in many respects, just the opposite of Morocco. Where Moroccans tend to be devout Islamists, Tunisians are often skeptical about religious ritual. Where Moroccans are passionate and easy to anger, Tunisians are gentle and take minor disputes in their stride. Where Moroccans speak of the glories of their past, Tunisians become enthusiastic about the modernization of their society. Where Moroccans worry about European ways destroying their traditional Islamic culture, Tunisians rush to embrace everything that is new and Western in origin.

History and geography help explain much of this difference between the two peoples. While Morocco lay rather isolated on the western fringes of the Arab world and developed her own unique culture, Tunisia was at the very crossroads of the Mediterranean. The ancient city of Carthage (now a suburb of Tunis, the Tunisian capital) was once the great rival of imperial Rome. Tunisian merchants spread through Africa, southern Europe and the Middle East. Cargo ships from Spain to Phoenicia set down at Tunisian ports, bringing rare goods and heady ideas to the Tunisians. Tunisians have prided themselves for centuries on being open to the world, on being flexible and on being modern.

Tunisia today, under the leadership of the greatest statesman of the Arab world—Habib Bourguiba—is a testing-ground for an exciting experiment in political and economic development. It is the most modern, the most European, the most democratic, and in many ways the most appealing of the North African states. Tunisia today is very much the product of Bourguiba's vision. He led the nation to independence and he has guided it every step of the way since. To speak of Tunisia is to speak of Bourguiba—and they are both exciting to watch.

In the first article of this section the editors of the *Atlantic* view the phenomenon of Bourguiba's Tunisia. Nora Beloff recounts the progress of Tunisia since independence, and Jean Lacouture, correspondent of the Paris daily *Le Monde,* draws a portrait of Bourguiba. The editors of the *Financial Times* (London) assess Bourguiba's efforts to achieve unification of the Maghreb economy. In the final article John Ardagh reports on the remarkable renaissance of the arts in Tunisia.

BOURGUIBA'S TUNISIA [1]

At home, Tunisian president Habib Bourguiba is immensely popular, while in the rest of the Arab world, he is all too frequently berated as a colonialist jackal or a tool of Zionism. The ostensible reason for the name-calling is that . . . [in March 1965] Bourguiba suggested negotiations with Israel based on the 1947 and 1948 United Nations resolutions on Palestine. However, Nasser has on several occasions made similar suggestions without being called any nasty names by his Arab brethren. Therefore, something else about Bourguiba rankles. It is probably that at heart he considers Tunisia a Western nation, part of the Arab world by geographical accident rather than vocation. He said in a speech last June: "Tunisia freed herself centuries ago from the ties that bound her to Baghdad, Damascus, and Istanbul."

Tunisia has also been freed from the Islamic mystique which other Arab leaders use to stay in power, Nasser most of all. Its basic elements are demagoguery, religious fanaticism, and prestige politics. The great demagogic hoax is that the Arab world is going to rise as one to reconquer Palestine. As Bourguiba points out, the anti-Israel crusade has been imminent for seventeen years.

In reality, the Arab leaders are bent on preserving the status quo which keeps them in power. The liberation of Palestine, far from being a program of action, becomes nothing more than a propaganda device to maintain the illusion of Arab unity. If it went beyond that, the illusion would crumble under the weight of Arab differences and lack of preparedness.

What most annoys Bourguiba about his fellow leaders is their hypocrisy. Publicly they attack his Palestine position, but privately they admit he is right. King Hussein of Jordan told Bourguiba . . . : "Our great mistake was to ask for Britain's de-

[1] From "The Atlantic Report: Tunisia." *The Atlantic.* 216:24+. N. '65. Reprinted by permission.

parture from Palestine. At least then Jewish immigration was limited and the Palestinians remained on their land." Bourguiba replied, "So now we have come to the point of regretting British colonialism in Palestine."

Religious fanaticism is another Arab instrument of political control which Bourguiba has scorned. In most Arab countries, the Moslem festival of Ramadan (which celebrates the revelation of the Koran in the ninth month of the lunar year) is strictly observed. Anyone who breaks the daylight fast, even by smoking a cigarette, can be fined or arrested. The result is serious absenteeism in factories and offices. Last year, on the third day of Ramadan, Bourguiba drank a glass of orange juice in the middle of a speech to a group of workers. "Eat or fast," he said, "take your choice, as long as production does not suffer." He has also advised his people against making the annual pilgrimage to Mecca because it affects the country's balance of payments.

And while other overpopulated Arab countries prohibit birth control (in Morocco and Algeria the French colonial anticontraceptive laws are still enforced), Bourguiba began a highly successful family-planning experiment a year ago. The strong opposition in Moslem families to contraception had to be overcome. The man considers a large number of children the tangible expression of his masculinity as well as an eventual source of wealth. For the woman, the birth of a child is a festive event which all her female relatives attend. . . .

After a year-long propaganda program which reminded Tunisian women that there is nothing in the Koran against birth control, family resistance is weakening. Health officials plan to administer . . . [contraceptives] to 50,000 women a year for the next four years. They hope to treat most Tunisian women who have had more than three children and keep the population under 5 million.

Unlike his Arab neighbors, Bourguiba is not interested in military might. Tunisia's 1965 budget spends 6 per cent on defense and 25 per cent on education, while it costs Nasser half a million dollars a day to finance his military expedition in the Yemen, and Algeria earmarks one fifth of its budget for its army.

"If Tunisia were attacked," says a Western ambassador, "its 18,000-man army would be able to resist just long enough for Bourguiba to lodge a complaint with the Security Council."

Nor does Bourguiba see much point in prestige industries. Nasser has poured millions of dollars into the production of an Egyptian automobile, the Ramses, and has to import steel to manufacture it. Tunisia imports cars, but has just opened a steel mill to process its small quantity of high-grade iron ore. Habib Bourguiba, Jr., Tunisian foreign minister, says, "We would be happy to sell Nasser our steel for the production of his car."

Despite all this unorthodox behavior, Bourguiba has shown that he is the only Arab leader with a strong enough political base to challenge Nasser's oracular commands. When Nasser broke diplomatic relations with West Germany, he naturally expected the rest of the Arab world to emulate him. Only Bourguiba did not comply, because preserving the trade agreements Tunisia has with West Germany was more important to him than placating Nasser.

Indeed, it can be said that aside from Egypt, Tunisia is the only viable Arab state. The regimes of Syria, Iraq, and Yemen exist only with the support of Nasser; Kings Hassan of Morocco, Hussein of Jordan, and Mohammed Idris of Libya are forced to align themselves with Nasser because they cannot count on the complete allegiance of their own people. In Saudi Arabia and Kuwait, political stability is bound to oil interests. Algeria has yet to show that it can escape what its own leaders disparagingly call "Congolization." And Lebanon's pluralist society is under constant pressure from a pro-Nasser minority.

And yet, what is Tunisia? A country which seems to have been created to prove Arnold Toynbee's theory that civilizations are founded in defiance of nature—small, underdeveloped, half Saharan waste and half coastal farmland. "Tunisia," a foreign ministry official explained, "has no oil, no minerals, no coal, no gas, twenty-two kinds of poisonous snakes, and four kinds of scorpions." Its annual budget, $160 million, is less than what General Motors spends on advertising.

It is not powerful enough to play Eastern and Western blocs against each other for aid, as Egypt has done. Its weight is scarcely felt in the international scale. Its importance lies perhaps in the fact that a country which has been independent for ten years can point to political stability and economic improvement instead of chaos, coups, corruption and economic bewilderment, the lot of too many other emerging nations.

Tunisia's progress is related to its manageable size, which has made it possible for Bourguiba to operate the country like a family business. No aspect of national life is unworthy of his paternal attention. On a recent Sunday afternoon he scolded Tunisia's two best soccer teams after a championship match. "The game was faulty because of lack of coordination," he said. "The play was disjointed and choppy. I hope the quality of the playing will improve and that in the future you will play with your heads as well as your legs."

Bourguiba spends three months of each year inspecting his domain. In each town and village, he knows the principal families by name. He listens to grievances and suggests improvements. Bourguiba's visits have been as responsible for slum clearance and school construction as have his economic programs. The other side of the "Supreme Combatant's" personality is that he cannot tolerate resistance to the team spirit.

Bourguiba also keeps tight control over the Socialist Destourian Party, the country's only legal political party. Its 300,000 members spread his gospel, give the good example, and denounce heretics. The gospel is socialism, but it is less a doctrine than the answer of a pragmatist to the aspirations of the masses. Bourguiba's socialism is simply the belief that the state must step in where the individual falters. Thus, he does not recognize the absolute right to private property. "It's a way of saying that society respects your right as long as you don't abuse it," he says. "No one will take your property as long as you are working."

State departments control mining, industry, agriculture, fishing, and tourism, and in the last few months there has been a tendency to increase state control in other areas. Bourguiba does not want a strong labor union questioning his decisions and disrupting his four-year economic plans with demands for higher wages. He is encouraging the development of party cells in factories and offices to sap the authority of the union.

At the same time, Bourguiba's state-controlled economy is trying hard to attract private capital, with some success. Krupp is interested in building a shipyard, and in the last year, a Danish factory for diesel engines and a Swedish factory for superphosphates have opened. In underdeveloped countries, the borders of capitalism and socialism are often blurred. When Tunisia sought a long-term loan from the International Monetary Fund in 1964, the loan was granted on the condition that the dinar be devaluated and that wages be kept at the same level; this was not Socialist but banker's *dirigisme*.

Tunisia's main economic problem is that it has little to export besides wine, olives, wheat, vegetables, and flowers; it finds it difficult to sell its products to European countries, which already have Common Market agricultural agreements. Until last year, Tunisia could sell its wine and its wheat to France at the interior French market price. But in May 1964, Bourguiba abruptly nationalized 850,000 acres of foreign-owned land, 90 per cent of which belonged to the French. France suspended its $20 million-a-year aid and its preferential trade agreements. It was a serious blow to the economy, for wine makes up one fifth of Tunisia's exports. In 1964 it brought in more than $20 million, but by the first quarter of 1965, only 10 per cent of the 1964 vintage had been sold, and there is no market for wine in a Moslem country.

Because it has to import such staples as dairy products, meat, and most manufactured goods, Tunisia has an unfavorable trade balance. In 1964, for example, it imported $220 million worth of goods and exported about half that much. It will be years before Tunisia can successfully diversify the colonial, one-market economy inherited from the French, and in the meantime, the economy is relying heavily upon American aid. As President Johnson has noted, two thirds of United States aid goes to seven countries, and Tunisia is one of them. Since the beginning of the aid program in 1957, Tunisia has received a total of $413.8 million. The gross aid in 1964 was about $100 per capita, the highest in Africa, although lower than Jordan ($192) and Israel ($450).

Bourguiba's Secretary of State for Planning and the Economy, Ahmed Ben Salah, left for Washington last May 9 [1965] and returned to Tunis eleven days later with assurances that the level of United States aid would be maintained. Tunisia then embarked on an $800 million four-year plan, about 40 per cent of which will be financed by foreign (mainly United States) aid. Tunisia hopes to maintain a rate of growth of 6.5 per cent a year and raise the per capita income from $77 to $100 a year by 1970.

United States aid pays for such varied projects as the construction of a law school and a long-range reforestation program; 45 million trees have already been planted, mainly Aleppo pines and eucalyptus, in the hope of restoring Tunisia to the fertile times when North Africa could be crossed in the shade.

Tunisia also has the largest Peace Corps contingent of any African country. Its director was the butt of some ridicule when he arrived two years ago because he insisted on riding a bicycle everywhere, which the Tunisians interpreted as a concession to their underdevelopment. . . . After showing what it can do, however, the Peace Corps has been given high marks, and its tractor-repair teams have been particularly successful.

Skeptics attribute Bourguiba's solid pro-Western stance to the amount of aid he receives from Washington. But beyond the helping hand it offers, Bourguiba has been drawn to the West out of disappointment with its alternatives. He turned away from communism when he was a young revolutionary struggling against French colonialism.

What Marx wrote was true of the nineteenth-century industrial revolution in England and France [he says]. It was true in that conjuncture. But afterward, things were not that way. His previsions for the proletarian revolution were not realized. There was no class struggle. I saw man as a moral being who escapes the laws of rank. I wanted to lift him in a climate where there would be no oppression and no chaos, where the balance between liberty and anarchy would be kept.

Bourguiba has also found pan-Arabism and pan-Africanism a burden. Those of his policies which have been prompted by the fear that he was not keeping up with the revolutionary pace of his neighbors, such as nationalization of foreign-owned lands, have proved economically disastrous. In many instances, Tunisia's efforts to maintain Arab or African solidarity have backfired. "Since we are no longer able to use ships on the Arab League blacklist," an official explained, "we have to pay more for freight, which often has to change ships at Genoa."

When Nasser calls him an American stooge, Bourguiba replies: "Don't tell me that to be a good Arab I have to fight America." While other Arab leaders visit Moscow for guidance, Bourguiba visits Scandinavia. He finds that the Scandinavian countries have problems similar to his own and practice the kind of socialism he would like to adopt.

Bourguiba is fond of saying that Tunisia is at the same time nonaligned and "the best friend the United States has in Africa."

INDEPENDENCE: TUNISIAN STYLE [2]

Are the people really better off now that the French have gone? The answer is a circumspect yes. The loss of capital and skills has been severe, but this has been made up for by the release of energies and enthusiasms of the entire Tunisian educated classes, previously engaged in obstructing the French. It is true that in real terms the basic wage is slightly lower than it was under French rule. . . . On the other hand, the worst-paid workers, particularly on the farms, are receiving more, and there is relief for the unemployed, more housing and more schools, plus the intangible advantage for the people of feeling that Tunisia is at last being run with, for, and by Tunisians.

The old French view, so often expressed when I visited Tunisia ten years ago, that Tunisia was too poor, too devoid of natural resources, and the people too indolent to manage a modern state, has proved unfounded.

Most of the Europeans have gone (a trickle are coming back, but on a contractual rather than a colonial basis), and it would be hard to find a Tunisian who really regrets them.

[2] From "Tunisians Found Better Off," by Nora Beloff, *Observer* correspondent. New York *Herald Tribune* (Paris edition). D. 25, '63. Copyright Observer Foreign News Service. Reprinted by permission.

Many leaders of post-colonial states have tried to compensate for their initial political and economic troubles—and Tunisia has many—by adopting blustering and revolutionary forms of nationalism. Partly for ideological, but also perhaps for temperamental reasons, Mr. Bourguiba has adopted the opposite course. His compatriots proudly call him "the Supreme Combatant." But his natural inclination is for compromise rather than conflict.

His policies of studious moderation and unideological pragmatism are in fact so unique in the newly independent states that a special word, "Bourguibism," has been invented to describe them.

At home, Bourguibism is a kind of little-by-little Fabian socialism. Tunisia is—emphatically in principle and embryonically in practice—a welfare state with full employment. In fact the country is far too poor to provide anything approaching Western standards, but the aims are identical. The unemployed are gathered into groups and put on to public works—digging, road repairing, planting—in return for board and bed. There is higher priority for education than in any other Arab state—25 per cent of the national budget, and the number of children at school has doubled since the French left.

There are also family allowances to keep the Tunisians above the hunger line, but they are relentlessly turned off after the fourth child. Tunisia has no military yearnings and therefore no incentive for decorating especially prolific mothers. On the contrary, it wants no more babies than it can feed. Contraception is officially encouraged, and the government authorizes sterilization, though not abortion.

Bourguibism provides for a fixed economy, with the state controlling "the commanding heights" and quite a lot of the hillocks as well, but also doing its best to induce the chary Tunisian moneyed classes to change their habits and invest their wealth productively. The semicapitalist regime might seem to bring Bourguibism nearer the Western type of social democracy. On the other hand, the political machinery, founded entirely on the single-party system, is much closer to communism.

The Neo-Destour party, closely modeled on the Communist pattern, has totalitarian control over press and propaganda and serves as a government agency to organize popular participation in national affairs. Mr. Bourguiba himself is the leader of the party as well as the government, and it is a tribute to his political genius that he has managed to install and preserve a single-party system without recourse to the brutal methods of a police state.

Communism itself was outlawed . . . [in 1962], but only a handful of the Communists then arrested for anti-regime activities are still in prison. None of the rightist opposition is under arrest, and the deposed Bey died quietly in his bed. The immense revenues of his large family were cut off, but they were encouraged to work their passage back. One of the cousins, I am told, is now a policeman.

The former trade-union leader, Ahmed Ben Salah, once regarded as a possible rival to Mr. Bourguiba for power and now working as his Minister of Finance and Planning (most potential rivals have been given key jobs), told me that the educated Tunisians know they cannot afford to fight each other. "We are too scared of being infected by what we people here call the Middle Eastern virus," he said.

Mr. Bourguiba's socialism is not of the kind that frightens off foreign capital. . . . The problem is only to provide sound investment projects in a country short of skills and resources.

In fact, the ten-year development plan on which the government's hopes of expansion rely depends for as much as 50 per cent on foreign loans and grants. Mr. Ben Salah told me that for the first three years the money is already committed. Mr. Bourguiba confidently said: "Come back and see us in ten years' time."

Mr. Bourguiba has, in fact, filled the vacuum left by the French by making his country into what looks to the outside world—including the French—like a politically and economically sound place to put their money into.

TUNISIA'S GEORGE WASHINGTON [3]

Last March [1965] on a tour of the Middle East, President Habib Bourguiba of Tunisia visited a refugee camp for Palestinian Arabs. Afterward, he remarked that "the search for peace" was becoming urgent for these poor people. He also said that it was essential to contemplate "cooperation" between Arabs and Israelis.

The words "peace" and "cooperation" produced an uproar in the Arab press, much of which, as Bourguiba says, is "more Nasserian than Nasser." The Tunisian Embassy in Beirut arranged a press conference which turned into a mass debate. . . . His eyes flashing, the color of dawn over the Mediterranean, Bourguiba stood up to the assembly.

You can continue to drug the masses with provocative slogans and unfulfilled promises [he told them] but at the rate things have been going for the last seventeen years, the Arabs have not made an inch of headway. It is time to abandon demagogy. War with Israel is impossible. The great powers, guarantors of the Jewish state, would stop us. I propose a solution without either winners or losers, for—and let us not forget this —we are at present in the position of losers.

A courageous political strategist, Bourguiba is often a poor tactician. He is determined to bring the Arabs back from the wasteland of mysticism and eloquence to the domain of political reality. His scheme is to have them accept the partition agreements of 1948 with Israel, thus getting the law—and world opinion—on their side. It is a bold and liberal idea, and a clever one.

But Bourguiba is tactless in his choice of words. For example, that "losers" irritated the Arabs. His plan is going to be thwarted by this error in tactics. Already it has put him at loggerheads with the most powerful leader in the Arab world, President Gamal Abdel Nasser of Egypt. Still, it gives the measure of the Tunisian leader and reveals his personality: pride, sensitivity, a passion for independence, nonconformity and realism—that is to say, a realism that fits the end pursued to the means at one's disposal. . . .

[3] From "Bourguiba: Portrait of a Nonconformist," by Jean Lacouture, correspondent of *Le Monde* (Paris). New York *Times Magazine.* p 26-7+. Je. 6, '65. © 1965 by The New York Times Company. Reprinted by permission.

Several years ago, one of the best-informed British diplomats said to me of Bourguiba: "I've never seen anyone outside of France so near to France. I've never seen anyone in the Arab world so remote from the Arabs."

Bourguiba knows France well and remains attached to her intellectually. *Le Monde* is the paper he reads most carefully, his jokes keep the flavor of the Latin Quarter, half of his best friends live in France.

An incident last month gave dramatic proof of his desire for French friendship. Tunisia had just nationalized farm land, much of it owned by French citizens. Bourguiba sent a personal message to President Charles de Gaulle assuring him that the action was not meant to offend "either France or her president." For a man of Bourguiba's sensitive pride, it was an explanation that must have cost him dear.

Yet Bourguiba is not to be counted a 100 per cent Francophile. His policy is essentially Tunisian, no longer founded on the Tunis-Paris axis, but on the Maghreb-Europe complex. . . . He is also anxious to maintain friendship with America and at the same time not to cut Tunisia off from the Eastern Arab world.

His relations with the Eastern Arabs are colored by an experience of some twenty years ago. The French, who had already imprisoned him several times for his nationalist activities, were again feeling fed up, and he fled secretly aboard a small boat at a remote Tunisian beach. He landed in Libya, and went on to Cairo and other Middle Eastern capitals, where he remained in exile for more than two years. He retains unpleasant memories of his stay in the heart of the Arab world. As an orator he knows the dramatic power of words, but he wants them to correspond to realities. What he could not bear in the Middle East was the contradiction between words and action. . . .

Bourguiba derives his political skill from his modest origins, which forced him to work hard in order to win his lawyer's diploma; from his stay in Paris, where he was a brilliant student at the School of Political Science. He owes it, also, to his experience as founder, then leader, of a party, to his prison sentences (1934-36, 1938-42, 1952-55), when he had time to think things out thoroughly, and to his interminable negotiations with some of the most capable French statesmen and diplomats, from Pierre Mendès-France to Edgar Faure, from Roger Seydoux to Georges Gorse, and to his international contacts from Washington to New Delhi.

As an example of his political style, here is a scene that I remember:

Bourguiba is watching the crowd massed in a square in Tunis to listen to him. It is midday during the month of Ramadan, a month of rigid fasting from dawn to sunset, required by the Moslem religion. He takes a glass, pours some orange juice into it and drinks slowly, his magnetic glance still fixed on the wondering people. He knows that he is taking a risk, for conservatives are numerous. But by this gesture of challenge to tradition he wishes to dramatize emancipation. He then delivers a long explanation of the duties of a believer who no longer observes the rites. The duty now, he says, is to be aware of the need to struggle against poverty and build a stable country. "The holy war is no longer against the infidel, but against underdevelopment," Bourguiba exclaims.

There are two men within him. First, a Mediterranean realist, one of those who founded the Phoenician trade posts, made the laws of the Greek cities and built the Roman empire. This man is the inventor of "Bourguibism"—a philosophy that might be described roughly as (1) believing in realism, the substitution of politics for self-delusion; (2) not trying to do everything at once, as in Tunisia's dealings with France; (3) being conscious of the bonds between Tunisia and both Europe and the West in general; and (4) above all, adapting the end to the means. "When I have to get a sideboard through a door too small for it, I prefer to take the sideboard to pieces rather than pull down the wall." This is Bourguiba's favorite formula. He has taken the Tunisian sideboard to pieces when faced by French colonialism, and by Egyptian imperialism. Now he is apparently trying to dismantle it in front of Israel's wall. Perhaps, in fact, he is the one man for the Jewish state to dread. Certainly, Israel has more cause to fear a comparatively restrained opponent with a record of getting things done than wild shouters whose policies have no chance of being put into practice.

But this realist who knows that Rome was not built in a day is at the same time a tribune who sets the crowds in the forum vibrating. This statesman, whose contribution to contemporary Arab history will probably prove to have been the substitution of politics for prophecy, can transform himself into a prophet—into a muezzin—and declaim in so vibrant a voice that his own eloquence supplants his political ends. Sometimes he forgets himself and says things which go too far. Then, since, unlike other Arab leaders, he does not want to create too wide a gap between words and acts, he finds himself dragged into an adventure which he has possibly not foreseen. . . .

To avoid the danger of seeing your prophetic words sink into oblivion, you must not be alone. Your must have constructed a system which may be able to resist your death. Bourguiba is not alone, because he has built up the sole truly coherent party of the Arab world, the Neo-Destour, which . . . became the Destourian Socialist party, ("destour" means constitution). In thirty years, this weapon against French ascendancy has been transformd into an organism of government—and has survived that test, which destroyed or divided the Egyptian Wafd, the Syrian Baath, the Algerian FLN [National Liberation Front] and the Moroccan Istiqlal.

Bourguiba's party has been through only one serious crisis, that of 1955-56, when Salah Ben Youssef, secretary general, rebelled and denounced the Bourguiba strategy of "stages." Ben Youssef found himself in exile; finally he was assassinated in Germany under mysterious circumstances.

Apart from this sanguinary episode, the history of the Neo-Destour is that of a group of competent men directed by a leader of exceptional prestige, and acknowledging his supreme authority. Bourguiba is undoubtedly a despot, but an enlightened one. And his party organization is such that Tunisia is the only country, except for the U.A.R., in this part of the world where a government order is certainly transmitted to the villages—and probably carried out.

The "Supreme Commander's" general staff comprises four principal members. First, Bahi Ladgham—tall, solid, going gray, silent—he stands for stability. As secretary of state in the president's cabinet and minister of defense, he is the heir presumptive. It is he who knows all the dossiers, and who works twelve hours a day. He lacks charm and is not close to the people. But perhaps Tunisia is waiting for someone austere and reserved.

Many people would prefer the president's charming son, Habib Jr., who is minister of foreign affairs. "Bibi," former Ambassador to Rome, then to Paris, then to Washington, has countless friends in the West. His wife and he were personal friends of the Kennedy family. He is popular, but very young—not yet forty—and is considered rather "rightist" in a political set-up where Socialist influence is growing with the pressure of the rising generation.

Taïeb Mehiri has been the irremovable minister of the interior for nearly ten years. He knows everything about everyone, is energetic, is a fine organizer, is influential in the party and has the approval of the left and the Arab wing. But he is too taciturn to be popular with the crowds and suffers from a grave illness which limits his field of action.

Ahmed Ben Salah, younger, brilliant and now recovered from a long period of disgrace (incurred in 1956, when, as leader of the unions, he refused to hand them over to the authority of the party), controls all sectors of the Tunisian economy. He represents the "opening to the left" and the intellectual classes. But he is distrusted by the senior cadres who still control the party.

Bourguiba remarked recently: "Democracy's problem is that of the succession." He is preparing it carefully, persuaded—like de Gaulle—that he has no real heir, that power will have to be split into several balanced sectors.

However brilliant Bourguiba's career, it has experienced several serious setbacks. He is often reproached with his failure to come to an understanding with the Algerian and Moroccan leaders in order to bring about a union of the Maghreb. He is considered to have had as much responsibility as General de Gaulle in the tragic misunderstanding of Bizerte—the impact of two proud men. [In 1960 the Tunisians attacked the French base at Bizerte and suffered heavy losses in the counterattack. At the request of the UN France later abandoned the base.—Ed.] And still another grievance against him is his excessive sensitivity toward Egypt, which has widened the gap between Tunisia and an important center of culture, and has cut Tunisia off from profitable alliances.

More generally, Bourguiba's critics say that he acts too much as a dictator—at least, his system is too centralized—that he stifles initiative and will not allow full discussion of a subject. On the other hand, they say that his recent initiative in social and economic problems—he has put down polygamy, given legal equality to women, abolished child labor and paved the way for agrarian socialism—goes no further than paternalism.

What are the forces that drive him: There is the wish to give Tunisia a standing greater than its small size (4 million people) and feeble resources (wine, dates, grain, phosphates) would suggest. There is a desire to rescue from destitution more than 50 per cent of a people of whom he likes to think himself the father. Because Tunisia is small and poor, he feels he has to make a great din to have it taken seriously.

Bourguiba unquestionably loves Tunisia passionately. He also loves his own image. A recent incident shows that his taste for grandeur can prevail over political interest. While his declarations about Israel were earning him a thousand insults in the Arab press, the French magazine *Réalités* published an interview with Nasser supporting almost the same point of view. That should have made Bourguiba "safe." One of his aides rushed to show him the article but Bourguiba was only annoyed. "What's come over Nasser?" the President of Tunisia demanded. He had been robbed of the glory of being the only one to dare speak the truth.

Bourguiba's supporters insist that his personality has raised Tunisia to a far higher international level than its feeble resources would normally permit; that his rationalism gives his country the role of a pilot nation in the search for an Arab-Moslem civilization adapted to the modern world; and that, thanks to the foundation and progressive consolidation of the Neo-Destour party, Tunisia possesses the cadres and the discipline which make it the best-governed country of the Third World.

He will never make a great power of Tunisia. But an outsider may observe that his patriotism and his talent, summed up in the one word "Bourguibism"—which will remain a synonym for realism—have made of Tunisia one of the laboratories where the men of the second half of the twentieth century are seeking the solution to a major problem—the relations between great industrial powers and peoples in the process of development.

A MAGHREB COMMON MARKET? [4]

Bourguiba's motives for supporting the Maghreb ideal [of economic cooperation] are primarily political. He hopes to extend Tunisian influence along the North African coast, and believes that Tunisia can avoid being swallowed by its burly, more aggressive neighbor. But he is also sure that Tunisia would derive economic advantages from closer cooperation with Algeria.

Free trade would assist Tunisia's very ambitious program of industrialization, by opening a market of 20 million people instead of a mere 4 million, and joint planning would enable the three countries to develop larger individual plants.

The biggest single investment in the country, the steel industry . . . might well have been larger if there had been easy access to Algeria; as it is the project is considered to be useful, in that it saves foreign exchange. A variety of other industrial projects would undoubtedly have been planned on different lines if relations with Algeria had been closer—for instance, the 50,000-ton sugar mill at Beja, the 1-million-ton oil refinery at Bizerte, and the esparto pulp plant at Kasserine. . . .

Cooperation with Morocco in, perhaps, marketing and research, might well have led to some changes in Tunisia's only large export industry, the mining and enrichment of phosphate

[4] From "Will Bourguiba's Ideal Come to Life?" *Financial Times* (London). D. 12, '63. Reprinted by permission.

deposits in the southern desert—Morocco is an even larger producer. The prospects of the industry are good and the head of . . . Sfax Gafsa [Company], M. Abbassi, states that production is rising at the rate of over 10 per cent a year. Phosphate enrichment has attracted the only large private foreign investment to come to the country since independence in 1956, the $6 million share of the Swedish firm, Forenade, in the plant at Sfax. . . .

It might be thought that Algeria's poor economic performance since independence and disposition to violence would discourage Tunisia. But Bourguiba clearly believes that this is only a temporary phase and the result of the French withdrawal.

There is certainly little concern in Tunis that foreign aid sources will be scared away by a move towards Algeria. Foreign governments appear to place considerable faith in Bourguiba's firm leadership; and there has never been any doubt about the President's strong attachment to the ideal of Maghreb unity. The United States has virtually underwritten the early stages of the ten-year plan with a $180 million loan, one of the most generous civil aid programs in the entire United States foreign aid budget. . . . And the Russians are sponsoring one faculty of the new university at Tunis, as are the Americans and the French—as well as providing some technical aid.

Western governments thus appear to accept that "Bourguibism" is very much alive—though many observers argued that it had died at the time of the Bizerte "accident" (as Tunisians prefer to call it). The austere, pro-Western policies supported by Bourguiba and other top leaders like M. Mongi Slim, the foreign minister, and M. Nouira, the governor of the Central Bank, appear to have been firmly maintained.

Nor does it seem likely that closer relations with Algeria will discourage private foreign investors. For there has always been a strong tendency to associate the two countries in Europe, and to assume that what goes for one applies to the other as well. While firing could still be heard on the border it was not, perhaps, surprising that private investors were chary.

Foreign investors should, in fact, be impressed rather than the reverse if cooperation increases in the Maghreb. For it should be read as a sign that hot-headed nationalism is on the wane. As a result the Tunisians could find it easier to attract foreign funds into the development of their long beaches and oases for tourism. So far no foreign interest has been willing to buy an hotel in Tunisia; and Tunisia searched in vain for a foreign owner for the $5.6 million Tunis Hilton . . . built by the U.K. [United Kingdom] firm, Cementation. The interest which breaks the ice might get excellent terms, and obtain exceptional opportunities since the government has a program to make Tunisia the fastest-growing tourist area within easy reach of Western Europe.

President Bourguiba believes that if there is to be unity in the Maghreb then progress must be made soon, before the differences harden.

THE ARTS IN TUNISIA [5]

When I was in Tunisia recently, I saw the beginning of a new experiment that seems to be the first of its kind in Africa or the Middle East. In a white villa amid cypress trees, on the coast near Tunis, the Tunisian have opened an International Cultural Center, where scholars and creative artists from East and West can meet and exchange ideas. The aim is to help to bridge some of the gap of ignorance and suspicion that exists between European and Arab cultures. It is something that many educated Tunisians feel strongly about. Today, throughout the Arab world, they see the reawakening of Arab civilization after centuries of decline; and they want a platform where they can express this to Europe. They also want to keep contact with European ideas and art—especially with French culture, which has given them so much. So for them the new center is a step towards fulfilling President Bourguiba's ideal that "Tunisia must form a cultural bridge between East and West." It is a phrase I heard continually from Tunisians. "Our country," they told me, "is an open window on the world." Other nations, too, have this kind of ideal—but nowhere else is it so much an article of faith. The Tunisians, as everyone finds, are a remarkably gentle and un-xenophobic people, with a tolerance that one does not

[5] From an article by John Ardagh, *Observer* correspondent. *The Listener* (London). p 792-4. N. 19, '64. Reprinted by permission.

always associate with Arabs. They are even called *"les femmes du monde arabe."* Maybe it is because they had been occupied by almost every Mediterranean power in turn, from Phoenicians to French, and so have become a more fully integrated racial mixture than most Arabs. "Above all," they tell you, "we are Mediterraneans. That is why we feel close to the French. We are especially suited by history and geography for the role of cultural mediators."

Their new Center, at the chic resort of Hammamet, southeast of Tunis, is supported and financed by the Tunisian government and by the Ford and Gulbenkian foundations. But it is more or less privately run by a shy Anglo-Lebanese scholar called Cecil Hourani. . . . Bourguiba bought him an elegant villa as headquarters for the Center, which opened officially in July with a Pan-Arab production of *Othello* in Arabic—the main Arab contribution to Shakespeare year. Each summer there will be a modest arts festival, drawing talent from Europe and the Arab world and making use of a spectacular new open-air theatre by the beach, where part of the auditorium swivels round at the press of a button to provide a natural change of scene. For the rest of the year the Center is open for conferences, concerts, and private visits. . . . An international symposium has been held on Mediterranean music, and another is planned soon on Arab architecture.

All this I found stimulating and exciting. But there are great difficulties. The gulf between European and Arab cultures is very real, and building that cultural bridge is not going to be easy. Arab civilization has suffered from a long neglect and is still not readily equipped for an equal confrontation with the West. For instance, it has virtually no theatre tradition. Arab music has little in common with Western classical music. Arab literature and philosophy of the past hundred years are meager compared with Europe's. Many Tunisians realize this. Often they find it easier to learn from Europe than to express their own culture to Europe. And most European intellectuals and artists, unless they are specifically Arabists, may not feel they have much to learn from modern Arab culture. Gone are the days when people like

Burton, T. E. Lawrence, and Gide looked in the mystic East for a projection of their own Western complexities.

All this may sound harsh. But I think it is true, and many Tunisians would admit it. It is a situation that can only be changed gradually, by a long period of mass education and national development. So, much though I admire all that Mr. Hourani is doing for intellectual contact with the West, I was even more impressed by the mass *popular* reforms, social and cultural, of the Tunisian government. Under President Bourguiba this government is omnipresent and autocratic—but as benevolent and enlightened as any in Africa. It is trying, deliberately, to forge a modern Tunisian cultural identity out of the mixed elements of French colonial heritage and the older national traditions and personality which Tunisians feel the French buried and distorted.

Consider the theatre. There is little Arab theatre tradition, as we know it, largely because narrow interpretations of the Koran put a ban on "representation." But now, with religious taboos removed in Tunisia, the government is trying to create a tradition. It has set up new amateur drama groups in several towns, and has started weekly drama classes in many secondary schools. Bourguiba says: "We want to make the theatre part of people's daily lives." Emancipation of women helps. In the holy city of Kairouan, last bastion of Moslem conservatism, I saw a girl of eighteen taking part in an amateur drama rehearsal; by Kairouan standards this was a social revolution unthinkable more than a year or two back.

Tunisia's leading actor-director, Ali Ben Ayed, has had some success in Tunis and other towns in wooing popular audiences to Arabic adaptations of Molière, Camus, and Shakespeare. He and other directors have to rely heavily on foreign material. There are few Arabic plays, owing to the lack of tradition, though some good modern ones are now being written in Egypt and Lebanon. Extreme nationalists tend to criticize Ben Ayed for using foreign plays rather than doing more to stimulate Tunisian playwrights. He and the government argue that only by first building up popular drama in schools and clubs can you create a natural climate for local playwrights.

The same applies to music. In an ornate Arab palace of Kairouan's ancient *medina* [native quarter], while the girl of eighteen was acting in one room, in another I listened to a troupe of musicians practicing *malouf*. This is Tunisia's classical music, which was taken by the Moors into Spain and back many centuries ago, and has links with *flamenco* though it sounds more like plainsong. It is very popular, and *malouf* groups have been springing up everywhere under government sponsorship. It is melodious but, to Western ears, rather monotonous. The Tunisians are proud of it, and the government is trying to develop it at the same time as increasing the teaching of Western classical music in Tunisian schools. Bourguiba's son . . . told me he thinks it is possible to appreciate both types of music, with practice, incredibly different though they are. But, for the moment, the number of Tunisians who really enjoy, say, Mozart or Beethoven is very small. Mr. Hourani has a fine new orchestra that plays Western music at Hammamet and Tunis—but the audiences are mostly European and the players entirely so.

The palace I visited in Kairouan is one of a chain of Maisons de la Culture that the government has set up even in quite small towns. Here, film shows, folklore, and handicrafts are all booming. In Kairouan I found the Neo-Destour (government) Party offering locally an annual £500 [$1400] poetry prize! And in Tunis the young minister of culture, Mr. Klebi, said to me:

We lay special emphasis on popular arts. We know that their strict aesthetic value is often slight, but they are close to the people, and we are building up Tunisian culture from the grass roots. It is no use imposing operas from Paris. After all, we have a hard task to raise the prestige of the arts in a country where theatre, for instance, has always been associated with debauchery. . . .

This policy goes closely with the government campaign, since independence eight years ago, to modernize the Moslem religion. Mr. Bourguiba, junior, told me: "We are trying to get back to the sources of Islam, which later teachings have obscured. In reality it is a very flexible religion, well adapted to the modern world." The government's approach to Islam, I found, is remarkably pragmatic. It has closed down the old Islamic college of Zitouna, run by the mullahs, and it now teaches Islamic thought in a much more secular way, as a branch of philosophy at Tunis University. It has even waged a campaign to stop Ramadan—the month of daylight fasting—from harming people's work. It is now illegal to plead Ramadan as an excuse for bad work or absenteeism. As a result, strict observance of Ramadan has certainly declined—if not as much as the government would like. The government's hardest task, however, in trying to modernize Islam, is to wipe out the deeply ingrained Moslem sense of *mektoub*—the fatalistic Arab belief that man has no power to better himself. It is this that underlies so much of the apathy and listlessness of the modern urban Arab. Only generations of material progress and education can change it.

It is here, in education, that the dilemma of Tunisia's dual culture, Arab and French, is seen most clearly. The Tunisians still bear the French a grudge for having neglected popular education under the Protectorate, as they certainly did. Tunisians even believe that the French deliberately tried to "destroy the Tunisian personality" by teaching French rather than Arabic in schools. In many *lycées* Arabic used to be taught as a foreign language. Now, of course, the Tunisians are gradually Arabizing their education system. But everyone still learns French, and in many classes French is still the main language for teaching subjects like history and mathematics. Many Tunisian children still find it much easier to do their lessons in French, because of the confusing differences between spoken and written Arabic.

But during the next few years French will cease to be used as a "vehicular" language (that is, one in which other lessons are taught) and will become instead the primary foreign language, with everyone also learning English. Even science will be taught in Arabic, and Tunisians claim that whatever Europeans may believe, Arabic is in fact a perfectly suitable language for expressing scientific terms.

So what should be the place of the French language and culture in a free Tunisia? The Tunisians carry on the same kind of love-hate relationship with the infuriating French that so many of us have. The Tunisians are mesmerized by the French. And in some ways, with their subtlety and slight femininity they are at least closer to the French than Algerians or Moroccans are. Many of the pale-skinned young students wandering around Tunis seem every bit Parisians. And Tunisians, unlike many ex-colonial nations, never deny the good side of what the colonizer gave them. A Tunisian professor of philosophy told me: "The French have taught us independence of thought, a fine critical sense, and a capacity for totalization"—and he then went on to draw some very French-type diagrams to explain the dynamism of Islamic thought. In fact, a lot of the apparent anti-French feeling among young people in Tunisia is really due to the emotional need to forge patriotic legends out of the only chapter of glory available to them—the battle of Bizerte. That may explain the proud display of bloodthirsty anti-French battle-scenes that I saw painted by a group of schoolchildren in Sfax. They were not necessarily any more anti-French than the murals of Yorktown and Bunker Hill in America are anti-British.

But the very closeness of Tunisians to the French, the very strength of the hold that French culture has over the educated ones, are reasons why their intellectuals have difficulty in forging their own identity. A young sociology student complained to me that he felt still colonized because he spoke no English and was forced to swallow all his sociology with a French slant.

Several young novelists told me how hard it is to develop modern Tunisian writing, when the traditions and techniques for expressing modern ideas are European rather than Arab. "We want to Tunisify the novel," they said. "But we find it hard to steer between simply imitating Western novels—as some of us do —and falling back on classical Arab literature, which hasn't much to offer us."

For many centuries there has been little Arab writing. The golden age, before that, was full of richness—but naïve and formal by modern standards. It is as if an English writer had Beowulf and Chaucer for his models—but no one else from Shakespeare till today. Classical Arab writing has tended to be general rather than individual in its expression: stories or poems about love, or ideas, have been stylized and formal. This can put modern Arab writing at a disadvantage in the face of the more complex and inquiring West. These are the problems that face Tunisians today as they try to build their cultural bridge. It may take them a long time. But, in the long run, their dual heritage may prove a blessing. Mr. Hourani said to me: "We Arabs do form part of Mediterranean civilization. Our roots are the same as yours, though we've been separated for a long time. I believe that the Arab world will one day produce its Dante, its great genius— and he will be the man who perfectly blends the two cultures."

V. ALGERIA

EDITOR'S INTRODUCTION

Of the four countries of North Africa, Algeria is probably the best known to most Americans. This is not only because she is the largest nation in the Maghreb, but because she was the scene of a tragic war that lasted for eight years and did not end until 1962. During that time half a million Algerians were killed or wounded and even more were left homeless. Algeria finally gained her independence, but the cost was a frightful one, and the price is still being paid today. Most of the French colonists have departed, taking with them desperately needed skills and capital. As a result, independent Algeria is faced with a grave economic crisis—a crisis which would be even worse if France were not supporting her former colony with massive subsidies.

Algeria's economic woes are matched by political troubles, which came to a head in the summer of 1965 when the government of Ahmed Ben Bella was overthrown by the army under the leadership of Colonel Houari Boumedienne. Under the new regime Algeria is less interested in fomenting revolutions abroad, and more concerned with improving her own economy. This may be welcome news to many Algerians, but the problems remain enormous and very little has yet been done to bring Algeria to the point where she may be able to stand on her own feet. But if the picture is gray, it is not necessarily black, and the potential riches of Algeria—dramatized by the oil wells gushing in the Sahara desert—indicate that this latest of the North African nations to win its independence may yet have reason to be optimistic about the future.

The articles in this section represent an attempt to put today's Algeria into perspective. The first article shows that independence is no panacea, while the second article, from the *Atlantic*, suggests that the changes of regimes in Algiers have not solved the nation's basic problems. In the following articles Peter Mansfield analyzes the Algerian scene after the fall of Ben Bella, William H. Lewis discusses the change in Algeria's political orientation, and Robert

Shaplen of the *New Yorker* draws a vivid portrait of today's Algeria from a political, economic and above all, a human point of view. Peter Braestrup and David Ottaway analyze the elusive personality of Colonel Boumedienne and J. H. Huizinga draws a pessimistic list of the Boumedienne regime's shortcomings. In the final article Peter Braestrup paints a fascinating sketch of the Algerian Sahara which is now being transformed by the discovery of oil.

ALGERIA'S COSTLY FREEDOM [1]

Algeria, a large Moslem land of mountains and desert and arid soil, achieved her independence from France in 1962 after a costly eight-year war.

But independence ushered in, rather than ended, many political and economic problems. . . .

On the political side, President Ahmed Ben Bella moved increasingly toward one-man rule in a one-party regime. On the economic side, Algeria was faced with serious problems in rebuilding an economy damaged by war, and in adjusting to the loss of the hundreds of thousands of French Algerians who left during the war. They had provided much of the professional and agricultural skill on which pre-independence Algeria depended.

In this situation Algeria has depended heavily on foreign assistance. France and her allies have provided much economic aid. The United States has sent food, physicians and technicians, giving 300,000 tons a year of surplus wheat and other commodities. Britain has financed a $22 million pulp mill, and West Germany has reconstructed the port of Bône and provided equipment and technical assistance for irrigation.

The Soviet Union provided $100 million in purchase credits at low interest. China remained aloof until the fall of 1963, but then Peking . . . [offered] $50 million in credits. . . .

[In 1964] an Algerian mission to Moscow came away with an additional loan of $127 million, largely earmarked for completion of a steel mill near Bône. The following September the Russians

[1] From "Algeria Finding Freedom Costly." New York *Times.* p 5. Je. 20, '65. © 1965 by The New York Times Company. Reprinted by permission.

opened a petroleum institute in Algeria and helped to modernize and standardize the Algerian army's equipment.

Two French companies and Sinclair Oil operate the oil wells in the Sahara. France still has a missile and atomic test headquarters in the Sahara and a naval base at Mers-el-Kebir near Oran. But France is shifting nuclear and missile testing to French territories in the Pacific.

Algeria is a country of 952,000 square miles. It is populated by more than 10 million Moslems. They include the Berbers, the original inhabitants, who have been largely hostile to President Ben Bella, and Arabs who are descended from the conquerors of the seventh century.

In the sixteenth century the Turks took suzerainty but left control of the capital to the Dey of Algiers and the hinterland to local lords. France's involvement dates from the 1820's when a trade dispute led to a three-year blockade and finally a French invasion in 1830.

France began colonizing the country with French, Alsatian, Maltese, Spanish and Italian settlers. The Constitution of the Second French Republic in 1848 declared Algeria French territory.

In time the Europeans, who numbered 1.2 million by independence, came to think of themselves as Algerians. They formed a class of landed proprietors known as the *colon,* colonists or settlers, and built roads and railroads, schools and other institutions. But an integration of the French and Moslem worlds was not achieved.

After World War II bloody clashes broke out and thousands were massacred. The Moslems organized an independence army, which President Ben Bella led from exile in Libya from 1952 to 1956, when he was arrested.

With 800,000 troops the French tried unsuccessfully to crush the rebellion. Finally, President de Gaulle developed a plan for self-determination to end a war that was sapping French national strength. The plan prevailed in a vote in France in 1961, and in Algeria on April 8, 1962. The following July 3 the French handed over sovereign power to the Algerians.

NEW BOSS: OLD PROBLEMS [2]

A good way to see the Algerian problem is from the air. A two-hour flight southward from Algiers covers geographically the whole range of difficulties. The good lands are filled with poverty, while the desert land in the neighboring Sahara is filled with riches. In three years of independence the Algerian government has made very limited progress in bringing the desert riches to the help of the poor in the cultivated green fields and in the cities along the coast.

Except for the oil and gas discovered in the desert, Algeria is not endowed with great resources. The cultivated land and small mines in the Mediterranean coastal belt would at best provide only a scanty living for the population of ten million. Instead of these oil resources coming into quick use in the country, they were held to a trickle by nearly two years of negotiations between Ahmed Ben Bella's government and the big French, British, American, and Dutch companies which discovered the oil and have the means for developing it and selling it.

Meantime, production on the farms and in the small factories which the Algerians took over from the French is falling off steadily. Nearly half the working population is jobless, and foreign investors are steering clear of the place.

It would be easy to say that all these failings are the fault of Ben Bella, and that Colonel Houari Boumedienne, defense minister, was justified in staging the flash coup d'état that threw the president out of office and into imprisonment, and at the same time smashed the Afro-Asian conference on which Ben Bella had set such store. A more basic explanation lies elsewhere.

It is not that Algerians cannot perform well. They can. Thousands of well-trained and intelligent Algerians are spotted throughout the economy and in the government. They cannot begin to make up, however, for the loss of expert personnel resulting from the departure of 300,000 or more trained Frenchmen—businessmen, government employees, bankers, mechanics, and experienced farmers—who left the country after independ-

[2] From "The Atlantic Report: Algeria." *The Atlantic.* 216:14+. S. '65. Reprinted by permission.

ence in 1962 and during the harassment and disorder that followed. The loss of their experience affects almost every sector of Algerian life. It was perhaps in handling this problem that Ben Bella's government appeared at its worst, for it discouraged people who were ready to come in and replace the departed French with capital and know-how.

Despite the economic and political difficulties in the country, a foreigner in Algiers gets an impression that things are not altogether bad. The city is clean. Sidewalk cafés are gay and as crowded as in Paris. Streets are washed regularly, and shop owners are required to sweep off the sidewalks in front of their stores at least twice a day. Boy scout troops carrying placards saying "a clean city, a symbol of Islam" periodically remove trash from neglected alleys. Radio and television announcers plead with housewives to stop hanging out their laundry on the front balcony because the festoons of panties and shirts give some of the French-built apartment houses the appearance of slum settlements.

The old Aletti Hotel, a favorite hangout for people making more or less regular trips to Algeria, has come out of a thorough face-lifting with two good dining rooms, a well-stocked bar, and a casino that brings in a surprising number of Algerians with money to play. Moslem girls and boys meet in coffeehouses, as free in spirit as in European or American cities. The number of women in Arab dress seen on the streets is decreasing. Under French influence, Algiers long ago became a near-Western city. Under independence it is even more Western, for the Algerians enjoy their newfound freedom.

Moreover, out in the Sahara, five hundred miles by air, the new oil city of Hassi Messaoud is a garden spot among the sand dunes. Water brought up along with the oil or in separate wells irrigates acres of flowering oleander bushes, palm and eucalyptus trees, orchards and grass. If every place in Algeria were as prosperous as the oil cities, nobody would go hungry or jobless. Hassi Messaoud has become one of the most livable spots in North Africa for its five thousand engineers and technicians. There is one drawback, however—the city has only forty women.

Behind these signs of moderate well-being are the grimmer marks of social and economic difficulty. There are many beggars, men and women, with ragged children. No ambitious hotel chains have promised to come in to build up the beautiful beaches into resort spots to compete with those in Europe; perhaps none will come until they know just what kind of Socialist or other regime is likely to show up in the end. Boumedienne's friendly gesture to the French and Americans, and his expulsion of the Communists after his coup, might invite some reconsideration by foreign investors. But many already there are losing money hand over fist, and are not excessively optimistic.

On the farms, wheat production dropped from the 1962-1963 crop of 1.6 million tons to 1.1 million tons in the following season. This year it promised to be a bit better, but not much. Production of wine, which is Algeria's principal cash crop, has fallen from 12 million hectoliters (about 317 million gallons) a year under the French to a point where last year the country could not fill the quota which the French agreed to buy, about 8.6 million hectoliters. This year promises still less.

Heavy industry, such as automobile and truck assembling, cement manufacture, and oil refining, remains in the hands of the French and is doing fairly well. By contrast, small industries which were taken over by the Algerians, sometimes by agreement, sometimes by nationalization, have gone downhill steadily.

In the face of the growing distress in the country, Ben Bella continued his somewhat expensive program of making Algeria a leading light in African politics. He set up military camps to train guerrilla fighters for rebellions in the Congo and Portuguese Africa. He talked big about sending troops to help the Arab states "liberate" Palestine and destroy Israel. These were heady projects for a man whose biggest job before the revolution had been that of a very efficient adjutant noncommissioned officer in the French army. But he had charm, and ambition.

He told interviewers that he counted on getting the oil money flowing fast enough into the sluggish economy to provide fresh capital for equipping the farms, to rehabilitate the old factories and build new ones, and to look after the poor. But the economy had slipped for so long that something had to happen.

Boumedienne and the army struck June 19, ten days before the Afro-Asian conference opening, when Ben Bella was rising to his showiest if not biggest hour. A few foreign delegations were already on the scene, and others were converging on Algiers with great fanfare, such men of prestige as Chou En-lai of China, Nasser of Egypt, and Mohammed Ayub Khan of Pakistan.

Despite the postmortem claims of many who said that they foresaw the take-over, virtually everybody was caught by surprise: diplomats, foreigners, Algerians—and Ben Bella. There had been grumbling about the hard times, but always there was the promise that oil money someday would fill up the national treasury.

In the weeks before the coup d'état, Ben Bella appeared as relaxed and confident as was Khrushchev in Moscow before his fall. He even freed some of his former associates whom he had imprisoned for criticizing his regime. Only after the coup did the stories begin to come out about conflicts in the cabinet. Evidently there had been heated disputes over Ben Bella's expansive dreams of African leadership, and there had been clashes between him and his agricultural specialists. The farm experts claimed that the ill-coordinated management committees which had been put in charge of the huge plantations taken over from French settlers were ruining the countryside.

While many of the leaders in and outside the government were Socialists, like Ben Bella, some felt he was leaning further than they liked toward the Soviet Union—and perhaps toward Nasser's Egypt. Also, Ben Bella was surrounded, especially in the areas of press and information, by Communist advisers from France and elsewhere. One of Boumedienne's first acts was to sweep them out.

Boumedienne's own army journal, *El-Djeich*, declared after the putsch that the country was destitute. It reported that farm production had fallen to half what it was under the French, that farmers were quitting the land for the cities in search of something to eat, that the ports were idle and the rail system little used.

The magazine also viewed with alarm the flow of workers abroad, although this matter certainly could be looked at from two sides. For years Algerian workmen have flocked to France for the higher wages there. Their remittances to their families have been an important contribution to the nation's income, for since the revolution some 600,000 Algerians have continued to find jobs in France.

Boumedienne, supported by Chou En-lai, tried to rescue the Afro-Asian conference, but his putsch did it in. The new Algerian leader gave assurance to the amazed delegations that the national policy was not changed, that only a traitorous and power-hungry leader had been deposed. But the score of foreign ministers who had been called to meet a few days before the conference voted to postpone the meeting until November 5, then hurried out of the unhappy capital. They could hardly have done otherwise. Not only had the atmosphere been poisoned by removal of the rather popular man who had invited the sixty-seven nations to come, but someone had effected a punctuation mark by exploding a bomb in the new auditorium. Algerians said Egyptians had done it out of sympathy for Ben Bella.

The army had organized the coup so expeditiously that it was over in a matter of hours, and Ben Bella was carted away to detention. Reacting to a wave of foreign indignation, Boumedienne gave personal assurance to such leaders as Egypt's Nasser and Haile Selassie of Ethiopia that Ben Bella was unharmed and would be tried for crimes against the revolution. Promptly, a flood of denunciation of Ben Bella appeared in the Algerian press to justify the putsch.

Having made the move, Boumedienne could not find any among his colleagues to take Ben Bella's job as premier. Finally he took it on himself. An almost hermetically sealed personality, he dislikes life in the public eye. Where Ben Bella was easy and relatively relaxed in company, Boumedienne is stiff and reserved, a poor mixer. Once at a government reception in Algiers, it is related, he sat alone at a table for four hours, inviting no one to talk to him, occasionally signaling for a fresh cup of coffee.

On a visit to Moscow two years ago he greeted Soviet officials with a forced smile, made a routine speech, cold and uninspired. Boumedienne has none of Ben Bella's magnetism; both Easterners and Westerners seem mystified by him. He rose to the top as a fighter in the revolution, which began in 1954. He fought viciously against a tough French army, and when it was over, sent his own men to track down and kill Algerian sepoys who had fought with the French against the revolutionary forces. Yet this summer he launched a new campaign to enlist the sepoys in the army.

He started off well as a new leader by stating that all agreements with France, the country's principal benefactor, would be fully respected. President de Gaulle reciprocated with equally strong guarantees of support. To American embassy officials in Algiers, many of whom had hardly seen him, he indicated that relations would continue normally. He sent a Fourth of July message to President Johnson phrased more warmly than any sent by Ben Bella in the past.

Evidently he recognized that whatever his own political leanings might be, he needed continued foreign help. Had it not been for large-scale French aid, about $200 million to $250 million a year, and the lesser aid of the Soviet Union and the United States, the country would have suffered real hardship. As it is, nearly a third of the population lives in part on American surplus food.

The American Presence

The surplus food is the principal direct American influence in Algeria. Part of it goes to feed Algerians working on a reforestation project that has covered tens of thousands of acres of barren hills with young trees. The Arabian armies, twelve hundred years ago, had brought goats with them, which in the following centuries have eaten the greenery down to rock level. The last shipment of American wheat for this operation comes in September, after which the Algerian government takes over.

Whatever limited influence the American Embassy and the United States Information Service have in the country was largely offset under Ben Bella by an unrelenting press campaign against United States activities in Vietnam, Cuba, and Santo Domingo. Embassy officials could only get up in the morning and read ulcer-breeding articles in the newspapers while they hunted in vain for a tiny mention of the food deliveries.

Except for the French, other embassies have little better to report. The French, despite the truly atrocious seven years' war they waged to forestall independence, have the best relations of any. Part of it is the old school tie; the French in the embassy and the Algerians in the government in many cases went to the same schools in Paris or worked in the same departments in Algeria before independence.

Boumedienne's fast coup left him all the slow-moving problems Ben Bella had not solved. . . . [The 1965] budget of $840 million carried a built-in deficit of $83 million.

The dragging oil negotiations were bequeathed to him. The oil has been choked off out in the desert where it comes up under high pressure, boiling hot, but far from the refineries and tankers awaiting it along the Mediterranean coast. The wells at Hassi Messaoud could produce three times the amount the few available pipelines now haul. Haggling over terms for building them and over terms for continuing the leases has brought great loss to the country and frustration to the oil companies. Neighboring Libya to the east, with fewer ideological preoccupations, quickly came to profitable terms with the big world producers and now is selling more oil only two years after it was discovered there than Algeria delivers after seven years of development.

With the putsch over, Algeria, at least superficially, again took up its regular way of life. People streamed to the beaches on Sundays. Beggars were in the streets. The government continued to try by various methods to get Algerians to pay rent to the state for the thousands of French apartments they had crowded into, often as squatters.

Boumedienne has promised that the new government will look after Algerians first, the rest of the world later. Whatever long-term effect the sacking of Ben Bella and postponement of the Afro-Asian conference will have on Algeria's relations with other countries will emerge only with time. The operation has undoubtedly chilled the once warm contacts between Algeria and the Soviet Union, and has created a rift between Algiers and Cairo, and other Middle Eastern capitals.

The colonel announced to a graduating class that he was building Algeria on Algerian Socialist principles and did not need any coaching from Socialist states on the outside. Algiers, he said, would no longer be a broadcasting center for Communist propaganda.

If the country truly settles down, though, many will be surprised. Several of the leaders who made the revolution against the French still choose to remain in exile. Boumedienne after the putsch called Ben Bella a despot. Nobody could be certain whether the epithet would come to fit Boumedienne.

ALGERIA AFTER BEN BELLA [3]

When the Algerian people became independent . . . their revolution had caught the imagination of the whole world and the new republic started out with an immense fund of good will from all sides, including President de Gaulle himself. But there was always the danger that this would go to the Algerians' head and that they would fail to tackle with sufficient energy the staggering problem of running the economy left behind by the French with only a handful of trained administrators or technicians.

It is easy to see now that this is just what happened and that ex-President Ben Bella must bear much of the responsibility. With ten times Boumedienne's charm he made Algeria cut a dash in the world while persuading most Algerians that things were getting better at home, even when they patently were not. This explains lingering pro-Ben Bella sympathies among students and women, even when they have greatest difficulty in explaining what he actually did for them.

Now Boumedienne is at last beginning to emerge into the public eye. As President of the revolutionary council he could hardly remain a mysterious recluse, but even now few Algerians can tell you where he lives or even if he is married. Painfully

[3] From "Algeria Catches Up on Ben Bella" by Peter Mansfield, *Sunday Times* correspondent. *Sunday Times* (London). N. 21, '65. Reprinted by permission.

shy, he blushes slightly as he talks with averted eyes and nervous gestures of his graceful hands. But occasionally he turns with a smile of improbable charm or a frighteningly penetrating glance.

Since Boumedienne and the army removed Ben Bella the new regime has made no major policy statements. This is partly because of absorption with a problem of the Afro-Asian conference, but more because time was and is still needed for study and rethinking of the country's problems. These would have been vast enough in any circumstances but they were made much worse by the previous regime's policies.

Out of the male population of about 5 million, 2 million are unemployed or underemployed. About 80 per cent of males are illiterate; nobody bothers to count the women.

Yet in many ways Algeria isn't a typically underdeveloped country. Before independence it had a 10 per cent minority with high West European living standards existing side by side with a majority as poor and ignorant as anywhere in Africa.

There are now about 90,000 French in the country compared with a million before, but of these probably less than one third are *pieds noirs* or French Algerians and the rest are teachers and technicians on temporary contracts. When most of the minority left, the Moslem Algerians were able to move in and take over what they had left—rich farms in the country, luxury flats and factories in the cities.

But they were not trained to manage this high-grade economy which, in most ways, is unsuited to their real needs. Today, Algeria's problems are made worse by the gleaming shop windows, the silk ties and suede jackets, which give the capital a false air of prosperity.

Algerians have no sympathy with Communist austerity and puritanism and they want the bourgeois living standards their country's potential resources could eventually provide; but there can be no short cut to the long, hard road to reach them.

Ben Bella's answer to the problem created by the departure of the French was Algerian socialism or workers' self-management. Not surprisingly, this was a disastrous failure in most cases but it is fair to say that at the time there was no alternative. The French managers had gone and were unlikely to return, while the Algerians hadn't trained men to replace them.

Boumedienne is insistent that self-management is fundamental to the revolution and must stay. All he can do is to try to make it more efficient and pay its way.

Some young Algerians are beginning to return after management training in Yugoslavia and their numbers will increase. Already the government has appointed its own *commissaires* in some factories where things were going especially badly. Another scheme is to train several thousand government auditors to supervise self-management committees, many of which have been taking self-management as synonymous with self-government and treating the factory's budget as their private concern.

One positive move the regime has been able to make to set right its predecessor's mistakes is to hand back some small businesses—shops, cafés, cinemas—which according to Boumedienne were nationalized out of personal spite rather than for any economic purpose. Also, it has removed the fear of imminent land nationalization which hung over small Algerian farmers during the last months of Ben Bella's regime.

Because Boumedienne is the first Algerian leader to speak good Arabic, Ben Bella sympathizers spread the rumor that he was an Islamic reactionary and wanted to make Algerian women who had discarded their veils put them on again. In fact, today, there are fewer unveiled women in Algiers than in any Arab capital outside Arabia. Also, the more superficial aspects of Islam such as the law issued in Ben Bella's time forbidding public sale of alcohol to Moslems has been noticeably relaxed.

What any Algerian leader must be concerned with is a revival of the Islamo-Arab culture which was either suppressed or ignored by the French. Most Algerians have no desire to remain second-class Frenchmen, although it is sometimes difficult to believe it seeing the Algerian student dressed for the Left Bank, devouring *Le Monde* with his *café crème*. The country will remain bilingual probably forever, with French the language of higher education, and therefore of most intelligent conversation. Ben Bella did his best to put Algeria at the head of the anti-imperialist liberation movement in Africa. The Boumedienne regime repeats the same slogans but the tone is more sober and the leader of any Africa liberation movement who comes shopping in Algiers will have to submit to a long, cool scrutiny.

And Boumedienne is lowering his sights. There are high hopes in Morocco that he will be easier to work with than Ben Bella towards Maghreb unity, which is astonishing in view of the dislike and suspicion he used to arouse among Moroccans.

Relations with both Russians and Chinese are likely to remain friendly on the official level and government spokesmen have repeatedly expressed determination to avoid involvement in the Sino-Soviet quarrel. But direct influence of either bloc has been reduced by the removal of unofficial advisers Ben Bella had collected around him.

Internally, there are few countries where it is harder to put statements of intention into effect. The regime wants to give the people more bread and fewer circuses, but unless it can produce results fairly soon, they will forget that circuses were about all they ever got from Ben Bella.

ALGERIA CHANGES COURSE [4]

Algerian political society remains a series of parts; the whole is an abstraction that is yet to become a reality. This state of affairs results from two interrelated factors—the upheavals generated by seven years of brutal conflict, and the inability of the Ben Bella administration to come to grips in a sustained and coherent fashion with the attendant dislocations.

The costs of independence were higher in Algeria than in any other African country to date. Between November 1, 1954 and mid-1962, almost 250,000 Algerians were killed, 500,000 wounded, and more than 2 million made homeless. In addition, more than 300,000 Algerians fled to neighboring Morocco and Tunisia as refugees awaiting the outcome of the war, anxious to

[4] From article by William H. Lewis, visiting professor of African studies, Department of Political Science, University of Michigan. *Africa Report*. 10:8-16. N. '65. Reprinted by permission.

return if the FLN [National Liberation Front] should succeed in slipping France's colonial moorings.

The final paroxysm of mindless violence and destruction wrought by French members of the Organisation de l'Armée Secrète (OAS) from March through July 1962 had a devastating effect. Important government files were destroyed or carried abroad; property damage through sabotage rose to over $1 billion; finally, and perhaps most crucially, the psychological gulf between French and Moslem Algerians grew to seemingly unbridgeable proportions.

The *coup de grâce* sought by the OAS came with the panicky exodus of more than 85 per cent of Algeria's one million French residents. Their departure spelled the loss of skills needed to maintain the modern economic sector during a critical transitional period, as well as a net decline in revenues, productive capabilities, and managerial talents required for the effective maintenance of government services. Thus, Ben Bella and his fellow nationalist leaders were confronted with a virtual *tabula rasa*. The situation called for the application of all the talents of a united, resourceful, and dedicated leadership, but united action was not forthcoming.

During the summer of 1962, intramural rivalries erupted among the top echelons of the FLN and carried Algeria to the threshold of civil war. Essentially an eclectic movement, the FLN had managed to contain its numerous political differences within the framework of wartime imperatives and through rigorous application of the principle of collective, or collegial, leadership. However, the ceasefire and the signing of the Évian Agreements with France in March 1962 unleashed . . . [the divisive forces] which had been latent. In rapid succession, Ahmed Ben Bella and his four fellow detainees were freed from French jails, a major dispute broke out over concessions made by Belkacem Krim and Provisional President Ben Youssef Ben Khedda to France at Évian, and contention arose over the role and prerogatives to be assigned Ben Bella in the post-independence regime. . . .

The intervention of more level-headed "neutral" Algerians who were weary of bloodshed and eager to get on with the problems of postwar reconstruction, averted what could have been a tragic *dénouement*. In time, a Political Bureau was installed at Algiers under the aegis of the Ben Bella faction, and it set about the task of subordinating the various leadership factions and moving Algeria toward a one-party constitutional government. In 1963, Ben Bella was elected president in a popular mandate, the FLN was enshrined as the sole political instrumentality of the state, and Colonel Boumedienne was accorded the dual assignments of vice president and minister of defense.

The atmosphere of political passion slowly gave way to hopeful anticipation as a result of these steps, but the basic divisions remained. The forces which had carried the brunt of the conflict with France—the *wilayists,* or internal guerrilla forces—chafed at the controls imposed by the Ben Bellists and Boumedienne, who had led the so-called "external army" that was subsequently transformed into the present Armée Nationale Populaire (ANP). In addition, the Islamic traditionalists dominated by the *ulema* [the mullahs], bourgeois conservatives inspired by Ferhat Abbas, urban labor federations, youth groups, and veterans' organizations watched with mounting anxiety Ben Bella's dramatic march to power. This process reduced politics in postwar Algeria to conspiratorial and extra-constitutional levels, for Ben Bella moved ruthlessly to humble other potential leaders and reduce any rival citadels of power.

The scion of a poor peasant family of western Algeria, Ahmed Ben Bella had first achieved national prominence as a co-founder of the Organisation Secrète and the Comité Révolutionnaire d'Unité d'Action (CRUA), forerunners of the FLN. Captured by French secret service agents in October 1956 as a result of a clever ruse, Ben Bella languished for the next five and a half years in French detention. During this period he gained the status of a martyr and his political star rose in Algeria; at the same time, his intellectual horizons changed and broadened on a prison diet of French Communist and Marxist literature.

A brilliant political tactician, Ben Bella was eminently successful in mastering the apparatus of power; however, as the architect of a society desperately concerned with the problems of postwar reconstruction, his skills were wanting. Neither an ideologue nor the representative of a special class of Algerians, he developed his political platform from certain simplistic beliefs. Among these were a deeply held conviction that transferring the means of production to "the people" would place the country on the road to recovery; that the FLN could serve effectively as Algeria's revolutionary vanguard; and that Marxism and Islam could be reconciled to form a new philosophic guideline for economic and social action. Above all, Algeria's first president remained vitally concerned with the preservation of Algeria's Homeric revolutionary image among Arab and African nations.

In reality, Algeria's political health did not improve. The FLN did not recover its revolutionary élan; its ranks were inflated with postwar opportunists, its leaders divided into client blocs of supporters, and its discipline eroded by disillusionment at the enormous problems of governing. As a result, the FLN could not fulfill the functions assigned to it under the September 1963 constitution, to "define the politics of the nation" and "inspire the action of the state." In short, the FLN was unable to transform itself from an eclectic wartime movement into an effective governing party. . . .

As a result, power in Algeria was diffuse. . . . There were few interlocking lines of interest and authority which could effectively pull together all segments of society. Government consisted largely of tactical improvisations, and the gulf between policy pronouncements and actual achievement widened each year.

Foreign Policy

While grappling with this array of domestic problems, Ben Bella also concerned himself with fashioning an Algerian *Weltanschauung* toward Africa and the rest of the world. Anxious to perpetuate Algeria's revolutionary image abroad, the Ben Bellists adopted a radical posture in Africa and the Near East on such questions as Palestine and the liberation of colonial territories in southern Africa, the Tshombe regime in the Congo, and Western "neo-colonialist" influence in North Africa.

President Ben Bella made a major contribution to the tone of the Addis Ababa founding conference of the Organization of African Unity in May 1963 in a brilliantly improvised speech calling upon Africans to "die a little" for the final liberation of their continent from colonialism. In addition to their public declarations, the Ben Bellists actively intervened in several areas: (1) shipping arms to the Congo rebels early in 1965 in defiance of several UN resolutions; (2) providing safe haven and guerrilla training for nationalists from Angola, Mozambique, and South Africa; and (3) permitting political dissidents from Morocco and Tunisia to use Algiers as a base of operations.

Though it proclaimed an official policy of nonalignment, the Ben Bellist group increasingly identified itself with the Communist world on major international questions: Cuba, Berlin, South Vietnam, and a number of related issues. . . . In the military sphere, Soviet assistance flowed to the ANP in heavy volume following the signature of an arms aid agreement in October 1963, and more than one thousand Algerian cadets and technicians were sent to the U.S.S.R. for training. Although the army thus became dependent on Moscow for its equipment and organization, its officers have seemed much more concerned with transforming the ANP into an effective professional force than with Communist ideology.

Paradoxically, French-Algerian relations prospered during this period. Despite the lengthy and bitter conflict over independence and Ben Bella's strong views on neo-colonialism, an intimate relationship existed between the Algerian president and French officialdom, including General de Gaulle. The foundations of this relationship rested partially in Algeria's need for French subventions, which exceed $200 million annually, and for the eighteen thousand French teachers and advisers who staff local schools and much of the civil administration. France, on its part, has a considerable interest in maintaining a first claim to Algeria's petroleum and continued access to strategic military installations such as Mers-el-Kebir and to the Saharan testing ground for its atomic energy program.

These factors were reflected in the respect shown by both parties to the Évian agreements of March 1962, which defined the terms of independence and Algeria's subsequent relations with France. While some vendettas occurred against French residents in the immediate post-independence period . . . the rights and obligations of both parties have generally been observed. French economic and technical aid has been maintained at a high level, the French military presence has been reduced at a rate in advance of that prescribed at Évian, and the French-Algerian partnership in petroleum exploitation was recently perpetuated in a new agreement negotiated mainly during the Ben Bella period. Algerians residing in France continue to be protected as agreed in Évian.

The congruence of interests led to a number of incongruities in Algerian foreign policy. While calling for the removal of foreign military bases from African soil, for example, the Ben Bellists quietly accepted a French military presence. In the forefront of nations appealing for the denuclearization of Africa, Algeria nevertheless allowed French atomic testing to continue undisturbed. Although it condemned European economic hegemony over underdeveloped nations, Algeria consistently sought preferential status within the European Economic Community.

The consequence of these apparent contradictions was perplexity and cynicism at home, and collisions with various African and Arab leaders abroad. The Saharan border warfare with Morocco during September and October 1963 left an expanding residue of suspicion and animosity against Algeria. Moderate statesmen below the Sahara exhibited increasingly negative reactions to what they termed Ben Bellist "adventurism"; even within the Arab League, Algeria's radical approach to the Palestine problem proved irritating. By early 1965, Algeria was almost isolated from the rest of Africa and the Arab world.

The Economic Scene

The vacuum created by the departure of French settlers had to be filled. Into their places moved a large number of Algerians eager to gain a footing in the modern world and earn salary and status at a time of economic uncertainty.

Propelled by these and perhaps other more personal motives, these elements have formed themselves into Algeria's "new elite." Springing from diverse parts of Algerian society, they now dominate the modern, erstwhile French sector of the economy. . . .

By no means a coherent entity, the new elite nevertheless played a crucial role in filling the gap between President Ben Bella at the apex of Algeria's power pyramid and the broad mass of Algerians at the base. While their credentials have varied from individual to individual, they have been indispensable in providing rudimentary government services, policing areas of insecurity, and attempting to restore to the shattered economy a semblance of operating efficiency.

For example, as a result of the flight of French *colons* from their farms, the entire modern agricultural economy—embracing more than 6.25 million acres of land and accounting for almost 40 per cent of gross exports—was threatened with collapse. Under a series of decrees promulgated in March 1963, the vacated lands were turned over to the Algerian laborers on the erstwhile French estates, who formed themselves into self-management committees *(comités de gestion)* with governmental assistance.

Whatever the technical deficiencies of these committees, they have proved effective in salvaging the vital agricultural sector, providing needed revenues, and reducing somewhat the political pressures placed on Algiers by the rural proletariat. In this manner the new elite has helped to hold Algeria together at a time when political leaders were distracted by personal rivalries and factionalism.

The primacy of politics has overshadowed not only the emergence of Algeria's new interest groups, but also has contributed to the malaise that gripped the Algerian economy following the traumas of war. A vast country of 920,000 square miles, 800,000 of which are arid and semi-arid Saharan territory, Algeria has limited capabilities to support its proliferating population. Eighty-five per cent of the 11.2 million inhabitants live on but 15 per cent of the land, essentially the Mediterranean coastal belt.

Demographic pressure, land hunger, and the shocks of war have contributed to a burgeoning urban population. Between 1960 and 1964 alone, 800,000 landless peasants flooded to the cities in search of work, raising the national percentage of urban Algerians to one third, straining the resources of the cities, and engendering a wide range of health, housing, and educational problems. Moreover, according to recent estimates, the birth rate has increased by one third since 1960; 400,000 births were recorded in 1963 alone.

Within rural areas, the problem of social and economic disequilibrium is particularly troublesome. Vast areas of farmland were ruined during the liberation struggle, livestock and implements lost, wells sanded over, and distribution systems uprooted. Since 1962, the government has been confronted with the formidable problem of fashioning plans for a more equitable allocation of arable lands to farmers. Under existing arrangements, 1 million Algerians own and maintain 7.5 million acres of land, while 8 million of their brethren subsist on the remaining 10 million acres, which are largely arid and infertile.

A net decline in agricultural productivity has further clouded the outlook for recovery. Wine production, for example, which accounted in the prewar period for 50 per cent of the output of the modern economic sector, amounted in 1964 to less than 10 million hectoliters—3 million less than in 1962. Similar shortfalls have occurred in cereals production and citrus fruits. Overall, the value of annual farm output has fallen by some $100 million, reducing government revenues and straining the resources of the administration.

These setbacks have had a multiplier effect with a strong impact in both the rural and urban sectors. Rural unemployment has produced a floating manpower pool of about 1.2 million Algerians, and the surplus of manpower has in turn depressed wages and increased popular dissatisfaction. In the cities, disillusionment and restiveness are the hallmarks of an essentially refugee population uprooted by war and uncertain of its future. In the department of Algiers alone, 160,000 housing units are occupied by squatters who cannot pay rent. The eminent French sociologist, Germaine Tillion, has characterized this process as the *clochardisation* (pauperization) of at least one third of Algeria's population.

The sector which has generated unrestrained optimism is Algeria's petroleum industry. Active exploration, which began in 1951, uncovered promising fields in the region of Hassi Messaoud and Edjele. In addition, a vast natural gas field has been discovered at Hassi R'Mel in the Sahara. The total known reserves currently are estimated at 4.8 billion barrels of crude oil and 35 billion cubic feet of natural gas, and these projections are regarded as conservative by some specialists. Crude oil output has grown from approximately 15.7 million metric tons in 1958 (the first year of full operations) to 26.5 million tons in 1964. The gross value of Algerian oil production now exceeds $400 million annually.

Under the terms of an agreement signed with France on July 29, 1965, Algeria is to receive a substantial share of petroleum and gas revenues. Concluded after twenty months of spasmodic and sometimes brutal negotiations, the agreement provides for a French-Algerian "cooperative association" in exploiting Algeria's oil resources, a five-year $400 million French assistance program for Algerian industrial development, and a substantial increase in Algerian taxes on French companies operating in the Sahara. Over the next five years Algerian royalties are expected to treble from their present level of $80 million.

As against this windfall, demands on the government's financial resources are multiplying. The army alone commands more than $100 million annually for its training and reequipment programs; aid to the socialized agricultural sector probably will exceed $20 million; support for other government operations probably will rise beyond $300 million during the coming year. The austerity program introduced by Colonel Boumedienne may eliminate some excesses (Algeria imported some $38 million worth of cars in 1963) but existing conditions would seem to warrant a rise in government expenditure to bolster the sagging economy, rather than retrenchment.

The Road Ahead

Algeria remains a young nation by most standards. More than half of its people are less than twenty years of age. But Algeria's youthfulness can be measured in other terms as well. The large majority of the population retains an awareness that anything is possible in the modern age, that responsible leadership can ameliorate the country's woes, and that the real revolution lies in the future, rather than the past.

LETTER FROM ALGERIA [5]
ROBERT SHAPLEN

[In] July [1965] a few weeks after the fall of Algeria's President Ahmed Ben Bella, the Algerians were given their first major policy speech by Colonel Houari Boumedienne, the taciturn and ascetic Army commander who had led the coup against Ben Bella after three years of quietly holding up the pedestal from which Ben Bella noisily ran the country. It was announced in advance that Boumedienne's speech would be not only broadcast over the radio but also televised, and those relatively few Algerians who had access to television sets looked forward to getting a closeup view of the new strong man. What they saw on their screens, though, was a loudspeaker, from which issued Boumedienne's measured and largely expressionless phrases. To a visiting foreigner, the event seemed Orwellian and not a little scary, but if the Algerians were disappointed they did not say so. They accepted the telecast, like a great many other things in contemporary Algeria, as simply another manifestation of their country's distinctive political and psychological climate. As it happened, Boumedienne's method of introducing himself to his countrymen was both typical of his own desire to remain in the background and part of a carefully thought-out program. Since the fall of Ben Bella, who had flamboyant aspirations to be a leader of a never-defined "Third World," Boumedienne has been trying to achieve something called the "collegial principle," originally enunciated by the Algerian revolutionaries during their country's seven-year

[5] Reprinted by permission from an article by Robert Shaplen. *New Yorker*. 41:147-8+. O. 30, '65. © 1965 The New Yorker Magazine, Inc.

fight for independence, won in 1962. In accordance with this principle, Boumedienne is working chiefly through a Revolutionary Council of twenty-six members, of which he is the head, and which includes many men who were military leaders in the struggle against France. A number of these men are still using their wartime underground aliases, and this, in conjunction with Boumedienne's faceless voice, suggests another circumstance of the new regime—an almost compulsive clinging to the clandestine way of life that its leaders developed during their prolonged and painful underground experience, in the course of which many of them spent years in prison and were subjected to various forms of torture. . . .

. . . In many respects, Algeria is now more closely tied to France economically than it ever was when it was actually a part of metropolitan France; on the other hand, instead of the million French civilians and half a million or more French soldiers who were here a decade ago, there are only ninety thousand persons of French nationality now and the departure of the others has left a tremendous vacuum. The vacuum is all the more apparent because so many bureaucratic and cultural legacies of the French remain, like colonial ghosts, to haunt the Algerians, whose respect for France and French ways has outlived the hatred they used to feel for the oppressive and contemptuous *pieds-noirs* colonists. The continuing French presence is not in fact entirely ghostlike, since among the ninety thousand French still in the country there are some fifteen thousand so-called *coopérons,* mostly teachers and technicians, who are playing a significant part in Algeria's efforts to rebuild. The dependence on these Frenchmen and on nearly a billion dollars' worth of French aid poured in during the last three years, which has kept the country from going bankrupt, has done much to put the Algerians on the defensive, for although they emphasize their relationship with the Socialist countries of Eastern Europe, there is no denying that they have been not only unable but unwilling to cut the umbilical cord to France. In the eyes of the Marxist world—and especially China, which has made a number of acerbic comments on the matter—Algeria's acceptance of so much French aid stamps her as unable to endure any degree of hardship in building a new nation and lays her open to charges of "bourgeois Socialism." A Yugoslav diplomat here remarked to me, somewhat self-righteously, "There's still too much evidence of French corruption here. Just look at Algiers. Except for the Casbah, it's still a French middle-class city, with French luxury shops, fine hotels, a luxurious swimming club, and so on. Just look at all the automobiles!"

The evidences of a century and a third of French influence mingle and often compete with disparate influences out of Algeria's disordered past—the influences of the indigenous mountain Berbers and of Romans, Carthaginians, Vandals, Arabs, Spaniards, and Turks, who preceded the French. It is only to be expected that the Algerian personality should be a many-faceted one, and that it should now be undergoing a process of adjustment—a process both fascinating and exasperating to both Eastern and Western nations. . . .

. . . It seems to be no accident that in its initial search for national models to follow Algeria turned to those revolutionary mavericks Yugoslavia and Cuba, even though neither of them had much in common with Algeria in respect to race, religion, economic conditions, or historical development. Each represented to the Algerians—and especially to Ben Bella—boldness in theory and action combined with the colorful, dynamic stamp of personality epitomized by Tito and Castro, whose style Ben Bella, as the would-be ideological leader of the new African nations, sought to emulate. Compared to either Tito or Castro, though, Ben Bella was a hollow man. Those who knew him best say that, despite his showmanship and his demagogic exhortations, he had no genuine revolutionary philosophy. This appraisal of Ben Bella accords with the belief that Algeria actually underwent less a full-scale revolution than simply an exhausting physical and spiritual crisis, in which its people were near defeat before Charles de Gaulle made his far-seeing decision to call off the war, on the ground that even if the French won they would obviously have to garrison the country indefinitely, at a prohibitive cost. One of the most perceptive analysts of Algeria, Charles F. Gallagher, of the American Universities Field Staff, has written, "The end product of the colonial period . . . was that Algeria . . . was a series of bustling boomtowns and destroyed villages, a huge concentration camp, and a gigantic slum inhabited by millions of despairing, desperate, displaced persons. It was hell on earth."

Most Algerian writers are busy dealing with the theme of a stricken, oppressed people who have fought valiantly, with a mixture of hope and Muslim fatalism, against enemy forces intent on bombing and burning their villages and destroying the old patterns of family life. In much of this literature, survival is the keynote and individual heroism is the motif. These two themes are also being emphasized in the first full-length motion picture ever to be made in Algeria by Algerians. This is "The Battle for Algiers," in which some of the hardest resistance fighting went on, and which served as a hideout for guerrilla leaders all during the war. It is also interesting that there is a continuing preoccupation in Algeria with the late Frantz Fanon, a Negro psychiatrist from Martinique who became an Algerian citizen and whose books— particularly "The Wretched of the Earth," which   still sells heavily here and is reserialized from time to time in the government-controlled newspapers—by explaining the process of depersonalization that colonialism always causes, helped the Algerians understand themselves. . . .

. . . Most of the contemporary Algerian leaders have read Fanon, and have felt that he described their own political and social predicaments. Although a number of them—most notably Ben Bella—became semi-skilled latter-day Marxists as the struggle continued, they were never able to inculcate any meaningful ideology into the Algerian people. One reason for this was that during the revolution the Algerian partisans fought in six separate regions, called Willayas, and each was led by a cadre of officers to whom they gave their main allegiance. The men in the Willayas constituted the spearhead of the resistance, and did more fighting than the units of the Liberation Army, which was organized on a nationwide basis but most of the time served only as a screening force on the borders of Morocco and Tunisia. So in fact there was never any single, unified revolutionary organization, nor was there any mass uprising until just before independence was won. The Communists, especially the French Communists, who might have been able to create a unified political organization, refrained from doing so, because, for their own reasons, they had opposed the Algerian guerrilla movement at the outset and never subsequently gained an important role in it, though ultimately they became strong backers of Ben Bella. At the time of the signing of the truce agreement with France at Évian-les-Bains in June, 1962, no individual Algerian was recognized as a national leader. It was not until the next month that Ben Bella outwitted the comrades who had shared exile with him and, with the help of Colonel Boumedienne's Army units, seized power. But while Ben Bella proved himself a master political tactician by eliminating his remaining rivals one by one and breaking up the semi-political, semi-military organizations in the Willayas, many members of which were consolidated into the national army under Boumedienne (although two or three rebel leaders took to the mountains and led opposition elements until they surrendered or were captured), he never really became a popular national figure. His travels around the country seldom took him outside the western area, where he was born and where he felt at home, and even there, toward the end, his speeches, full of promises and threats, were received without much apparent interest. All this helps to explain why his disappearance and his replacement by the far less flamboyant and talkative Boumedienne have caused so little stir. . . .

. . . In trying to establish a mass base where none had existed, Ben Bella made the mistake of failing to consolidate the old revolutionary elements that did exist—the local and regional partisans and military leaders, and the members of the underground National Liberation Front who had remained in Algeria. He tried instead to use a group of urban intellectuals, including a handful of doctrinaire Marxists, as the nucleus of a farmer-labor type of political organization. "The city mice were to educate the country mice and show them the way to Socialism," an American I know who has been here for many years said to me. "But it didn't work out that way. In the first place, the rural people who seized the large French farms immediately after independence did not welcome Ben Bella's administrators when they were sent out to help reorganize and operate the properties. The seizure in itself was an interesting manifestation of the peculiar Algerian revolutionary outlook. The peasants who had worked the land for the wealthy French owners made no attempt to divide it among themselves, as peasants in similar situations have done in other countries; they simply took each farm as a whole and set about running it as an autonomous unit. I suppose this might be regarded as a perfect demonstration of the impact of French bourgeois thinking."

My American friend went on to explain that Ben Bella had never been able to reach the rural people the way the Army had. Boumedienne always made a point of maintaining the Army's political independence, and he had always stressed the fact that the Army, which was garrisoned throughout the country and made up of people from all classes and all regions, depended on the common people—the peasants—for its existence. When Ben Bella belatedly tried to counter the Army by creating a people's militia, in the manner of other Socialist and Communist leaders, the idea never really caught on. His effort to create a dynamic national party also failed. Under his leadership, the National Liberation Front was never more than a paper organization, most of its eight thousand members being nothing but well-paid governmental hacks and hangers-on, whose presence in the villages and towns was either accepted passively or, more often, resented as an autocratic, interfering, and corrupt influence. "Ben Bella failed to consolidate the areas he should have consolidated, and he extemporized too harshly and too quickly in others," my friend continued. "His loudly trumpeted Marxist ideas got to be a bore, and they made even less of an impact because newspapers, magazines, and books from France and elsewhere gave the people—especially the people in the cities—a clear idea of what they were missing economically. The Algerians want to be amused just as much as anybody else, and they soon realized that Ben Bella's form of Socialism didn't have much sex appeal. Ben Bella got his kicks by involving himself in all sorts of foreign adventures, by being fêted everywhere and getting awards like the Lenin Peace Prize—but the folks back home got nothing." . . .

. . . Boumedienne has said that Algeria intends to "turn inward"—that is, concentrate on domestic problems—in contrast with Ben Bella's compulsion to involve himself in left-wing causes abroad, but relations with other nations are by no means being neglected. In dealing with the Soviet Union (which had supported Ben Bella and which initially called the new regime "militaristic") and with the East European Communist countries, the Algerians have emphasized that while they will maintain their "Socialist options"—a favorite term—and will welcome continued Communist assistance, they will not brook any "interference" in their internal affairs, nor will they any longer permit the unlimited dissemination of Communist propaganda. What this signifies, essentially, is that Boumedienne intends to combine a continuing "revolutionary" foreign policy and a more independent policy of Algerian nonalignment with any of the existing blocs and front groups led by Russia and China. "We have no need of advice from abroad on how to build Socialism," Boumedienne has said. It has also been made clear that Algeria will pay more attention than before to its neighbors Tunisia and Morocco, which with Algeria form the so-called Mahgrib nations of Islam. "*Mahgrib*," in Arabic, means "the West," and the languages and customs of these three nations are much alike, and quite different from those of the eastern Arab countries. . . .

. . . In the general area of relations with the United States— aside from the Vietnam issue—the Boumedienne government seems eager to reverse the long process of deterioration that began soon after Ben Bella came to power, when, having visited President Kennedy in Washington, he went to Cuba to see Castro just as the missile crisis there was coming to a head. In spite of this apparently unfriendly gesture, the United States continued a large-scale Algerian aid-and-relief program, under which wheat, vegetable oil, and powdered milk were distributed to orphans, war widows, disabled veterans, and other needy persons. In late 1962 and early 1963, between three and four million Algerians—a third of the total population—depended almost entirely on this American aid for their basic subsistence, and today about a million and a half are still totally dependent on such help. In all, some eight hundred thousand tons of surplus American food, worth about a hundred million dollars, has been sent to Algeria, where it has been distributed through CARE and through Protestant and Catholic welfare organizations. As Ben Bella became increasingly anti-American in his attitude, Washington was tempted to cut off the program, but it decided that Ben Bella's diatribes did not represent the general feeling of the Algerian people—a belief that I have been able to substantiate—and the program, though it was cut down early this year, has been kept going. Because the need for supplementary food is still widespread, Boumedienne has now asked that the food supplies be increased again, and he has also indicated that he is eager to receive other forms of American assistance. Under Ben Bella, the only other official aid offered Algeria was a million and a half dollars for a rural rehabilitation program, in which soil-conservation experts were supposed to use some sixty thousand unemployed Algerian workers to build earth dams, small ponds, and other useful projects. The workers were to be paid in American food and in cash provided by the Algerians, but the Ben Bella regime was unable to supply the cash for more than twenty thousand workers. (A reforestation scheme initiated by several world Protestant groups and also supported by American food donations proved more successful.)

There is a tremendous need in Algeria for many sorts of technical and agricultural aid, but in this area the peculiar Algerian attitude comes to the fore. In the opinion of some highly placed American aid officials, the Algerians "want the aid and the privilege of attacking us, too." Algerians have privately pointed out that we take political differences more seriously than they do, and that they look upon their criticism of American foreign policy as an inherent right, which should not interfere with any economic relationship. Since Boumedienne has come to power, criticism of American policy in the Congo and in Cuba, among other places, has died down, leaving Vietnam as the principal sore point, but the fundamental difference in attitude is a deeper one, and one that may require some reorientation of American as well as Algerian thinking. "We've got to decide, once and for all, that any offers of assistance we make have no political strings attached, and

that our interest is solely in helping people and in making a country or an area, such as North Africa, economically viable," an
American at our embassy told me. "If we do that, the political
advantages may or may not come later, but the risk is worth
taking." It is difficult, however, to determine whether the Algerians will be able to make good use of our technical aid. One
disillusioned aid official observed, "I'm tired of telling these people
what they need and of starting things they won't coöperate on.
I've discovered there's no correlation between need and what will
work, especially in Algeria. As things stand, the Americans have
agreed to Boumedienne's request that all existing assistance programs be continued and that discussions be held regarding additional American aid.

If things really *are* to work, all qualified observers agree, they
can be made to do so only by properly trained Algerians who are
given their heads by the politicians. Under Ben Bella, the few
experts available were shunted aside and the Marxist theoreticians
ran the show, or, at least, interfered enough to keep it from running efficiently; under Boumedienne, the government is showing,
for the first time, some respect for the opinions and methods of
young technical specialists who have received training in the
United States, England, or France. A growing number of such
people are filtering back to Algeria, along with some who went to
France to live in 1963 after disillusioning experiences with the
low salaries and the Socialist bureaucracy at home. "These young
technicians are the hope of the country," a French administrative
planner working with the Algerian government said to me the
other day. "Unlike the politicians, they deal in facts and are not
the prisoners of formulas."

Agriculture is the base of the Algerian economy, and after
three years of independence it is still in a state of confusion.
Prior to 1962, French landlords owned nearly seven million acres
of Algerian vineyards, orchards, and wheat fields, or about a
third of the arable land. These holdings, known as the "modern"
sector of the country's agriculture, netted the French owners at
least two hundred and fifty million dollars a year, though they
employed only a sixth of the rural labor force. The yield from

these lush farms was anywhere from three to five times as high as that from the farms in the larger but much poorer "traditional" agricultural sector, in which a million illiterate Algerian families struggled on tiny plots to produce enough food to survive. Between the summer of 1962 and the spring of 1963, the French settlers fled and thousands of Algerian farm workers moved in to occupy the big farms, whereupon the government took over and began the process of consolidating a total of twenty-two thousand former French properties into about three thousand "Socialist production units" under a National Agrarial Reform Office. A decree in March of 1963 defined the terms under which these units were to be operated. Each was to have a general assembly of workers; a smaller, elected workers' council to serve as a self-management committee, consisting of from three to eleven workers; and, finally, a director appointed by the central government, who was to oversee technical and financial matters.

From the start, these *"auto-gestion"* farms, as they were called, ran into trouble. The workers' self-management committees proved incapable of running the big units, because their members lacked sufficient technical knowledge, especially when it came to raising grapes for wine, which was the chief source of revenue. The various interested bureaucrats began squabbling over the farms, many of which, lacking proper equipment and proper direction, quickly went into the red. The inadequate profits, aggravated by a shrinking French market for Algerian wine and increasing competition in the citrus-fruit market from Italy, Spain, Israel, and Morocco, led many of the peasants on the *auto-gestion* farms to hoard their crops or sell them surreptitiously on the free market. This year, though the farms are supplying more than two-thirds of Algeria's agricultural output, they are still not making a profit, so the government expects only about twelve million dollars in revenue from them, which won't be of much help in reducing the expected budget deficit. Still to be dealt with, and in many respects much more difficult, is the problem of improving the yield of thousands of marginal farms on which most of the rural population dwells. Land-reform efforts have had virtually no effect; talk about distributing large tracts of government-owned land to the peasants has remained just talk; and some twenty-three million acres of wasteland that could be reclaimed for cultivation or pasturage have not as yet been utilized. Though there has been a sizable effort to transfer people to the *auto-gestion* farms, only about a hundred thousand are now employed there while a far greater number of *fellahin* remain on their small ancestral plots, where they live lives steeped in ignorance as well as poverty.

With the population increasing at the rate of two and three-quarters per cent a year and with a quarter of a million people annually reaching the age of twenty-one, there seems to be little prospect of finding permanent jobs for the half of the potential Algerian working force that is now unemployed. During a ten-day trip I made through the south and east, there was hardly any sign of life in the small, drab, dusty villages and towns, while in such larger cities as Constantine and Bône I saw groups of poorly dressed young and old men sitting aimlessly in outdoor cafés, talking, playing games, or simply staring out into the glare of the sun, because they had nothing else to do. Such conditions are not likely to change until Algeria's birth rate is reduced. There is no formal Muslim proscription of birth control, and Algerian women are beginning to demonstrate some desire to obtain birth-control information; however, the men continue to pride themselves on the size of their families, and, as in most countries with a high degree of illiteracy, the poorest families seem to have the most children.

It is hoped that as educational opportunities increase—and two encouraging recent developments have been a rise in primary-school attendance and the institution of a broader secondary-school program—some of the rural population will be siphoned off into new industries, creating a better industrial-agricultural balance and, ultimately, increasing the productivity of agriculture by making better equipment and fertilizers available. The French have tried to stimulate this movement through what they call the Constantine Plan—named for a speech that de Gaulle made in Constantine in October, 1958—whose first phase, covering the years 1958 to 1962, was to concentrate on industrial development in the mining of iron, lead, and zinc, the manufacture of steel, and the building of fertilizer, plastic, and cement plants. French assistance got the industrial program started and made possible the creation of a number of secondary industries, including textile factories and tanneries, but under Ben Bella the scheme suffered from a lack of consistent planning and organization. Much of the promised French financial aid was withheld because of lack of precise technical agreement between the two countries, and in many cases the Algerian government was too poor to put up needed capital. Thousands of people left the countryside in hopes of finding better jobs, but they simply increased the numbers of the unemployed in the towns and cities. In Algiers today, many of these peasants are now super-squatters, living rent-free in fine, modern twenty- and thirty-story apartment houses abandoned by French tenants in 1962. The government has tried to temporize with the unauthorized flat-dwellers, and has put up notices promising to continue to operate the utilities if the tenants will pay as little as fifteen per cent of the rentals, but little headway has been made in collecting anything. Elevators frequently break down, with the result that many people—especially the elderly—live virtually isolated lives on the upper floors, where a visitor willing to make the long climb will very likely come across former peasant families with hordes of relatives occupying a three-room apartment, on whose balcony a goat or two will be nibbling at home-grown grass or uncollected garbage.

Under Ben Bella, it was never made clear how much business the state intended to take over, how much would be allowed to manage itself under state supervision, and how much would be allowed to remain in private hands. The labor unions urged Ben Bella in the direction of Socialism, for while they encouraged what they called the "self-management" of commercial and agricultural enterprises, they wanted to do the managing. Today, only about five hundred companies, employing some fifteen thousand workers—that is, less than a quarter of all small production units—are under *auto-gestion,* and most of these, among them such varied enterprises as laundries and metallurgy plants, are suffering as much from poor management techniques and lack of proper equipment as the *auto-gestion* farms.

Currently, the big hope is that the Algerian economy will be literally energized by a new oil-and-gas agreement between France and Algeria and by a five-year, four-hundred-million-dollar industrial-development agreement, which is sometimes referred to as the second part of the Constantine Plan. In the decade since oil was discovered in the Sahara, Algeria has become the world's tenth-ranking producer, its production for 1964 totalling twenty-six million metric tons. The country has an estimated two per cent of the world's oil reserves and—even more important—an estimated twelve per cent of the world's natural gas, which means that in potential production of the latter fuel it is second only to the United States. Under the new agreement with France, the Algerian government's share in the proceeds from the Sahara oil will increase from approximately forty-one per cent to fifty per cent, and it retains the right to impose further taxes on the French share of future production. Between now and 1969, Algeria's total revenues from oil are expected to rise from eighty million dollars to two hundred and forty million. Foreign oil companies, including three major American ones, will be allowed to maintain concessions that they now operate and also to prospect for new wells, but they will have to pay higher taxes and accept a gradual reduction in the percentage of the profits they may take out of the country; in return, they will be given a fifteen-year guarantee against nationalization of their wells. As for natural gas, the new agreement gives the French and Algerians a monopoly in its production, outsiders being essentially no more than contractors. The Algerians now have three pipelines from the Sahara to Mediterranean ports, and in the port of Arzew, east of Oran, they have a large plant for liquefying natural gas. So far, the Algerians have made relatively little use of the gas, but it is hoped that under the new coöperative plan a whole petrochemical industry will be developed to turn out fertilizers, synthetic rubber, and other industrial materials. What the Franco-Algerian agreement actually does is replace part of France's outright financial aid to Algeria with a pledge to help the Algerians market their oil and gas and any new products that are developed.

On a recent trip through the northern and central Sahara, I visited the big oil center at Hassi Messaoud, about five hundred miles southeast of Algiers, where the two major Franco-Algerian companies have a hundred and fifty working wells spread over many square miles of dunes. The sight, by day, of the rigs rising from the endless expanse of sand against the pale-blue desert sky and, by night, of the shooting flames from excess gas being burned off gives the impression of a huge offshore oil development rather than one on land, and the sense of being at sea is heightened if one spends a night at the plush camp of the Société Nationale de Recherches des Pétroles Algériens, or SNREPAL, which resembles a huge, self-contained naval base, a twentieth-century air-conditioned sanctuary in the middle of a broiling vacuum. Some five hundred workers—fifty of them with their wives and children—live in the camp, which has handsome modern cottages, communal dining rooms that serve excellent food flown in from France, recreation rooms providing movies and games, an outdoor swimming pool, and floodlit tennis courts. Approximately five thousand workers are employed in the whole Hassi Messaoud area, somewhat less than half of them by the oil companies. The remainder work for various smaller construction or transportation contractors or for the Organisme Saharien, a Franco-Algerian government organization that has done a remarkable job of building the so-called Sahara infrastructure, with special emphasis on a network of hard-surfaced highways and gravel roads connecting a score of oases, some of which contain full-fledged towns with populations as high as eighty thousand. Life at SNREPAL is a monotonous one, consisting of hours of work in the searing desert heat, where the daytime temperature rises as high as 145° F., followed by recuperative hours in the air-conditioned haven of the camp. Except for the men on the oil rigs, who work eight-hour shifts around the clock, the oil-company employees' hours are from six to eleven in the morning and from three to six-thirty in the afternoon. In order to keep going, they drink as much as five gallons of water a day. (I myself, without doing any manual labor, drank about two gallons a day during my week in the .desert, and I was constantly thirsty.) Fortunately, there is a good water supply from local wells. The lowest paid workers at SNREPAL—manual laborers—receive a hundred dollars a month, which is twice as much as the annual per-capita income of the three-quarters of a million Algerians living in the Sahara. From all over the desert, every week hundreds of men come to Hassi Messaoud (which means "Lucky Well") in search of work. Those who aren't lucky enough to be hired are allowed to spend three days and nights in the company dormitories before starting the long trek home.

The Sahara occupies four-fifths of Algeria, stretching from the belt of mountains near the Mediterranean down to Central, or Black, Africa. It also reaches into Morocco, in the west, and into Tunisia, Libya, Egypt, and the Sudan, to the east, but most of it is in Algeria. Since prehistoric times, the desert area has gone through many transformations. Nearly a million years ago, it was a tropical country of rivers and swamps, inhabited by elephants, giraffes, antelopes, hippopotamuses, and crocodiles. Then, when Europe was covered by a heavy icecap, the area dried up. Toward the close of the Paleolithic period, the dryness receded, and as the moisture came back man began to hunt and fish in the region, as is evidenced by artifacts found in the desert sands. As civilization reached the Sahara, men moved in from the Near East across Egypt; others came from the shores of the Mediterranean, and there was also some migration of African Negroes from the south. By 5000 B.C., the country was well populated; it was verdant, and large herds of cattle grazed over it. Art flourished there, and delicate wall carvings and paintings depicting the life of those days in astonishing detail are valuable guides for archeological and anthropological data. Then the climate changed once more; it grew hot, and the Sahara became savanna country, lush and damp. The Egyptian influence became paramount, and camels were introduced as the chief means of transportation. As the heat increased, the humidity decreased, until the area became a desert, except in the north, where there were some large bodies of water, including an inland sea that covered part of Tunisia and the area south of Constantine. Men shunned the expanding desert, though the Romans reached its northern rim and built cities there, among them Timgat, which is near the present-day Constantine and is now being excavated. The successive waves of Vandal, Byzantine, and Berber warriors who crossed North Africa left the Sahara unexplored for centuries. The Berbers, however, gradually moved south, and the Tuareg tribes that now occupy the southern part of the Sahara are their descendants. Trade across the desert began; sugar, cloth, brass, and coral were carried south by caravan and exchanged for gold, ivory, ostrich feathers, and slaves. Not until the nineteenth century did the Europeans begin to explore the Sahara. The first European to reach Timbuktu, in what is now Mali, was a young Scottish officer named Alexander Gordon Laing, who survived the rigorous climate and several attempts on his life to get there in 1826, only to be murdered on his departure. At this time, much of the desert was inhabited by warlike and suspicious Tuaregs and by equally unfriendly Chaambas, whose forefathers had migrated from Syria in the fourteenth century, and who conducted a desultory caravan trade but preferred to pillage other people's caravans.

The Sahara is not likely to undergo any more great natural changes soon, but man-made economic changes are imperative if the present inhabitants of the area are to subsist, let alone prosper. The production of oil and gas and the building of roads have lately afforded irregular employment at high pay for a few workers, thereby spoiling these workers for the traditional and far less remunerative forms of labor, and have tended to drive the most highly skilled north in search of more permanent jobs. Until 1962, the biggest employer in the Sahara was France, and especially its Army. Now the Organisme Saharien offers parttime work in the desert to about a thousand laborers, most of whom spend their time cleaning sand off the roads after sandstorms, but out of three hundred thousand employable males in the region approximately a hundred and fifty thousand have no work at all, and the majority of the others do little more than tend a few date palms to keep themselves and their families alive.

During the war of liberation, many of the oases were abandoned, and what little cultivated area there was reverted to wasteland; wells dried up, and herds of cattle were left to die or else were killed and eaten by the fighters. Consequently, much, if not most, of the desert region is worse off today than it was ten years ago.

There is a choice of two possible solutions to the problem of the Sahara—to move practically the whole population north, or to start new agricultural and commercial projects in and around the oases. Since it will be some time, at best, before the economy in the north is stable and prosperous enough to provide for the people who are already there, the Algerians and their French advisers have determined to improve conditions in the desert to the point where the population will be able to survive on its own. The task—as I could readily see during my trip, which took me to five of the principal oases—is a monumental one. It requires, among other things, a new study of all the possible ways of obtaining more water and for expanding irrigation; a means of giving a widely scattered population of illiterate peasants enough technical knowledge and assistance so that they can grow better and more varied crops; a restoration of herds and the application of modern grazing techniques; and the development of local and regional commerce to complement the essentially agricultural economy. All this, as the French and Algerian government workers I spoke with were quick to point out, will take a lot of time, a lot of patience, and a lot of money. The key to the problem, they agreed, is to raise the general educational level of the population, and this is closely related to the improvement of health conditions, which, as a result of malnutrition and a high incidence of tuberculosis and trachoma, are extremely poor throughout the area. . . .

. . . Most of the prefects and sub-prefects I met were little better educated than the peasants they dealt with, being simply loyal members or supporters of the National Liberation Front who had been rewarded with jobs. The task of replacing them was one of the first that Boumedienne set for himself, and it is proving far from easy, for not only is the number of Algerians with administrative qualifications extremely limited but a sizable

proportion of them feel a natural disinclination to bury themselves in the desert for three or four years. In the peculiar post-
colonial climate of Algeria, I discovered, the continuing role of
the French is even more vital in the desert than it is elsewhere.
For example, when independence came, there were virtually no
doctors left in the desert. In the spring of 1963, the French and
the Algerians signed an agreement creating a French Medical
Mission in the Sahara. Today, the mission consists of fifty-four
doctors, fourteen nurses, four dentists, and a varying number of
midwives, and, with the exception of a few of the midwives, all
of them are French. In El Goléa, an oasis in the central Sahara,
whose population of seventeen thousand is part Chaamba and
part Negro, and which is almost totally dependent on its sparse
date groves, one of the French doctors told me he treated a thousand or more men, women, and children a month at his small
hospital, where he and another French doctor often worked
around the clock. Most of his patients suffer from malnutrition.
"I try to keep them in the hospital for a couple of weeks and
build them up," he said. "But we feel like sailors polishing the
brasswork while the ship is sinking." Among the most active
workers in the desert are members of the Order of White Fathers
and the Order of White Sisters, two century-old Catholic organizations. In El Goléa, Father Desharlet, a White Father who has
spent thirty years in the Sahara and is now running a trade
school there, told me that thirty youngsters come to his class each
morning, of whom twenty are so undernourished that they are
unable to concentrate. "If we didn't feed them lunch at our can-
teen, they'd probably have nothing to eat all day," he said. "It's
pretty hard to teach even elementary mechanics under such conditions." Father Desharlet was certain that the only help for the
desert population lay in educating the children, but he believed
the economic prospects to be so poor that the best solution was to
"educate them as well as we can and then get them out of here."

Poverty-ridden though it is, the desert contains some people
who are well off. Among them there are a few individuals—such
as the operators of transportation companies who made minor
fortunes when the French Army was here and who still do well

out of carting things from one oasis to another—and there is at least one whole tribe, the Mozabites. The Mozabites are sometimes called the Puritans of Algeria, and they trace their religious dissidence back to Mohammed's son-in-law, Ali, who, they claim, misinterpreted the Koran. Persecuted as heretics by other Muslims, they came to the desert in the eleventh century, and today they are concentrated in one of five towns that occupy the oasis of Ghardaia, about three hundred miles south of Algiers. The town of Beni Isguen, which, like the four other towns of Ghardaia, is built atop a hill, is regarded by the Mozabites as a holy city, and it is probably the richest enclave in the desert, too, being something of a tourist trap for visiting Europeans, who like its exotic atmosphere. Most of the young Mozabite men traditionally go north to Algiers and elsewhere, where their people have long prospered as grocers; they send money back to their families regularly, and return for visits three or four times a year, and when they retire they come back home to live. Beni Isguen, consequently, is inhabited almost completely by women, children, and old men. The women go heavily veiled after the age of twelve, and above each veil one eye barely shows as its owner moves through the lanes and alleys of the town. So strict are the Mozabites that a woman is not allowed to see her sister-in-law unveiled, nor is a man allowed to see his daughter-in-law unveiled. No Arabs except Mozabites are allowed to pass through the town gates, which are closed at dusk, at which time the market place is open for a time, and old men dressed in immaculate white robes drift down the hilly streets after their evening prayers and squat along the white walls of the shops and houses to exchange gossip. From a Mozabite tower on the crest of the hill of Beni Isguen, I was able to gaze down on the entire large oasis of Ghardaia and on its four other towns, which are much less prosperous and look it. In between and around them and their groves of palms I could see the tents and small fires of nomads who were encamped with the flocks they had been tending far to the south. Beyond Ghardaia, the desert stretched out endlessly in the hot evening haze, and it was difficult to believe that man could grub out any kind of existence here. . . .

. . . I had seen the privations and problems of the desert, and the bleakness and emptiness of village life in the plain, and as I passed through Constantine and the nearby port of Bône, with a harbor that had once been filled with French merchant ships but was now almost deserted, and with the streets and cafés full of aimless crowds, it seemed obvious that Algeria would need a lot more than a belief in Allah's will in order to survive and progress. Lannon Walker, the young American consul in Constantine, spoke hopefully, though. "These people are still strongly pro-American, despite all the Marxist propaganda and all the anti-American talk," he said. "I feel that we Americans have to learn to live with this Socialist structure in Algeria. We have to do what we can, and do it through training people and fostering self-help projects, rather than through handouts, to make the country productive."

One of the most beautiful drives in the world must be the one between Constantine and Algiers. The long, wild mountain chain of the Kabylia drops from a height of seven thousand feet to the rocky Mediterranean shore, where sea and sky are a blend of azure and cobalt. The Algerians have talked about promoting tourism along this coast but have done nothing about it yet, and the potential blessings of such a move seem highly questionable. The place all but shrieks to be left untouched. Besides, there is a suspicion that the proud and remote Kabyles in the hills not only would resent the incursion of tourists but might take matters into their own hands—with guns, if necessary. In their villages, in the ravines and on the mountain slopes, the red tile roofs are still shell-marked from the onslaughts of French bombs and guns.

In the Kabylia, I was reminded again of the great contrasts of Algeria—contrasts of geography and climate, and of people with different racial backgrounds and characteristics—and then of the contradictions that almost all Algerians harbor within them. There is one quality, however, that runs consistently through the country and its people—a sense of isolation and apartness, which can be felt everywhere. I had seen it in the desert, in the expressions of solitary turbaned Arabs sitting in the blazing sun by the roadside and waiting, it seemed, for nothing, or perhaps simply for a plane to pass overhead or a diesel truck to rush by on the highway and then leave them alone once more with Allah or whatever it was that possessed them. I had seen it in the empty eyes of beggars, many of them shell-shocked from the war, as they moaned their pleas in the streets of the cities. Now, in the Kabylia, I saw it in the almost sullen faces of brightly dressed Berber women herding their flocks into the hills, and in the silent, staring, defensive Berber men in little stone cafés as they watched the white faces of the strangers in the car flicker by. And, most memorably of all, I saw this sense of loneliness, transcending warfare, politics, history, and time itself, in the face of a small Berber boy we passed. He was sitting by himself on a knoll by the roadside, his back to the sea and his head, on which was perched a small red hat, lifted toward the sunset over the hills. In his hand he held one pink flower. He took no notice of us as we rode by, but just sat, as immobile as an icon. I wondered whether he would be there tomorrow or forever, in hope or in fear or simply in endless passivity, waiting for fate to deal with him in its own way.

WHO IS BOUMEDIENNE? [6]

Last June 19 [1965], early risers in . . . [Algiers], on their way to work downtown, found two big Soviet-made T-54 tanks stationed in front of the Moorish-style Central Post Office. . . . After thirty-three months of euphoric speeches, political juggling and helter-skelter "socialism," Ben Bella had been ousted. He was now a "traitor to the revolution." Ben Bella's former ally, Colonel Houari Boumedienne, had taken over—in the name of a mysterious "Revolutionary Council." . . .

There were no spontaneous demonstrations of joy over the downfall of Ben Bella. His successor drew no shouts of "Yah, yah, Boumedienne"; the colonel was no crowd-pleaser and he knew it. His well-paid army was respected but not popular. Thanks to the 1954-62 war for independence, most Algerians were

[6] From "In Algeria It's Not 'Yah, Yah, Boumediene!' but 'Wait and See,' " by Peter Braestrup and David Ottaway, correspondents. New York *Times Magazine*. p 36-7+. F. 13, '66. © 1966 by The New York Times Company. Reprinted by permission.

tired and fearful of soldiery. And, after three years of a disillusioning economic slump and surrealistic slogans, most Algerians had become numb to political crisis.

In the busy cafés around the Place des Martyrs, on the Casbah's edge, the ragged coffee-drinkers traded rumors, exchanged news of job-seeking relatives in France, and, when asked about the new regime, murmured, "Wait and see."

The people of Algeria have been watching and waiting ever since.

Everyday life in the capital, with its French architecture and a spectacular view of the Bay of Algiers, has not changed noticeably. During Ramadan, the annual month-long Moslem marathon of daytime fasting and all-night feasting, prices of tomatoes and potatoes rose, as usual; as usual, the authorities threw a few dozen unlucky merchant "profiteers" into Maison Carrée prison. The government has ordered yet another census of Algiers housing, including thousands of new "nationalized" apartments abandoned by the French in 1962-63 and now occupied by indigent squatters. Under the arcades, the street venders still hawk Hollywood-brand chewing gum, combs and shoelaces, despite intermittent police harassment. The sidewalk crowds have lost none of their aimless bustle; except for a few government secretaries, the women still wear veils and shawls like sheets. The new regime, like the last, has promised them "emancipation" from child marriage and from confinements at home.

On the waterfront, waiting to board the *Ville d'Oran* for the overnight trip to Marseilles and a low-paid job in France, are the same refugees from Algeria's economic doldrums: files of thin, shabby, patient men with proud mustaches and cardboard suitcases. On the Rue Michelet, young bureaucrats and students in Italian-cut suits and tinted sunglasses cluster at café tables for lively gossip in a mélange of French and Arabic, just as they did under Ben Bella. The Boumedienne effort at "austerity," if it has discouraged Sunday driving in government cars, has not ended traffic jams or brought Calvinist working hours; the three-hour siesta remains the rule. On warmer days there are poolside bikinis and bikini-watchers at El Kattani, midday refuge for white-collar Algerians, the shrinking French colony, and diplomats of all persuasions. The French alarm one another with reports of burglaries, midnight arrests, and new currency restrictions in Algeria. The diplomats trade rumors and complain about the impossibility of getting anything repaired.

To be sure, to the distress of Marxist kibitzers in distant Paris, several of Ben Bella's most celebrated projects have been quietly scuttled or cut back—notably the bankrupt "Socialist pilot stores" and that futile counter to the regular army, the People's Militia. . . .

But so far the change is more one of style than of policy. The new regime accuses Ben Bella only of having been a power-mad "deviationist" and an administrative fumbler, not of having erred in pushing the "worker self-management" doctrine on nationalized, formerly French farms and factories. Indeed, Boumedienne has doggedly pledged continued fidelity to Algeria's "Socialist option." But most diplomats here think that he has yet to make up his mind on how "Socialist" Algeria can afford to be. Some think his regime is merely a transition—to what nobody knows.

Boumedienne's direct personal impact on his fellow citizens has been all but invisible. He addressed his first major mass rally in November, on the eleventh anniversary of the start of the Algerian revolt against French rule. To Ben Bella's spectacular Castro-style public harangues, he prefers serious, get-down-to-business rhetoric, in closed meetings of the National Liberation Front (FLN) or the Revolutionary Council.

He has been accused by the French Communist party of leading a "Fascist junta," of sabotaging "socialism" and Algeria's "worker self-management" system, of being an ally of "neo-colonialism." He has yet to set anyone else's pulse racing.

Nevertheless, Boumedienne has replied to his critics—in speeches and in rare interviews, which he dislikes.

We are not an army of mercenaries. We are militants, children of peasants and workers, of intellectuals and nationalists worthy of the name [he says]. We took up arms without any military preparation in the classical sense—to fight the colonialists.

As for Ben Bella's ousted coterie of Algerian and foreign Trotskyites, Marxists and Communists, they were "foreigners who delight in empty words and play with Socialist slogans while totally ignorant of Algeria." Socialism, Boumedienne asserts, is not Ben Bella's "incoherent ensemble of improvised measures and personal reactions." He refers bitingly to Algeria's rival clans of "political careerists." He stresses "productivity," "a foreign policy within our means," "realism," and "civic duty." Algeria, he repeats, "must understand that it cannot continue to live indefinitely above its means."

Who is this gaunt, shy colonel, whose long red hair and intense green eyes make him look more like a starving Irish poet than a guerrilla veteran who stood silently beside Ben Bella for almost three years? Variously described since 1962 as a "fanatic," a "Moslem ascetic," a "pro-Chinese" (or "pro-Soviet") mystery man by the Western press, Boumedienne remains something of an enigma to most of his fellow countrymen.

He has not worn a uniform since he became Ben Bella's defense minister in 1962. In a land of would-be dandies, he favors sports shirts with the collar buttoned and loose-fitting ready-made suits, although he now wears more formal attire on state occasions. He walks somewhat stiffly, his hands clasped behind his back, and politely refuses to talk to most journalists who manage to corner him.

"Why should I smile just because a photographer is taking the trouble to photograph me?" he asked an Egyptian interviewer recently. "There may be nothing to smile about."

But his friends insist that portraying Boumedienne as a kind of North African Calvin Coolidge is unfair. If he is a demon for work and sleeps little, he can also take a Sunday off to visit the aquarium at Castiglione, play a merciless chess game, or spend all night over coffee in lively discussions with his old wartime associates. When one crony wagered that Boumedienne could not give up chain-smoking cigarettes, Boumedienne switched to Havana cigars and, laughing, collected the wager.

Above all, Boumedienne is a good listener, a patient seeker of "consensus" among his political allies, and a man who, unlike most Algerian leaders, believes in letting trained technicians work free of ideological fetters. He has never believed in gaudy display; the highest army rank is colonel, and Boumedienne often rides up front with the chauffeur. His office at the Moorish-style Defense Ministry, in Algier's Le Golf district, is unostentatious; its chief decoration is a portrait of the Emir Abdu-l-Kadir, Algeria's nineteenth-century national hero. Boumedienne's associates deny reports that he has ever been married. "His only wife," said one aide, "has been the army." For a time, Boumedienne employed an interpreter when he received non-Arab visitors, but, in private, according to a French interviewer, he "speaks better French than Ben Bella."

Unlike Ben Bella, Boumedienne is not a veteran of the quarreling post-World War II nationalist movements whose more determined members formed the National Liberation Front and launched the November 1, 1954, uprising against French rule. Nor is he a product of Algeria's long-implanted French education system that produced moderates like Ferhat Abbas, mystics like Hocine Ait-Ahmed, the imprisoned Berber leader, and most of Algeria's handful of latter-day Marxists. He was brought up in the Islamic tradition rather than on Descartes and the Jacobin glories of the French Revolution.

Indeed, Boumedienne has little in common with any of Algeria's "big name" politicians; he is of a different breed, the generation formed in the war itself. Boumedienne has one thing in common with his fellow nationalists; possibly out of habit acquired during the old clandestine days, he does not go out of his way to illuminate his own history. Even his age has been a matter of dispute.

However, interviewed by the writers this fall, the colonel's sixty-four-year-old father, a retired farmer, shed some light on his son's early days. He said that Boumedienne (family name, Mohammed Ben Brahim Boukarouba) was born August 23, 1932, in the tiny hamlet of Clauzel, not far from Guelma, in Algeria's poverty-stricken East.

The senior Boukarouba was a wheat-growing smallholder, a devout Moslem who still speaks no French, and the stern father of seven children. The future Colonel Boumedienne, his parent recalled, was a "shy, silent boy" who preferred reading to sports, or even to eating.

At the age of six, he was sent by his father to French elementary school at Guelma, and also enrolled in the local Koranic class for religious training. It was at Guelma in 1945 that he got his first glimpse of Franco-Algerian conflict, when club-swinging French police dispersed a Moslem street mob demonstrating in favor of an imprisoned nationalist leader.

Shortly afterward, at fourteen, his father sent him to the famed Kettani Médersa (high school) at Constantine, one of Algeria's few "islands" of Arabo-Islamic learning during 130 years of French rule. There Boumedienne stayed for six years, studying the classical Arabic, Islam, Arab literature and the Koran. It was an education common enough in neighboring Tunisia and Morocco, but rare in Algeria, which was officially considered by Paris to be as French as Brittany or the Côte d'Azur.

Young Boumedienne was at Kettani when he was called up for service in the French army in 1952. His father pleaded unsuccessfully with French authorities to leave his son, a bright student, in school. The plea was turned down, and, with four like-minded friends, twenty-year-old Boumedienne fled across the nearby Tunisian frontier and east to Cairo. According to French sources, he enrolled at Cairo's famed Islamic institute at El Azhar University in early 1952, just as Egypt's army colonels ousted King Farouk.

Just how long Boumedienne kept at his studies remains unclear. But much-echoed French press reports that he sandwiched in military training at (1) Moscow or (2) Peking in 1952-54 seem unfounded; the notion has been dismissed as absurd by the colonel's close associates. It seems more plausible that like other fervently nationalistic Algerian students at El Azhar, he soon got in touch with Ben Bella, Mohammed Khider, and the other Cairo-based "historic chiefs" of what was shortly to become the "National Liberation Front."

In any case, after the start of the FLN 1954 uprising in Algeria, Boumedienne dropped his studies and began guerrilla training at a camp provided by President Gamal Abdel Nasser at El Helouan, south of Cairo.

In early 1955, Boumedienne was sent to Morocco—then nearing independence from France—and from there, with eight other Algerians, made a night landing on a deserted beach near the western Algerian port of Oran. Thus did Boumedienne, a thin, taciturn ex-student with a smattering of small-arms training, begin his military career. He took his *nom de guerre* from the name of an Oranais mountain range, and was never known thereafter by any other.

Boumedienne had a tough mission. He was one of a small handful of "outsiders" from east and central Algeria who spread the guerrilla war to the rich vineyards of the Oranais, where heavy French settlement and Moslem apathy had discouraged local nationalists. By 1957 Boumedienne was head of Willaya (military region) 5, covering western Algeria. In June, 1958, he moved to the Algerian nationalist "sanctuary" in Morocco, as chief of the forces on both sides of the frontier. In March, 1960 . . . he took over as head of the National Liberation Army (ALN) general staff at Ghardimaou, Tunisia.

Unlike Ben Bella, whom French propaganda made a villain in France and a hero among Algerian Moslems, Boumedienne was a virtual unknown. He had no military triumph linked to his name (there were no Dienbienphus during the Algerian war). But according to his wartime associates, he was one of the rare ALN guerrilla officers who avoided personal feuds, showed a zest for organization, and a deep respect for the technical aspects of war.

After 1960, as chief of the twenty-thousand-man frontier armies, he was denied an active combat role by the French army's strong Algerian border defenses. But he developed homegrown political indoctrination for the troops, with less emphasis on Mao Tse-tung or Castro than on Arab culture and Algerian history. He also kept the loyalty of his subordinates through the periodic feuds that wracked the FLN leadership. He survived several efforts to depose him, and during one crisis his officers rejected his own offer to resign.

This loyalty, rare in Algerian politics, was important when the demoralizing post-independence struggle for power began in the summer of 1962. Boumedienne differed with the FLN politicians in Tunis on several counts. He opposed the Évian accords that ended the Algerian war as too favorable to France. He suspected the high-living Tunis FLN leadership of trying to walk off with the fruits of a victory won by the endurance of the army's *Djounoud* (GI's). The Tunis politicians, in turn, feared (rightly) that Boumedienne would try to dictate Algeria's postwar regime. In June, 1962, on the eve of independence, they abruptly fired him and two aides from the general staff. Boumedienne's officers remained loyal to their chief; and the provisional government, headed by Ben Youssef Ben Khedda, discovered that it had no military muscle to back up its orders.

No public figure, Boumedienne needed a "political" ally. Ben Bella, just out of French prison, was a national martyr-hero; he was ambitious and equally opposed to the Tunis politicians. Ben Bella needed the army's muscle. In what almost became a civil war, the peasant's son backed by Boumedienne's battalions, relatively well-trained and disciplined, finally came out on top. Ben Bella was installed as premier of the "Democratic People's Republic of Algeria" in September 1962. Boumedienne soon faded out of public view. His obsession was the conversion of the ragtag "Army of National Liberation" into a professional Soviet-equipped army second only to Nasser's on the African continent. He is still at this, to the concern of his Tunisian and Moroccan neighbors.

Beginning in late 1963, Boumedienne made the army a privileged "state within a state." Private's pay started at $40 a month, roughly half the annual revenue of an Algerian peasant. The officers got a $100,000 remodeled casino outside Algiers for their own club. All hands got new smart gabardine dress uniforms. The Soviets furnished tanks, jets and instructors. In addition, the army ran its own "cooperatives," its own printing plants, a chicken farm and a furniture plant, and published, for public consumption, the fortnightly *El-Djeich* (The Army), a local bilingual version of *Time*. The army had its own political commissars (kept outside civilian party control), its own literacy classes, its own premilitary high schools (one thousand students), as well as its own highly active secret police.

Although army propagandists made much of the slogan, "Pick in one hand, rifle in the other," the slogan's application in civic action was largely symbolic. However great his sympathy for "fellow revolutionaries" in Cuba, China or Yugoslavia, Boumedienne had no illusions about the role of the ANP as a "people's army." Its first task was to organize, unify and train along conventional lines, police duties permitting. On the side, the ANP backed up Ben Bella's "African Vocation" by training cadres for African liberation movements (some one thousand by January 1964, according to Ben Bella) and shipping arms to the south.

In the meantime, as always seems to happen in Algeria, the political marriage turned sour. Ben Bella's French and Algerian Marxist advisers warned the Algerian president that the National People's Army was a "Bonapartist" political threat. In public, Boumedienne said nothing. He dutifully arrested "counter-revolutionaries," suppressed several regional revolts against the one-party Ben Bella regime and bitterly watched his unprepared forces get mauled in a month-long Sahara border fight with Morocco in October 1963. But, privately, the colonel and his allies in the cabinet became increasingly uneasy about Ben Bella and his slogan-happy entourage. They resented the president's growing disregard for the FLN tradition of "collective leadership," distrusted his on-again, off-again alliances with Boumedienne's foes, and grumbled over the proliferation of costly "Socialist" experiments. In early 1964, Boumedienne offered Ben Bella his resignation, just before the FLN party congress.

Ben Bella promised to run less of a one-man show and to pay more attention both to the party central committee and to the growing economic crisis. He did neither. Instead he gathered more power into his own hands—the interior ministry, finances, foreign policy. He set up his own fifteen-hundred-man palace guard. He did his best to soothe Boumedienne with bigger defense budgets, and at the same time, tried to curb and divide the army.

The Marxists, backed by Algeria's legally outlawed but active Communists, got Ben Bella to set up a party-controlled People's Militia to offset the army's battalions. Boumedienne quietly talked with the militia commander; the militia really never got started, although Peking promised to arm it. In the fall of 1963, Ben Bella appointed an army chief of staff, Colonel Tahar Zbiri, while Boumedienne was in Moscow negotiating for arms; Boumedienne and Zbiri talked things over, privately agreed to frustrate Ben Bella's efforts to set them at each other's throats. But confident of his own growing prestige, Ben Bella, finally, sought to oust foreign minister Abdelaziz Bouteflika, Boumedienne's chief cabinet ally, two weeks before the climactic Afro-Asian summit.

Bouteflika refused to step down. Boumedienne backed him.

For more than a year, high-ranking army officers had been urging a coup d'état. Boumedienne, as usual, had been reluctant to take such an irreversible step (although, characteristically, he made contingent plans).

This time it was, as one of the colonel's aides put it later, "Ben Bella's head or Boumedienne's." Two days after the Ben Bella regime put out a communiqué denouncing foreign press reports of "rifts within the revolutionary leadership," Boumedienne acted. Shortly after midnight, on June 19, Ben Bella was arrested, spirited away to a still undisclosed location, and the twenty-six-man Revolutionary Council, including many of Ben Bella's former cabinet aides, was in power.

The new regime has given every sign of being profoundly impressed by the problems it inherited—among them the $88 million 1965 budget deficit, the twenty-million-hectoliter surplus of unsold wine, or the chaos in the nationalized, formerly French farm sector. . . .

Abroad, Boumedienne has apparently warmed up his relations with Soviet bloc nations whose leaders were surprised and upset by the ouster of "their man in Africa." During a trip last December [1965] to Moscow (his fourth), the Algerian President apparently got assurances that the Soviet economic aid commitment of $227 million would be maintained. The Soviets had already sent Boumedienne an estimated sixty aircraft, some surface-to-air missiles, and three hundred tanks, including those deployed in the June coup.

But Boumedienne's recent incarceration of Bachir Hadj Ali, former Algerian Communist leader, and his other far-left enemies, left the Kremlin with some reservations. The Soviet-line French Communist daily *L'Humanité* complained that it was impossible simultaneously to "build socialism and fight Communists."

In Paris, French officials privately speak of Boumedienne as an improvement over Ben Bella, even if the colonel is far less fascinated by General de Gaulle. French treaty rights (Sahara nuclear test bases, the naval and air complex at Mers-el-Kebir) have not been questioned; last July [1965] the two countries signed a long-negotiated oil agreement that gives Algeria a five-year $400 million loan-and-grant program for industrialization. Algeria remains General de Gaulle's biggest interest in the underdeveloped world. Despite flurries of mutual irritation, France remains Algeria's key source of aid (including 11,500 teachers and technicians) and its only important market for wine, oil, natural gas and citrus fruits.

The United States State Department has been impressed by Boumedienne's vows to concentrate on putting his ramshackle house in order. If the new regime has taken pains to declare that it is no less "anti-imperialist," "Socialist" or "revolutionary" than the old, Colonel Boumedienne has also seemed little tempted to take orders from Moscow, Cairo, or the indignant French Communist party. The United States has kept up its token food-relief shipments—some fifty thousand tons last year—pending agreement on a new program involving wheat but no dollar grants. As under Ben Bella, Washington maintains a "presence" here; a warmer embrace from Uncle Sam has neither been offered nor sought.

Can Boumedienne get Algeria moving again? Most short-range predictions are gloomy. There are still 2 million jobless here and 500,000 more are forced to seek a livelihood in France. The heritage of a 130-year-old colonial economy, of an artificial war boom, of 80 per cent illiteracy, of French consumer tastes but relaxed work habits would be hard to overcome under any circumstances. If the peasants of the Aurès and the Kabylia Mountains are fully conscious of their misery, it is difficult for Boumedienne's fellow countrymen in the modern coastal cities to accept the fact that Algeria is unable even to produce enough food for her booming population. The university students are restless; urban labor leaders are hostile. City workers protest economy layoffs and stage wildcat strikes for French-level wages and benefits; the government feels impelled to maintain three big money-losing television stations, a jet-equipped airline and scores of little-used airports—all inherited from the departed French. Boumedienne's administrative budget for 1966 is $30 million higher than last year's, despite the "austerity" talk. Even the expected new revenues from Sahara oil and gas will do little more than make up lost profits in the chaotic "Socialist" farm sector. From the colonial epoch, Algeria in effect got a Cadillac limousine which it cannot afford to keep in gas and tires.

Boumedienne has brought a measure of reason and stability to Algiers. But he is up against the same crushing problems as the man he reluctantly ousted. At least, he does not pretend the problems will go away.

NEW ALGERIA LOSES MOMENTUM [7]

At the time when the Charte d'Alger was formally accepted in April 1964, as the political, social and economic credo of the Front de Libération Nationale (FLN), it looked for a moment as if both the institutions and the policy of the New Algeria were set firm. The country was to be a single party state along the lines of a people's democracy and wedded to a policy rooted in orthodox Marxist analysis, but taking a leaf out of President Tito's book, as regards decentralization of economic power, as well as one out of President Nasser's book in rejecting Stalinist methods to compel capital accumulation.

Moreover, when Colonel Boumedienne ousted President Ben Bella in June . . . [1965] it looked as if his object was to bring Algeria back to the straight and narrow path of this credo, from

[7] From article by J. H. Huizinga, special correspondent. *The Times* (London). p 13. Mr. 31, '66. Reprinted by permission.

which it had deviated in the last phase of his predecessor's rule. He had made it not so much a one-party state as a one-man state and talked more about the Socialist revolution than implementing it. "Today," the new leader said a fortnight after his seizure of power, "the era of purely verbal socialism is over, we are now starting on the construction of the socialist economy."

It was true enough that, in spite of the Charte d'Alger and Mr. Ben Bella's brave talk, the country remained Socialist on paper only. After the takeover of the abandoned agricultural, industrial, commercial and residential property of the fleeing French he had rested on his revolutionary laurels. He had left even some of the French assets untouched, in particular the so-called "commanding heights of the economy" that any Socialist worth his salt goes for first, the banks. He himself recognized a few months before his overthrow that the private sector remained three times as large as the public sector and promised to undo this situation before the end of 1965, just as he promised—but did nothing about—agrarian reform aimed at the larger Algerian landowners.

So far, however, only the negative part of Colonel Boumedienne's promise that in future there would be less Socialist talk and more action has been implemented. He has shown himself a man of few deeds as well as few words. He has done nothing to carry out Mr. Ben Bella's promise of further encroachments on the private sector. Nor has he done anything more than his predecessor about agrarian reform. Not that there is much Socialist credit to be gained with that project. Algeria is no Egypt or Iran, with vast native-owned latifundia [estates] offering scope for a spectacular shareout of agricultural wealth. There are only a few landlords possessing extensive estates. Algeria's problem, therefore, is not so much to redistribute the land, to revolutionize its ownership, as to make it more productive by revolutionizing its cultivation.

It is partly because of this and partly because Mr. Ben Bella had pretty well exhausted the possibilities for "socialism without tears," that his successor had so little left to offer in the way of glorious revolutionary action. Hence, the impatience with his regime manifested by the students. Their rebellious mood has been officially attributed to that same "tiny and totally unrepresentative minority of agitators and troublemakers," which also used to be trotted out regularly by the former colonial ruler whenever he had a riot on his hands. But there is no need of this stock character to account for the students' unrest. Even after Mr. Ben Bella ran out of loot to nationalize, and thus no longer had revolutionary bread to offer, he still offered circuses, splendid visions of the Socialist future.

Colonel Boumedienne offers neither bread nor circuses. He not only does nothing about "the construction of the Socialist economy," he hardly ever says anything about it either. At first this verbal austerity was welcomed by many as a change from Mr. Ben Bella's noisy demagogy. But as the months went by and the strong silent man still failed to reveal himself as a man of action, impatience and disappointment became manifest.

This is felt not only among the young and the left-wingers. I have heard the same sentiments expressed by members of the business community. There, too, the ever recurring complaint was about the regime's immobilism. And in these more conservative circles it was inspired, of course, not by disappointment at the stagnating "Socialist revolution," but at the absence of any well-defined economic policy, whether Socialist or any other.

There is little doubt that the immobilism is due also to tensions within the regime. Colonel Boumedienne is no President Nasser, laying down the law to all and sundry. Perhaps he is only biding his time as the Egyptian leader did for a year. Or perhaps he will prove to be the Naguib of Algeria, pushed aside by a more resolute, ruthless operator. [Mohammed Naguib was ousted from power in Egypt by Nasser in 1954.—Ed.] These are subjects of endless speculation in Algiers. All one knows is that for the time being, out of weakness or conviction, in reaction against Mr. Ben Bella's personalization of power, he maintains a "collegial" form of government. And as neither the Revolutionary Council nor the government operating under its guidance is a homogeneous entity, but rather a coalition of various political persuasions and military clans, the consensus required for action is not easy to achieve.

Though the regime naturally tries to present a united front, enough is known of what happens behind the scenes to evoke memories of the situation in the summer of 1962. At that time, immediately after independence, a prolonged and confused struggle for power broke out between the rival personalities and groups that had been able to sink their differences only for as long as the armed struggle continued. They were divided not only by competing ambitions and class-based political views, there was also the division between those who had fought the war from outside, based on Tunisia and Morocco, and the *maquisards* [guerrilla fighters] in the interior, who had borne the brunt of the struggle and who themselves were again split up in regional clans.

It was Colonel Boumedienne who finally put an end to their protracted squabbles by imposing Mr. Ben Bella's rule. By withdrawing his support from him three years later and setting up his own "collegial" broad-based government, he has in a sense restored the status quo ante, with the difference that the squabbling now no longer takes place in the political market place but behind the closed doors of the Revolutionary Council and the government.

Thus, up to a point, Algeria is back to square one, with both the future of its institutions and its policy orientation once again in the balance, and the Charte d'Alger, which claimed to have resolved these issues, little more than a dusty blueprint.

As for the single-party state, it, too, exists only on paper so far. To become a reality instead of a façade for army rule, discreet as in the days of Mr. Ben Bella or avowed as today, it requires the existence of a party like President Bourguiba's Neo-Destour, disciplined, homogeneous, strongly organized and properly implanted, with grass roots in the masses. The FLN is nothing of the sort. After four years of peace it is still only the atrophied remains of a wartime resistance movement that, like all such movements, embraces the most heterogeneous elements, forms a small minority of the populace and in peace time has lost its grip on the masses.

Colonel Boumedienne has been no more successful than Mr. Ben Bella in turning it into an effective instrument of political power. In fact, the Colonel's political power—as distinct from the power he derives from the bayonets at his disposal—would, if anything, seem to be even weaker than Mr. Ben Bella's, as his attempts to "parachute" new leaders on to the trade unions and the student bodies have not helped to make him popular in these quarters.

Four years after independence there still hangs fundamentally the same question mark over Algeria's future, its choice of institutions, policy and ruling figures, as in the dawn of its hard-won freedom. Only one thing seems reasonably certain; in whichever direction the country may evolve, the brave document that so confidently gave all the answers in April 1964 is not likely to prove a very reliable guide.

BLACK GOLD IN THE SAHARA [8]

Little by little, the Sahara is becoming "Algerianized." Colonel Houari Boumedienne, like the man he ousted as president June 19 [1965], Ahmed Ben Bella, is slowly asserting "Socialist" Algeria's hard-won sovereignty over the most developed, most celebrated portion of the cruel desert that stretches across Northern Africa from the Atlantic to the Red Sea. Once more, the people of the Sahara are feeling the impact of change imposed by outsiders.

This time, the outsiders are fellow Moslems. As a result of Algeria's independence from France in 1962, the newcomers are also fellow countrymen, if not fellow "men of the desert." From Algiers, on the green Mediterranean coast, the new regime's "militants" and administrators, as well as unhappy lesser bureaucrats . . . have been sent to the south. They replace the French, whose soldiers first pacified the Sahara in keeping with France's *mission civilisatrice* fifty years ago.

[8] From "The Cruel Desert Is Algeria's Wealth," by Peter Braestrup, correspondent. New York *Times Magazine.* p 76-7+. N. 7, '65. © 1965 by The New York Times Company. Reprinted by permission.

As the French found out, governing the Sahara is no mean task: a 680,000-square-mile expanse (two and one half times the size of Texas) of bleak mountains and mesas, of waterless plateaus, of cramped oases, of great *ergs* (seas of sand dunes), with a scattered, largely illiterate, semidestitute population of perhaps 730,000, many of them nomads.

To most Algerians of the north, "the south" seems as unpleasant and strange as Greenland or Papua. Nevertheless, the symbols of the new order were put in place. Poster portraits of Ben Bella ("The Militant") graced the adobe walls of fly-ridden town halls in oases the Algerian president had never seen. The green-red-and-white colors of the Democratic People's Republic adorn a dozen vacated Foreign Legion *bordjs* (forts) from Tindouf, on the disputed Moroccan border, to Djanet, gateway to Niger.

In the larger northern Sahara towns, like Colomb-Béchar (population 45,000) or Laghouat (population 50,000), local officials of Algeria's ruling National Liberation Front have done their best to "mobilize the masses" for the periodic nationwide "days of solidarity" with "brother revolutionaries" in faraway Cuba or Vietnam or with the Palestinian Arabs exiled from Israel. Long run by France as a separate entity called "the Southern Territories," the Sahara is now to be fully integrated, according to Algiers spokesmen, into the nation's march along "the road to socialism."

Nevertheless, on their rare speaking tours in the Sahara, cabinet ministers, even under Ben Bella, eschewed the usual quotations from Lenin, *à la mode* in Algiers. Aside from seizing a few European-owned trucking firms, movie houses, hotels and date-palm groves, the government has warily marked time on "socializing" the Sahara, although reforms are contemplated. The regime's preoccupation is with the Sahara as a source—Algeria's only major source—of national wealth. On paper, at least, the potential is enormous.

The Sahara's known reserves of natural gas, barely tapped by new exports to the United Kingdom and France, are estimated at over 2,000 billion cubic meters, 10 per cent of the world's supply.

After nine years and almost $2 billion of French and other foreign investment, annual oil production has grown to 26.5 million tons (1964) with annual revenues to the new Algerian state of about $80 million. Completion of a third pipeline to the sea . . . is expected to increase both figures by more than 25 per cent.

In November 1963 Paris and Algiers began holding off-and-on secret talks on Ben Bella's demands for a new "revolutionary" Sahara oil and gas deal. . . . Last July [1965], shortly after Mr. Ben Bella's fall from power, Colonel Boumedienne's representatives finally reached a compromise agreement with Paris. Existing French oil company concessions and management were largely assured—at the price of heavier tax-royalty burdens and joint Franco-Algerian control over exploration and exploitation in the future.

Most welcome to the hard-pressed Algerians were the prospects, under the less-than-revolutionary July accord, of tripling annual oil revenues (to $240 million) by 1970 and of a five-year French government loan-and-grant aid commitment totaling $400 million.

"De Gaulle gave away the house," observed a French oil company executive, "but he saved the furniture."

The French government, itself a major investor in Sahara oil and gas, wanted—and wants—no rupture with Algiers. It has important interests at stake in the Sahara, affecting de Gaulle's quest for French independence and *grandeur*.

For one thing, de Gaulle currently satisfies about 40 per cent of France's petroleum needs from the Sahara fields. This oil, expensive to produce, costs as much as $2.30 a barrel as against $1.80 a barrel for oil from neighboring Libya. But France pays for Sahara oil in French francs, thus saving about $280 million a year in foreign exchange and strengthening her strong dollar holdings.

Secondly, as Paris sees it, a Franco-Algerian crisis over oil and gas might lead to abrogation of France's five-year rights—under the accords that ended the 1954-62 Algerian war—to elaborate atomic test sites and missile ranges in the western Sahara. De Gaulle needs these bases to develop his controversial nuclear strike force, pending completion of new test bases in the Pacific.

As the French and Algerian oil specialists, in their Italian-cut suits and pointed shoes, commute back and forth by jet between Paris and Algiers, other voices are heard. Under United Nations tutelage Algeria, Morocco, Tunisia, Niger, Mali and other African states bordering the desert are discussing a trans-Sahara highway to link the Arab North with Black Africa. Algiers newspapers this spring spoke euphorically of possible French help for a trans-Sahara railroad, reviving a twenty-seven-year-old dream. Experiments in neighboring Libya have shown that trees can grow in sand dunes stabilized by a coat of oil, and it might work in the Sahara. All these projects require cash; cash is scarce.

Meanwhile, the Sahara itself—or the several Saharas—are patiently adjusting to life under the star-and-crescent flag.

The Traveler's Sahara

No change of slogans, flags and administrators can alter the Sahara's *mystique*—its silence, its vastness, its astonishing physical variety, its harsh elemental grandeur.

As a veteran French specialist, Guy Philippe Fety, observed recently, the Sahara offers the Westerner both solitude and an escape from his "compartmentalized, hierarchized, intellectually conditioned" life at home. In the Sahara, Fety wrote, one is forced, willy-nilly, to contemplate "eternity and the infinite."

The Sahara has attracted anthropologists, geologists, archeologists—who have yet to determine, with any precision, how and when the Sahara became a desert.

It has also attracted its share of resident mystics, hermits and missionaries. There are teen-age French girls, in gray smocks, the Little Sisters of Père de Foucauld, novices of a Catholic contemplative order inspired by the famed scholar-missionary who was slain by dissident tribesmen in 1916. The girls tend goats in the barren Hoggar Mountains. An English Evangelical Protestant missionary at Tamanrasset has made only one convert, a local hospital attendant, in fourteen years, but he has translated the Sermon on the Mount into Tamahaq, the language of the

Tuareg nomads. Almost every major oasis seems to have its retired Foreign Legionnaire or middle-aged, sunburned French expatriate, in baggy black Sahara trousers and sandals, who has taken a native wife and become part of the landscape.

Least exotic, but perhaps most useful, are the nonproselyting White Sisters, Catholic nuns who have taught the three R's and rug-weaving to hundreds of otherwise neglected oasis women.

All these intruders have been tolerated by the new Algerian administrators, and by the Moslem population, since independence; the Saharans, secure in their own age-old traditions, never subjected to intensive colonization, little touched by the Algerian war, have few complexes about foreigners.

If the Sahara's *mystique* remains unaltered, the fading of the French "presence" has made travel there somewhat more painful, a process likely to continue. The oil boom, the French test bases and the influx of French military during the 1954-62 war brought the Sahara an unusually well-developed road system; but the southern two thirds of the area is still traversed by Land Rover or diesel truck over rocky *pistes,* or tracks, which, marked by pillars of stones, trace the route across sand and plateau. It takes five or six days to reach Djanet from Algiers.

The temperature changes as much as 60 degrees Fahrenheit in a few hours. Last February, camping in the desert south of Ouargla, I found icy slush in the water cans at dawn; by noon, one risked sunstroke without a hat. At sundown, I was shivering in a chill breeze. The air's dryness is phenomenal; one can drink a gallon of water a day without feeling a bead of perspiration, so quickly does body moisture evaporate. A fresh package of cigarettes, opened at breakfast, becomes a mess of crisp paper and dry tobacco shreds by evening. Sandstorms, added to dust, drastically shorten the useful life of machinery; after twelve thousand miles over the Sahara, a vehicle is often ready for the scrap heap.

Except for the fortunate few who can travel by cross-country vehicle, carrying their own canned water, provisions, sleeping bags and spare parts, most travelers come in by air. There are fifteen airstrips of airports in the Sahara; twice a week, from

October through May, barring sandstorms, the French-piloted Air Algérie DC-4 makes the swing through the Sahara, carrying mail, light cargo, newspapers and French technicians to the oases cut off like islands from the outside world.

Once on the ground, the air traveler finds austerity. The guides, the hospitable French garrisons, the cars for hire of yester-year are gone. The oases are poor. Transport costs make food prices double those of Algiers. Except in Ghardaïa, Bou-Saâda and Ouargla, hotels formerly run by Frenchmen have either closed or been "Algerianized." The service and cookery vary unpredictably from good (Béni-Abbès, El Goléa, Adrar) to flophouse (Touggourt, Djanet, In-Salah). At Colomb-Béchar, I had to help the friendly but semiliterate room clerk add up the bill; and all the hotel's breakfast coffee had been requisitioned by the prefecture at the last minute for a banquet in honor of a visiting cabinet minister. In the Sahara, as elsewhere in Algeria, the care and feeding of foreign visitors remains an art to be acquired.

The Oilman's Sahara

At the big centers of Hassi Messaoud and In-Amenas and a score of smaller isolated self-contained oil camps, the 3,600 French technicians and 6,000 Algerians live, as Claude Cheysson, director of the Franco-Algerian Organisme Saharien, wrote, "like the crews of submarines." Air-conditioned trailers, bars adorned by pin-ups from *Playboy*, nightly movies, food and wine flown in from France—these amenities ease the hard life of the drilling crews. The starting cash wage for the Algerians is $160 a month —good pay in Algeria. They get room and board and transportation. The crews may work four weeks of daily ten-hour shifts in the desert, then go home for a week's rest. "The pay is good," said a Frenchman at Hassi Tuareg. "But you blow it all in Paris on your leave."

Algiers' violent attacks on the status quo fixed by the 1962 Franco-Algerian oil agreements have had their effect in the Sahara. Uncertainty over the future of their $2 billion investment led the oil companies to halt most new prospecting and drilling, pending new accords. Pressure for "Algerianization" of the better-paying oilfield jobs has led to dramatic changes: 18 per cent of the 646 top "engineers and cadre" posts are now filled by Algerians, a sixteen-fold increase over the last two years.

Such "Algerianization"—and the prospect of more—has disturbed the French oil technicians, who wonder about their own futures. Yet the need for foreign help in the oilfields is unlikely to disappear soon. Not until 1970 will the first batch of Soviet-trained Algerian oil engineers graduate from the new technical institute, opened with fanfare by Ben Bella last year at Rocher Noir, east of Algiers.

The French Army's Sahara

Three years after Algeria's independence, the Algerian government has Africa's biggest remaining western military base in its own back yard. General de Gaulle, as one Algerian cynic noted, pays high rent: about $300 million in various forms of aid to Algeria last year alone. Despite their frequent condemnations of "foreign bases" elsewhere, neither Algerian press nor radio ever mentions the French army's striking presence in the western Sahara: the forward logistics base at Colomb-Béchar, the experimental missile center at Hamaguir, the "technological city" outside Reggane, the underground atomic testing site at In-Ekker in the Hoggar Mountains, and a dozen lesser posts manned by the Foreign Legion in between.

Yet in Colomb-Béchar, the tricolor flies proudly as of old. Dapper French officers in uniform stroll home from the office past the young olive-clad recruits of the Algerian National People's Army and posters decrying "neocolonialism." About three thousand French soldiers and technicians and their dependents live here in an air-conditioned, self-contained enclave, coexisting peaceably with a large Algerian frontier garrison and a growing Moslem slum population.

Along the paved highway south of Hamaguir, roadside signs bluntly warn the motorist that he is in a French army missile-firing range.

"I don't know how long we're going to stay," commented a Foreign Legion corporal at In-Salah. "But I guess the Arabs won't miss us, except for our money."

Whatever its psychic benefits, the French army's 1962-63 withdrawal from the eastern Sahara has not helped the local subsistence economy. The army's public works projects, its road maintenance, its housekeeping chores employed far more men of the Sahara than the oilfields of the north ever did. Now the French are slowly pulling out of the western Sahara. Officials in Tamanrasset, for example, are wondering what kind of jobs can be found for the fifteen hundred Saharans digging tunnels for underground atomic tests at In-Ekker.

The Saharans' Sahara

The French army's withdrawal (mandatory by mid-1967), the slackening of oilfield activity and the continuing postwar economic depression in the overpopulated north do not brighten the Saharans' economic prospects, which were never bright anyway.

Least affected by the change are the nomads, notably the Chaamba of Arab stock and the Hoggar's matriarchal Tuaregs whose veiled "Blue Men" still carry broadswords, speak their own Berber dialect and leave menial oasis labor to their Negro vassals. The Chaamba cross the great *ergs* from waterhole to waterhole with their black goats and short-haired brown sheep, moving to sparse pasture in the north in summer, the south in winter, ignoring the frontiers with Mali and Niger. If the camel caravans, once the mainstay of interoasis trade, have drastically diminished, they still carry dates, cloth, tea and sugar to the nomad tent encampments unreachable by diesel truck.

The nomads' routes often take them across the new macadam highways south of Ouargla and Touggourt. Little spare weather-honed men in flowing robes and sandals, they slide off their camels to squint amiably at the passerby, ask for bread and matches, and shake hands. Then they remount, move off easily across the low dunes. The brass food pans hanging from their saddles flash in the sun. Algiers might as well be on another planet.

But nomadism, as a way of life, is fading. The Tuaregs and Chaamba have even begun to drift toward the oases. And even in the big northern Sahara oases, life is far from easy, as population growth outstrips the food supply. Here, as elsewhere, United States relief food staves off starvation.

At Laghouat, on the Sahara's northern edge, local authorities can put on a good show for visiting officials: shotgun salutes fired by turbaned horsemen on prancing steeds, veiled Moslem women warbling the traditional *you-you,* a succulent *mechoui* (roast sheep) in the fragrant garden of the French-built subprefecture. Algerian sentries slouch on guard duty at the hilltop citadel dominating the palm groves and the low adobe houses, and Algerian gendarmes careen importantly through the streets in their new Land Rovers.

But the Mozabite shopkeepers, selling canned sardines and Polish hardware and cigarettes by the piece under the arcades, complain of rising prices and disorganization of transport. The cafés are full of ragged mustached Arabs, sipping the gritty, sweet Algerian coffee and exchanging rumors on prospects for paid employment.

"We have the roads and electricity and independence," said a local official. "But we need more irrigation, more teachers, more technicians and, above all, more jobs." He sighed. "Maybe ten years from now, things will be better, God willing."

During the past ten years, contact with twentieth-century Europeans gave young Saharans in the bigger oases a taste for cash wages, transistor radios and motorbikes. Many forsook the age-old cultivation of painfully irrigated gardens to work on the new roads and airports. As an Algerian official in Adrar observed, "Now they don't want to go back to their gardens. But there is nothing else."

In August [1965] an official Franco-Algerian study put Sahara unemployment at 120,000—or twenty times the total number of Algerians employed in the oilfields. The study's authors, moreover, predicted that the Sahara's population would grow by 550,000 over the next twenty years with no new food resources in sight. Unlike its Tunisian neighbor, Algiers has shown no enthusiasm for birth-control schemes.

Malnutrition, illiteracy (93 per cent among the women), tuberculosis, trachoma (afflicting 80 per cent of the people in the fly-ridden oases) add to the Saharans' distress. There are but 54 doctors for 730,000 widely scattered people. Like the Sahara's teachers, most of them are French, working under de Gaulle's aid program.

The regime's laudable drive to put every child into school is here handicapped by the reluctance of Algerian teachers from the north to serve in the south, and the traditional reluctance of Saharans to let their daughters out of the house.

"The school superintendent deplores the instability of the Algerian teachers," noted the Algiers weekly *Révolution Africaine* in a report on Adrar's problems. "But when the food supply is so difficult, the communications so unreliable, the isolation so total, can one ask the young city people, the 'Nordics,' to put down roots in this region?" Without the young Frenchmen, and a handful of Syrians and Egyptians, there would be no schools worth mentioning in the Sahara.

In strictly economic terms, "Algerianization" has ended the Sahara's favored position. The French government, as a matter of policy, gave the Sahara a break on consumer taxes, notably on gasoline. It consecrated its share of the oil royalties entirely to Sahara development. The hard-pressed Algiers regime necessarily had to end all this. The Sahara is now just one more distressed area among many in Algeria.

The joint Franco-Algerian oil regulatory board and development agency, the Organisme Saharien, has in effect kept the Sahara going. Financed by the oil companies and by Paris and Algiers, staffed largely by Frenchmen, the Organisme quietly has kept up most of the *pistes,* pushed the paved-road system a few miles farther south, and maintained the airports and telecommunications network. But its resources are meager (1964 budget: $26 million) and its future is uncertain.

According to a 1962 French government report, it would take a $223 million investment in the Sahara's agriculture alone just to double the per capita annual income of $40. It would take, the report added, a "general will to improve," a break with old traditions and reforms of archaic water codes, land ownership and marketing.

Such investments are beyond the capacity of Algeria's deficit-ridden treasury; Algiers is already hard-pressed to supply credits to rehouse several thousand oasis-dwellers whose adobe homes crumbled in freak rainstorms last winter. "We have submitted our plans and our requests to Algiers," said the In-Salah sub-prefect recently. "We are still waiting for a response."

In short, the Sahara's people, barring a miracle, are likely to benefit even less now than before from the riches under their feet. The old Sahara pattern has been broken; Algerianization as yet has brought none to replace it.

VI. LIBYA

EDITOR'S INTRODUCTION

The most enigmatic of the North African countries, Libya has recently come into international prominence as a result of the discovery of vast deposits of oil in her desert soils. Almost overnight this discovery has transformed feudal Libya from one of the poorest of the new African nations into one of the richest. The black gold of the Sahara has changed Libya's way of life, propelled the desert kingdom head-first into the mid-twentieth century, and sparked dramatic reforms in government and society. But the transformation has only begun, and it has not been an easy one. Today Libya lies between two worlds: between the traditional world of her past and the unsettling modern world she now faces, between a society based upon nomadic shepherds with flocks of camels and a society in which bootblacks have become oil millionaires and drive Cadillacs. Riches have been for Libya, as for most individuals, a mixed blessing, and if Libya today is the wealthiest of the North African states, she is not necessarily the most tranquil.

Dr. Philip Hitti of Princeton University fills in Libya's historical past, while in the second article the editors of the *British Survey* draw a portrait of Libya from ancient times until the present day. The following articles discuss the old problems that lie beneath the new wealth and the headaches that accompany oil riches. Hedrick Smith of the New York *Times* portrays some of the contradictions of Libyan oil riches, as does the article from the London *Economist*. The final article, from the *Financial Times* of London, recounts the growing pressures for reform which the oil boom has elicited.

FROM PREHISTORY TO INDEPENDENCE [1]

When the former [Italian-ruled] provinces of Tripolitania, Cyrenaica and the Fezzan were united in a sovereign constitu-

[1] From "Historical Highlights Over Three Millennia," by Philip Hitti, Professor Emeritus, Princeton University. *Afro-Mideast Economic Bulletin.* Spring 1965 Supplement: "Modern Libya." p 8-9. Reprinted by permission.

tional monarchy on December 24, 1951, they adopted the name *Libya*, which has a history stretching back three thousand years.

In the Egyptian hieroglyphic records of the second millenium before Christ, we read of a group of tribes named *Lebu* living to the west of Egypt in what is now Cyrenaica. The Greeks, noting that all of the tribes in the area from west of Egypt across North Africa to the Atlantic looked alike, called the entire region Libya. The Lebu are the people we now call Berbers.

The Romans borrowed the place name, but it fell into disuse from the Middle Ages until it was revived in 1934 to name the new colonial unit formed by joining the provinces of Cyrenaica and Tripolitania.

Tripolitania was the "land of three cities" founded by the Phoenicians about 800 B.C.—Oea (Tripoli), Sabratha (Sabratah) and Leptis Magna (Labdah). The Phoenicians were the first to realize the strategic importance of Tripolitania's location as a link between Egypt and the Near East on one hand and the Mediterranean Basin and tropical Africa on the other.

Through Tripolitania they tapped Africa's gold, gems, ivory and ebony. And, in addition to their merchant activities, Phoenician colonists developed agriculture. They introduced the olive tree, whose fruit is still a staple Libyan product.

The Phoenician colonies of Tripolitania looked to their older and more powerful sister-colony of Carthage (on the site of modern Tunis) for protection against encroachments from the Greeks, especially the Greek colonies in Sicily.

Carthage acted as champion of Phoenicia's cause and under its great son and hero Hannibal, contested with Rome for mastery over the Mediterranean. For fifteen years (218-3 B.C.) Hannibal conducted successful campaigns on Italian soil. The Phoenician era was the first Golden Age in Libyan history.

The second Golden Age followed immediately under the Romans and Byzantines, beginning in the middle of the second century B.C. It was an even more glittering era than its predecessor. The Romans built on Phoenician foundations, adding paved roads, public hot and cold baths, cisterns and dams, forums, theatres and monuments. Relics of these public works in

Leptis, Sabratha and Cyrene attract and amaze modern tourists. These are among the most impressive remains of those ancient empire builders and, next to Luxor-Karnak and the pyramids, the most impressive in all Africa.

They undoubtedly hide more than they display—their excavators having not yet more than scratched the surface.

An indication of the extent of Libya's trade has been preserved for us in the Bible, where Matthew (27:32) tells of a merchant named Simon from Cyrene who was on a business trip in Jerusalem at the time of Christ's crucifixion and was compelled to carry His cross.

The Roman emperor Septimius Severus (193-211 A.D.) was born in Leptis, which he endowed with several public works and monuments still in evidence. This was the emperor who married a Syrian lady, Julia Domna, from Hims and inaugurated the Syrian dynasty in Rome. Under him and other emperors the Libyan cities flourished as trading centers and starting points for caravans to the interior. They enjoyed an era of prosperity and peace unparalleled in their history.

With the Arab conquest, beginning in 643 A.D., the history of Libya took an entirely different course. Its culture was changed and so were its language, religion and population. In a few years the Arabs were able to do in Libya and the rest of North Africa what neither the Romans nor the Byzantines had been able to do in centuries.

The Roman culture in the area was but a thin veneer. Only the littoral was Romanized and Christianized. The hinterland, with its nomadic or seminomadic Berber inhabitants, was hardly touched. But with the Arabs, whom the wave of Moslem conquest spread, Berbers felt close kinship. Indeed, both Hamitic Berbers and Semitic Arabs are members of the same Mediterranian branch of the white race. The two peoples intermixed in the seventh century and later, early in the twelfth century, when the banu-Sulaym and banu-Hilal tribes migrated from Arabia, Cyrenaica received the largest influx of Arabs. Basically the population remained Berber, but, except in out-of-the-way spots, it became Islamized and Arabicized.

But the focus of the Arab world shifted westward to al-Qayrawan (Kairouan, near modern Tunis), founded in 670 by the Arabian general who conquered the area. Al-Qayrawan became seat of the caliphal viceroy and headquarters of the armies which overran Spain and threatened France.

The four centuries beginning in the middle of the twelfth were times of trouble including invasions from Norman Sicily and Spain, and occupation by the Knights of St. John. These were originally a religious order serving Crusaders in Palestine but turned military, occupied Rhodes and Malta and harrassed Turkey. The glory that was Tripolitania began to fade away.

Conquest by the Ottoman Turks, beginning in 1551, did not improve the situation. Libya, in common with its Arab sister-countries to the east—conquered by the Ottomans thirty-four years earlier—was cut off from vital contacts with Western Europe at a time when Europe was emerging from its dark ages and entering an age of unprecedented enlightenment and scientific and industrial development.

In the meantime, two history-making events—the finding of a shorter route around southern Africa connecting western Europe with India and the Far East, and the discovery of the New World—had worked to the disadvantage of the Arab East. The two events gradually diverted the international maritime trade routes from the Mediterranean to the Atlantic, bypassing the Arab world. Economic decline went hand in hand with the intellectual decline.

The thirty years of Italian occupation, beginning in 1912, were perhaps the unhappiest in the history of the Libyan people. The endurance and sacrifice which they displayed in their efforts to gain their liberty won the admiration of the world and, finally overcame the successive attempts to crush their spirits and colonize their land.

The Libyan people, led by Sayyid Mohammed Idris, formed the backbone of the resistance and eventually led the nation to independence.

In World War I, Turkish assistance enabled the Libyans to drive the Italians back to the four main coastal towns. But when the Turks withdrew after the defeat of the Central Powers, the Libyans were left to continue the resistance alone.

In a peace treaty with the Senussi in 1920, the Italians recognized Sayyid Mohammed Idris as Emir of Cyrenaica. But the Italian parliament failed to ratify the treaty. Libyan nationalists refused to compromise their demands for independence and active resistance to the Italian regime was resumed.

Sayyid Mohammed Idris turned over command of the Senussi troops to General Omar el-Mukhtar and went to Egypt, where he organized a line of supplies and arms to his fighting forces. Commander el-Mukhtar mobilized the tribesmen and city dwellers into a resistance army which held out against the Italians for nearly a decade.

In 1931 el-Mukhtar was captured by the Italians and executed. His heroism and martyrdom have been a powerful inspiration for the Libyan freedom fighters.

The liberation of Libya from Italian domination came in World War II. A Libyan battalion led by Sayyid Mohammed Idris fought with the Allies to drive out the Axis powers and the nation finally gained its independence.

The year 1951 marks the birth of the United Kingdom of Libya and signals the dawn of a new era of progress and prosperity. The nation has joined the League of Arab Nations, extended its relations with the Western powers and taken firm steps toward constitutional development. Before the end of the decade, an unusually rich and seemingly inexhaustible new source of national revenue—petroleum—was discovered. The extensive planning and remarkable development since then embrace all aspects of life and promise a new golden age for Libya and the Libyans. In this age Libya faces a unique opportunity to act as liaison between the Arab East and the Arab West—the Maghreb.

LIBYA: PAST AND PRESENT [2]

The name Libya has meant different things to different people throughout history. To the ancient Greeks it meant the continent

[2] From "North Africa." *British Survey* (London). 198:10-19. S. '65. Published by the British Society for International Understanding. 36 Craven St. London W.C. 2. Reprinted by permission.

of Africa and more especially that part of North Africa lying to the west of Egypt. But when we speak of Libya today we refer to the former Italian colony of that name which became an independent kingdom on December 24, 1951.

From 1951 to 1963 it was known as the United Kingdom of Libya and was a federation of Tripolitania, Cyrenaica and the Fezzan. After the Germans and Italians were driven out in 1943, these provinces of Italy's former colony had been under British and French military administration, but they became independent when the British Residents in Tripoli and Cyrenaica and the French Resident in the Fezzan handed over their powers to the Federal Libyan Government. On April 27, 1963, the federation was dissolved and since then the official title of the state has been "The Kingdom of Libya" (Al Mamlaka Al Libiyya). Libya is a hereditary monarchy, ruled by King Idris I, chief of a Moslem religious sect of Cyrenaica called the Senussi. He had previously been recognized by the British as Emir (Prince) of Cyrenaica and was the logical choice as ruler of the new Libya. King Idris (his name means "Enoch") is now seventy-five years old. He has no direct male heir and has designated a nephew, Hassan Rida es-Senussi, the youngest surviving son of his brother, as crown prince and heir to the throne.

Libya is bounded on the north by the Mediterranean (it has a coastline of some one thousand miles), on the west by Tunisia and Algeria, on the south by the republic of Niger and Chad, and on the east by Egypt and the Sudan.

The area is about 680,000 square miles, larger than the whole of Western Europe, but only a very small section, mainly near the coast, is suitable for cultivation; the rest is desert or semidesert. There are no rivers and, apart from wells, Libya depends for its water supply entirely upon the rainfall, which amounts to less than 9 inches annually over the country as a whole. Some areas of Tripolitania rival the Persian Gulf for the unwanted title of the hottest place in the world. Libya, in fact, holds the record for the highest shade temperature in the world, 136.4 degrees F., at a spot in the desert just south of Tripoli.

Libya supports a population of just over 1.5 million, most of whom are living in rural communities or are Bedouin nomads, and nearly all are Arabic-speaking Moslems. About 95 per cent live in the coastal strip. There are only two towns of any size— Tripoli (376,000) and Benghazi (nearly 280,000). The development of the oil industry is leading to a drift from the country to the towns and largely accounts for the rapid growth of Benghazi which ten years ago was only a quarter of its present size. When Libya first became independent, Tripoli and Benghazi acted as the two capitals of the country but a new city has been constructed at Beida in Cyrenaica and since 1961 this has been the official capital and the seat of parliament and the administration.

Three Countries in One State

One of the many problems facing this kingdom is the welding of three separate countries into one united whole. The Libyan national flag (a red, black and green tricolor with a white crescent and star in the center) flies over three areas which possess certain common fundamentals but are very different so far as the living standards and appearance of their people are concerned. They certainly share a common culture and language, Arabic, and a common religion, Islam. Most of the inhabitants gain their livelihood by a primitive form of agriculture or by raising sheep or goats. But racially there is a distinction between Tripolitania, with its preponderance of Berber stock, and Cyrenaica, the home of the Senussi, where the Arab is blended with the Berber. Furthermore, between these two key areas of the kingdom there are five hundred miles of desert and communications are none too good.

As a means of furthering the growth of unity in Libya, the three provinces of Tripolitania, Cyrenaica and the Fezzan were abolished when the federation was dissolved in 1963 and the country was divided into ten administrative districts.

Tripolitania, with a population of over a million is much more Europeanized and more advanced than the rest of the country. This is partly because it is close to Tunisia, where French influence became supreme towards the end of last century, and partly because of the money poured into it by Italy after Libya became an Italian colony. Today there are still about 35,000 Italians living in Tripolitania, mostly in and around Tripoli itself. They are mainly engaged in trade and farming and there are still considerable Italian investments in this area. These settlers have preferred to continue their new life in Africa rather than return to their homeland. As they are superior to the general level of the inhabitants in intelligence, education and industry, they exercise an influence out of all proportion to their numbers. In complete contrast there are few Italians in Cyrenaica, where they made themselves greatly disliked during the Italian occupation. In Tripolitania also there are several other minorities, all of which tend to give it a more cosmopolitan character than the rest of the country. There is, for instance, a group of Arabic-speaking Jews, although many of these have emigrated to Israel in the last few years. Then there are small communities of Greeks, Maltese and Turks.

Cyrenaica, on the other hand, has a much smaller population, about 450,000, most of whom belong to the Senussi sect. Historically Cyrenaica is linked with Greek civilization, while Tripolitania looks back more to a Roman and Carthaginian past. During the Italian occupation of Libya Italy was compelled to wage two wars against the Senussi before conquering Cyrenaica. In the Second World War much more of the fighting took place in Cyrenaica than in Tripolitania, and Benghazi itself endured more than one thousand air raids and changed hands no fewer than five times in the struggle between the British Eighth Army and Rommel's Afrika Korps.

Again in contrast we have Fezzan. Its capital is Sebha and its total population is less than 100,000, although its area is almost as great as that of Cyrenaica and Tripolitania put together. The Fezzan embraces the desert region to the south of Tripoli and communications with the remainder of Libya are very difficult. During the Second World War it was taken from the Italians by the Free French Forces under General Leclerc. For this reason the administration was carried out by the French until Libya became independent. In fact, until 1955 the French maintained a detachment of the French Foreign Legion in the Fezzan.

Recent History

Prior to the coming of the Arabs Libya had known a succession of settlers—Berbers, Phoenicians, Carthaginians, Greeks, Romans and Vandals. Then in the seventh century came the Arab conquest and from that day to this Arabic culture and the Islamic faith have been dominant in Libya, though there have been periods of foreign political rule. The Turks conquered Libya in 1551 and the country remained a province of the Ottoman Empire until invaded by Italy in 1911.

After Mussolini had entered the Second World War on the side of Germany (June 1940) Libya was used as a springboard for Axis attacks upon British positions in Egypt. . . .

The cold war between the Western nations and Russia, which so soon succeeded the collapse of Nazi Germany, bedeviled all discussions about the future of Libya. For a time it seemed as though the strategic needs of the victorious great powers (Libya has immense value as an air and naval base for control of the Mediterranean) were likely to weigh more than the welfare of the recently liberated inhabitants.

By the terms of the peace treaty which came into force in 1947 Italy renounced all claim to her former colonies; these were handed over to the Big Four—the United States, Russia, Britain and France. If agreement could not be reached after one year they were to revert to the trusteeship of the United Nations.

In an endeavor to solve the problem the Big Four sent out to Libya a Commission of Enquiry in 1948, which later in the same year reported to the United Nations. Both the report and the discussion which followed showed remarkable divergences of opinion.

Early in 1949 the problem was handed over to the United Nations General Assembly. A further attempt at a compromise was made with the Bevin-Sforza scheme, so called from the British and Italian foreign ministers who formulated it. This proposed that Libya should be partitioned into three trusteeships —Cyrenaica going to the British, Tripolitania to the Italians and Fezzan to the French. This was defeated in the General Assembly by only one vote. Finally, in November of the same year the General Assembly passed a resolution which placed the three territories of Libya, with their respective military administrations, under the supervision of a United Nations High Commissioner, assisted by an advisory council composed of representatives of Britain, France, the United States, Italy, Egypt, Pakistan, the three Libyan provinces and the principal racial and religious minorities.

After this step had been taken things moved more rapidly. In October 1950 the General Assembly passed a further resolution that a constituent assembly representing the three provinces of Libya should be called to draft a constitution, that Libya should become independent and should be admitted to the United Nations and that it should receive United Nations technical and financial assistance. It was this constituent assembly which met in Tripoli at the end of 1950 and resolved that Libya should become a federal kingdom with equal rights for the three provinces and chose as king Sayyid Idris el Senussi, who had previously (in 1949) been recognized by Britain as the Emir of Cyrenaica. A year later (24 December 1951) independence became a reality. Libya was accepted as a member of the United Nations in 1955.

Administration and Education

Libya is a hereditary constitutional monarchy. There is a central government with a prime minister and his cabinet responsible to two chambers, a Senate of twenty-four members, all nominated by the king, and a House of Representatives, elected on the basis of one deputy to every 20,000 inhabitants. There are 103 deputies, 68 from the western districts (former Tripolitania), 30 from the eastern (former Cyrenaica) and 5 from the southern (the former Fezzan). Elections take place every four years and since 1963 women have had the right to vote. The country is divided into ten administrative districts, each with a wide degree of local self-government. At the head of each is a *muhafidh*, chosen by the cabinet on the advice of the minister of the interior. In addition there are local advisory councils which assist the *muhafidh* on problems of health, education, agriculture, etc.

Libya is pushing rapidly ahead with an education program, and this is of vital importance in a country where most people still cannot read or write and where there is a great dearth of suitably trained men for the civil service and the professions. The most pressing need is for an extension of technical education. At present the country could not function efficiently without the help of foreign advisers and technicians, provided mainly by Britain, the United States and the United Nations. Primary and secondary schools are being built as fast as money becomes available and teacher training colleges, both for men and women, are providing the necessary staff. Since 1957 elementary education has been compulsory and is now almost universal both in urban and rural areas, though not in outlying oases. It is claimed that about three quarters of children of school age are now receiving some form of instruction.

There are two universities, a Moslem University and the University of Libya, which first opened in Benghazi in 1956, housed in a former palace of the king. There is now a branch in Tripoli (opened in 1957). Owing to the limited scope of this university, a large number of Libyan boys study abroad, principally in Egypt, and these will form an educated nucleus from which the country's future leaders will be drawn. In Libya's early days Egypt supplied the bulk of the staff in the schools and most of the textbooks, but there are fewer Egyptian teachers now that trained Libyans are becoming available. There are also a number of Italian schools in Tripolitania which accept other nationalities. A Franco-Libyan school was opened in Tripoli in 1956, and in 1957 Tripoli College was founded as an Anglo-Libyan school, run by the British Council in conjunction with the Libyan Government. English is the second language taught in all schools. One of the problems facing education in Libya is the unwillingness on the part of many Arabs to allow their daughters to go to school. In Libya the Arab woman still lives a much more secluded life than in most Arab countries where female emancipation has been longer at work. But long-established prejudices are gradually being overcome, as is shown by the granting of the vote to women in 1963.

Communications. One of the many reasons why Libya makes slow progress towards national unity is that there are such poor communications throughout the country. There are only 220 miles of railway grouped in two sectors, Tripoli and Benghazi, and serving only the immediate neighborhood. Communications between the eastern districts (the former Cyrenaica and the western districts (the former Tripolitania) are maintained by the coastal road, along which a bus service links Tripoli and Benghazi. It is also possible to travel by bus along the coast of Tripoli westwards to Tunis and from Benghazi eastwards to Alexandria. In 1962 a road was opened 400 miles in length, from Misurata on the coast south to Sebha, capital of the former Fezzan, and on to Ghat near the Algerian border. This has certainly improved communications with the interior but it is used more by the military and by government officials than by commercial vehicles. The chief means of communication with the interior are still by the caravans which follow the historical routes. The principal civil airports are the Idris el Awal Airport at Castel Benito, just outside Tripoli, and at Benina, near Benghazi. Many of the major international airlines use these airports and link Libya with Europe and many parts of Africa. A North African company, Tunis Air, runs a service from Tunisia to Tripoli and then on to Sebha. Plans are under way for the establishment of a national Libyan airline. Tripoli is the main port for sea-borne trade but Benghazi, where a new harbor is under construction, is of growing importance. For the transport of oil three loading terminals have been opened in the Gulf of Sirte.

Agriculture. Since independence much has been done through local effort and foreign aid to develop and increase the small area of land (about 8 per cent of the total) suitable for agriculture. This has a threefold purpose, to raise the standard of living which, until the discovery of oil, was lower than in any other country in the Middle East, to make provision for an increase of population and to stimulate Libyan exports. The former Tripolitania has three zones, the Mediterranean, subdesert and desert. The Mediterranean zone is the only one properly suited for agriculture. The oases along the coast are the richest in North Africa and produce dates, olives and oranges, and the steppe district, slightly inland from Tripoli, is suitable for cereals (mainly barley, the staple diet of the Arabs, and wheat) and for pasture. This is the area where Italian colonists have settled. Afforestation on a large scale is taking place, especially on the sand dunes to the east of Tripoli. In the former Cyrenaica there is a plateau called Djebel Akhdar (Green Mountain), about one thousand feet above sea level, suitable for cereals, olives and vines, and for grazing, which occupies a large proportion of the population.

Until oil was discovered the wealth of Libya lay almost entirely in farming and grazing. About 80 per cent of the people are engaged in some form of agriculture and for the most part still employ primitive and uneconomic methods. The area sown in a given year and the crop produced depend largely on the amount and timing of the rainfall. Once in every five or six years there is a pronounced drought. The average annual production of cereals is about 110,000 tons. Animal husbandry is the basis of farming. The country contains 2.5 million sheep and over 2 million goats. More than half a million camels and donkeys, together with over 200,000 cattle, provide animals mainly for draught and transport. About 3 million date palms and 3 to 4 million olive trees augment the local food supply and find a place amongst Libya's exports. Until oil was produced exports consisted almost entirely of agricultural products but these are now insignificant in comparison with oil. Libya, however, still exports a good deal of esparto grass (known also as "alfa"), which is widely used in the manufacture of good quality paper, such as bank-notes. A number of leading British paper mills obtain their supplies from Libya. Groundnuts [peanuts] and live sheep and goats are also exported in considerable quantities. On the coast sponge and tunny fishing have long been leading industries but these are mainly in the hands of foreigners.

Beginnings of industry. No large manufacturing industries exist in Libya. The country is lacking in coal and water power but oil is likely to foster industrial growth. Today there are tanneries, distilleries, soap works, cement works and a shoe factory, to name just a few activities which are supplying local requirements and cutting down the need for importing manufactured goods. But there is a great dearth of local artisans, technicians, electricians, etc. to provide the necessary labor force. Before the advent of oil Libya had to import much more than it was able to export. Coal and much of the necessary foodstuffs and manufactured goods still come from abroad, mostly from Italy, the United States and Britain. Until 1963 Libya could not export enough to cover its imports and there was what we call a "trade gap." As a result it depended on foreign aid, from the United States, Britain and France, to balance the budget. But today oil exports more than cover Libya's imports and the country is consequently less dependent on help from abroad. Formerly Italy was Libya's best customer, taking over 50 per cent of its exports. But the picture has changed, thanks to oil, about half of which is exported to Britain and Western Germany. Libya is in the sterling area. . . .

Foreign Affairs

Libya is an Arab country and since 1953 has been a member of the Arab League; consequently its people share in the hopes and aspirations of the Arab and Islamic world. For instance, there was much sympathy with their brethren in Algeria when the country was struggling for independence against the French, and there were anti-Western and pro-Egyptian demonstrations in Tripoli, Benghazi and other towns at the time of the Suez crisis of 1956. Egyptian influence in Libya has been powerful since the granting of independence, and especially since Nasser came to power after the Egyptian revolution. In 1953 King Idris visited Egypt (where he had spent twenty-one years of exile) and a commercial and cultural agreement was signed between the two countries. As a result of this many Egyptian teachers were seconded to Libyan schools and a group of Egyptian lawyers helped to codify Libyan law. There is plenty of evidence that Nasser is doing all he can to detach Libya from its Western alliances and bring it into his own orbit as an Egyptian satellite. From time to time Cairo Radio pours forth a spate of abuse, which aims at poisoning the relations between Libya and the West and between the Libyan people and their king. The Egyptian embassy in Libya has taken a hand and in 1957 the Egyptian military attaché was expelled from Libya for smuggling arms into the country to equip an underground army working for Nasser. More recently (1964) Nasser made a speech calling on Libya to close down the American and British bases and rid the country of the "imperialists." There is no doubt that Egyptian propaganda is having considerable effect among the young educated town-dwellers, many of whom have come under the influence of Egyptian teachers at school. But as long as King Idris remains at the helm Libya is likely to resist any temptation to toe the Egyptian line and will jealously guard its independence. As a means of countering Egyptian influence as well as extending its links with the Arab world Libya has signed a treaty of friendship and cooperation with . . . Morocco, Algeria and Tunisia. . . .

The chief danger to Libya seems to lie in the uncertainty about the succession to the throne. King Idris is an aging monarch but he is still very much the dominant figure in the country and commands general respect. It is known that his health is poor. In March 1964 he announced his abdication but withdrew it following large-scale demonstrations outside the royal palace in Tobruk, where he now spends most of his time, and assurances of loyalty both from the army and the security forces. Whether or not this announcement was aimed at testing public opinion, he must soon hand over the reins of power. It is a question whether the crown prince, the king's nephew, lacking as he will do the personal prestige of King Idris, will be able to command the allegiance of the country as a whole. It is possible that the king's abdication or death could lead to the breakup of the kingdom. It would be a tragic waste of time, money and effort if Libya were to disintegrate just at the moment when oil is pointing the way to a prosperous future. Libya will remain for some years to come in need of technical assistance so that the best use can be made of the oil revenues.

LIBYA'S NEW WEALTH AND OLD PROBLEMS [3]

Libya, that long strip of desert and sparse sown along the Mediterranean seaboard, with a population of little more than one million, is becoming a rich country. Oil revenues, negligible . . . [several] years ago, were . . . [$64 million] in 1963-64 . . . and are expected to exceed . . . [$196 million] in 1965-66. Whether the curve will flatten off then or continue its steep ascent depends on whether further important strikes are made—which with all the vigorous prospecting going on is far from unlikely. But the figures already in view represent a vast accretion of wealth to a country whose total annual budget is of the order of . . . [$182 million] and which has hitherto been largely dependent on foreign aid.

This wealth must in the long run change the whole outlook of Libya. So far it has had surprisingly little effect. Following the pattern set in Iraq and elsewhere, 70 per cent of it is earmarked for economic development, but comparatively little of the sums so far banked has been spent; Libya is finding, as other underdeveloped countries have found, that development is a plant whose growth is determined less by the amount of financial irrigation initially available than by the inevitably slow processes of planning, surveying, costing, and procuring which must first be gone through. In her case, lack of natural resources other than oil, and consequently of openings for development, is an additional complication. So the reserves rise.

Not that objects for expenditure are far to seek. Schools are badly needed to cope with the onrush of Libya's education-thirsty youth, and training facilities for teachers to reduce her dependence on politically minded Egyptians. The medical services can use all the money they can be given. Tourists must be attracted to Libya's magnificent Roman remains, and equally magnificent

---

[3] From article in *The Times* (London). Je. 11, '64. Reprinted by permission.

bathing beaches, by the construction of hotels and access-roads. Above all, agriculture must be expanded to combat widespread unemployment; but this necessitates an expensive program of tree-planting or oil-spraying on the sand dunes which, both along the coast and on the periphery of the Sahara, threaten to advance and blot out the exiguous area of cultivable land.

Economically there is hope; politically there must be doubt. Libya's obvious and desperate poverty can be overcome, but she has two serious weaknesses.

One is inherent in her geography. The two main provinces, Tripolitania and Cyrenaica, are poles apart. Between their respective capitals, Tripoli and Benghazi, lie seven hundred miles of desert. Their peoples have different outlooks, and tend to despise each other. The third province, the Fezzan, is merely a string of oases in a wilderness of steppe and waste, and is despised by both. The attempt to increase the cohesion of the country by substituting for these provinces twelve smaller ones ran counter to regional prejudices and seems to have been a virtual failure; and the only real unifying factor is King Idris, who in Cyrenaica is a venerated religious leader and in all three provinces a respected symbol of independence. His prestige, however, is personal to himself and cannot be inherited, and the ability of any successor regime to preserve the slender links which bind these disparate regions must be questionable.

The other weakness is human. Libya is a young country, whereas her present regime is dominated by an aging monarch and a group of men who, whatever their personal competence, are mostly drawn from the ranks of the large property owners. In the eyes of the younger educated town-dwellers, most of them avid listeners to Cairo Radio, the traditionalism of the regime unduly limits their own opportunities for advancement, in sharp contrast with the progressiveness they discern over their frontiers in Nasser's Egypt and . . . [in] Algeria. Against this latent but growing frustration the regime seems to have little to offer but repression which, misused during some relatively harmless student demonstrations in Benghazi . . . caused bloodshed and engendered hate. Here again the king's personal prestige is the main stabilizing agent, but its eventual disappearance from the scene must bring far-reaching changes which, in the short term at least, can hardly increase stability.

OIL: BOON AND HEADACHE [4]

Last summer parking meters had to be installed in Tripoli. Not that they are of much help to the motorist, for as he circles round the one-way traffic system in the center of town he will usually look in vain for a space. But they are one outward symbol of Libya's newly acquired wealth. Ten years ago it seemed extremely doubtful whether the country could ever become economically viable. Now, Libya is exporting 1 million barrels of oil per day (with further increases literally in the pipeline) and the government is hard put to it to find productive ways of spending its revenue.

Tripoli, one of the most expensive capitals in the world, is a prime example of a boom town. When I was there, the general atmosphere of suddenly acquired wealth was given a distinctly international flavor by the Trade Fair. Government representatives and businessmen from thirty nations—the majority of them from Arab countries and the Communist bloc—were trying to ensure that they would get their share of the rapidly growing Libyan market.

But while oil may have put Libya on the map it has also posed a number of formidable problems for the government. Most developing countries have too many people and too little money. Libya has a population of around 1.5 million and the government's oil revenues should amount to between . . . [$336 million] and . . . [$420 million] this year [1965]. How this money can be used to provide the people with a rapidly rising standard of living is the question which above all others preoccupies the government.

There is a very real danger, as one Libyan put it to me, that the country will become another Kuwait, the latter in this context being defined as a place where foreigners do all the work while the

<hr>

[4] From "The Libyan Scene: Too Few People, Too Much Money," by M. H. Fisher, foreign editor, *Financial Times* (London). *Financial Times*. Mr. 12, '65. Reprinted by permission.

local population sits back to enjoy the good things of life. Here indeed lies the crux of the problem. Agriculture, which in the past provided the main source of employment, is losing labor rapidly as Libyans either flock to the towns or seek to find highly paid work in the oilfields.

The government is trying to support agriculture, but so far has not succeeded in arresting the movement of population. In its Five-Year Development Plan it has allotted . . . [$84 million] out of a total of . . . [$476 million] to agriculture. But it will not only have to improve the infrastructure, social services and amenities in the countryside; it will also have to find a way of holding down the cost to the consumer of what is produced.

This applies not merely to agricultural production but to the industrial sector as well. Schemes are afoot to establish or expand a number of industries; food processing, fertilizers, building materials, textiles and glass. Difficulties, however, arise because the market is small and the cost of labor so high that it is hard to see Libya gaining wider markets abroad.

Prices have risen by more than 100 per cent in the last eight years and wages, if anything, even faster. A highly skilled workman in Tripoli will today earn up to . . . [$14] a day. Inflationary pressures are bound to increase further. For the next few years the government must pump money into the economy at a high rate on a whole host of investment projects—housing, schools, hospitals, roads, electric power—which initially will add little to productive capacity.

Unless the consumer is to be harshly squeezed by even higher prices, Libya will have to import foodstuffs and consumer goods in ever increasing quantities. She has the money to do it, and Libyan businessmen are demonstrating that they have the necessary commercial skills in high measure. But how are local industries to be established in the face of competition from imports? And in the absence of industrial development how is the government to achieve the distribution of its oil wealth?

That the population at large has benefited substantially already is quite clear. But there is considerable pressure on the government to speed the process of getting the money into the hands of the people. There is no point in increasing taxation. It might take some money from the very rich, but this would only swell the government's own overflowing coffers. As one economic planner put it to me: "The only way of distributing the cash quickly is for the government to employ more people." Yet the government already employs 60,000 of the total labor force of 380,000, not counting the police and the army.

In the face of these unique long-term problems the government is moving cautiously. Since 1963, the opening year of the Plan, allocations have been underspent, partly because of physical limitations, partly, as government spokesmen stress, because of the determination to get value for money. (Over the five years as a whole expenditure is now expected to reach $700 million, part of the rise being accounted for by higher prices.) It is cautious in its immigration policy, allowing in only the skilled labor which cannot be found in the country. . . .

The very extent of the "gold rush" has made it difficult to exploit some natural assets. Climate, scenery and Roman ruins between them provide powerful attractions for the tourist. But the high cost deters them. The government intends to build low-cost motels to overcome this particular snag. Altogether it is conscious that it is working against time, although there is now no political agitation in Libya in the sense in which this term might be applied in other Arab countries. The prestige of the seventy-five-year-old King Idris stands as high as ever. . . .

Whether the country will, in fact, become a showcase of all that is best in the Arab world—and that is the target the Libyans have set themselves—only the future can show. There is a tendency in some government quarters to seek the perfect solution rather than a quick but imperfect one.

Somewhat wistfully one Libyan remarked to me: "If only we had found water instead of oil." Another pointed out that all the discovery of oil could do was to resolve the balance of payments problem. But the realization of the problems ahead, implicit in these remarks, shows that at least in broad terms there are those in the country who know where they want to go, even if they are not always very sure of how to get there.

LIBYAN CONTRADICTIONS [5]

In the old days—and Tripoli takes it for granted that this means before Libya struck oil—cars were a luxury for Westerners and for a wealthy few.

Now it is common to see a much more humble and conservative Libyan, dressed in the ancient blanketlike *barracan* shawl and bright red fez of his forefathers, scooting around the city in a Volkswagen or Fiat, enjoying the sudden affluence of his country. . . .

Not only cars but also stores stocked with the best conveniences and luxuries the West has to offer attest that Tripoli, once a fading, war-ravaged capital, has become a city of conspicuous consumption.

Shop windows bulge with English woolens, Swedish crystal, Danish teak furniture, Italian textiles, Japanese transistor radios, British silverware and Western appliances from refrigerators to television sets and hair driers. . . .

Prices are higher than in New York or Paris. Taxies charge fares that would make New York cabbies jealous, and even old horse-and-buggy carriages, which once offered a leisurely ride around Tripoli's well-swept palm-lined streets, now charge steep rates.

But if downtown Tripoli seems overwhelmed by money, there are disquieting signs that many in Libya have not yet tasted its gaudy new affluence.

Thousands live without sanitation or electricity in shantytowns or *barrakas,* as they are called here, on the outskirts of the city. These are vast settlements of Bedouin squatters lured from their nomadic farming life to Tripoli by visions of sudden wealth.

The first of them came several years ago and settled in traditional mud huts with grass roofs. Now their settlements are more

[5] From "Tripoli Strikes It Rich," by Hedrick Smith, correspondent. *New York Times.* p 8. Ja. 23, '65. © 1965 by The New York Times Company. Reprinted by permission.

substantial. Boards, corrugated metal and tar paper have replaced mud huts, and community living is more organized.

In one shantytown, perhaps a mile long and several blocks deep, a visitor can see dirt roads trailing off into the Sea of Leantos. A whitewashed structure near a bus stop serving this barraka flies the green flag of Islam to mark a makeshift mosque.

Animals and people live together. A sleepy-eyed donkey blinks at a passerby from the door of one shelter. Sheep and chickens run by the roadside while children stuff sticks and stones through gunports of old Italian ramparts still topped by rings of rusty barbed wire.

More and more of the settlers have managed to find work in the booming construction industry or in oil fields. Occasionally a visitor can see one in coat and tie disappear into a barraka with a sack of groceries, or another emerge wheeling his bicycle.

Most of the Arab women live a circumscribed existence. In the lower classes many are forbidden to leave their homes except with their husbands. Shopping is done by houseboys and when children fall ill it is the fathers who take them to the doctor. Child marriages still occur.

In the middle and upper classes, men and women do not mix socially, except sometimes within family circles. Schools are segregated by sex, and even women who venture into public have their own matinee at local movie houses apart from men.

A few young women have discarded the barracan costume—through which the world is viewed from a peephole no larger than a half dollar—to take jobs as typists for oil companies. They show their Western clothes and wear heavy black veils over their heads. One young woman recently dropped her veil entirely to become an airline receptionist.

The visitor finds a sharp contrast to Moslem conservatism in Georgimpopoli, which some Libyans call "the American oil-man's suburb." There, Western women in skirts and slacks market at a shopping center which, except for Italian-style arcades and Libyan flags in the store windows, could be in Long Island or Oklahoma.

LIBYA'S OIL BOOM [6]

No Cadillacs—nor beggars either—are visible in oil-rich Libya. In Tripoli and Benghazi, the two provincial capitals, the motor cars jamming the streets and often outnumbering pedestrians are of medium or knockabout variety. The raggle-taggle boys who used to haunt the pavements were long ago put into shoes and whisked into schools or jobs. Behind cool arcades shops are stuffed with the world's goodies, from American refrigerators to Japanese transistor radios and elegant Danish furniture. But you must go in and find what you want. Window displays are still modest. Mammon is served discreetly and wealth—like most women—is veiled.

New housing estates are largely Italian-style suburban. One new palace with bright purple domes has appeared on Tripoli's seafront; but nobody can quite account for it. It was said to be built for the crown prince. But he seems to have thought it too showy and has stayed in his pint-sized villa. King Idris himself has given up living in palaces. He commutes between his two delectable but simple farms (one near Tobruk and the other just outside Tripoli), never uses his official Rolls-Royce, dislikes being called "His Majesty"—and remains the real power in the land.

The oil boom's most striking accomplishment is that it has firmly established a middle class that barely existed before. It is not just a matter of turning out little capitalists—truck drivers becoming contractors and lift-boys hotel proprietors. There has been a huge educational advance. Government officials and clerks, responsible oil company staff, suave military men and police have risen from a society that fifteen years ago was predominantly peasant and Bedouin. When Libya became independent in 1951, only fourteen Libyans existed with university degrees. Now there are fourteen hundred students at Libya's own university. The country's struggles have been all the greater through having to drop Italian and take up English as the second official language. Thanks to their Egyptian, Sudanese and Pales-

[6] From "Libya: A Sort of Freedom." *The Economist* (London). 218:1225-6. Mr. 26, '66. Reprinted by permission.

tinian teachers, Libyans speak and write a more assured Arabic than any of their Maghrebi neighbors.

The government is often taxed with pampering this new bourgeoisie and neglecting humbler workers. All education is free but older students get living allowances as well. Civil servants all get free houses—a hefty bonus since rents and most prices have doubled in the past five years. By contrast, the country folk who have swarmed to the cities in thousands, attracted by the high wages paid even for unskilled work, live without light or water in shantytowns built of packing crates.

Yet there was method in official priorities. Free housing for government servants counterbalances the much higher than government-level salaries with which oil companies lure away talent. The new middle class forms the sinews of a gradually modernizing state. It is this class and not the old families (who still hold the levers of power) that is breaking down crippling traditions, sending its girls as well as its boys to college, and holding its Libyan own with the foreigners in its midst. And the shanty dwellers, too, are enjoying the feel of money. With no rent or services to pay for, they can send back some of their wages to their former villages, buy bicycles, even second-hand cars. Their cost of living is minimal since the prices of basic foods—flour, sugar, tea and so on—are strictly controlled. It is only above this level that the pangs of inflation are felt. Moreover, two months ago the government bestirred itself and proclaimed a new "Idris" plan for building 200,000 people's homes.

Foreigners fill the gaps in Libya's society. Doctors from many countries, from Eastern Europe to Pakistan, keep a national health service going. The 26,000 Italians who stayed on in Tripolitania provide the main pool of skilled labor and retain a strong hold on commerce. The oil company people, with their powerful American contingent, set a pace with their high living standards. American investment in Libya is larger than in any other African country (barring only South Africa). All the same, Libya is not nearly so neocolonialized as a country like Algeria with its government-to-government oil and development agreements with France. By treaty with each of the eighteen oil companies separately . . . the Libyans keep the whip hand. Mr. Hussein Mazegh, the thrustful prime minister, gave the companies a rough ride when he forced them . . . to accept the new Libyan oil law bringing taxes and royalties into line with those paid to other oil-producing countries.

Since Mr. Mazegh came to office in March 1965 a spurt has been made in using the 70 per cent of oil revenues . . . that is set aside for development. From Tripoli all the way to the Egyptian frontier, schools and hospitals are rising in every town and village. More spending power has been given to local authorities. But planning and execution remain a formidable problem. There are too few competent administrators and the population of 1.5 million is too small to provide an adequate labor force. Official life is made more exhausting by the distances that have to be traveled between Tripoli and Benghazi, and to the new capital, Beida, which is two hours by car from Benghazi in the heart of the Cyrenaican hills. This extraordinary Libyan Brasilia now boasts splendid government offices and residences. But there is virtually no local community to do the cleaning and cooking; and the water supplies are still fitful. Officials return from sessions there with pained stories of shaving in mineral water or even being offered beer for their religious ablutions by their less devout friends.

Arabs from elsewhere who are serving as technical advisers declare that there is much more freedom in Libya than in any other Arab state. This is true for the individual. He may do and say as he likes, grumble or criticize the government without fear of being snooped on. But there is no kind of organized freedom in the Western sense. There is no opposition group in parliament. The ginger group of a dozen nationalists who were deputies in 1960 were conjured out of their seats in the 1964 and 1965 elections—a result of the campaign they waged, on Cairo's prompting, against the American and British bases in 1964. There is no general labor movement. Each trade has its own union, for which the government pays. Students have a myriad of youth clubs lavishly endowed by the government with everything for recreation and sport. But the new generation is growing politically restive. Students—and teachers too—are clamoring for their own independent unions; and younger men sourly complain that government remains the monopoly of old families and tribal chiefs.

Many Libyans say why change things, when life as it is is so peaceful and on the whole kindly? All the same, the Libyan government is in danger of being too out of touch with the people and so getting caught out in a crisis. The critical moment will come at the end of King Idris's reign. One safeguard would be to bring some younger men into government; as King Hussein has done in Jordan.

PRESSURES FOR REFORM [7]

The future of the British and American bases in Libya has attracted much foreign attention, but to most Libyans this problem is merely part of a much wider issue: how to modernize the Libyan economy and thrust the country into the forefront of Arab and African affairs. Libya's most urgent need is for a program of political, economic and social reform to ensure the proper spending of its oil wealth and a fairer distribution of national income.

A few years ago, the bases were seen as a potential instrument for reform. When Libya became independent in 1951, its national income was only about . . . [$84 million]; it desperately needed capital to develop its agricultural base, small though this was, and it thus seized the chance of earning money by exploiting its strategic situation in the southern Mediterranean and across Britain's vital Commonwealth routes. Today, however, the bases are seen as part of the old order that must be broken down before progress can be achieved.

Many factors have contributed to this change of attitude— the growth of Arab nationalism and dynamic neutralism within and outside Libya, the spread of education and the "transistor" radio, and the rapid rise in migration from the rural areas to Tripoli and Benghazi. But oil has been the catalyst which precipitated the effects of these developments.

The petroleum industry has grown remarkably quickly. Exports started in 1961 but will soon exceed a rate of over 1 million barrels a day. Three new fields have been found recently and the potential for further growth seems almost unlimited. The oil companies have poured millions . . . into the country—in 1963 they spent [$300 million] in Libya while in 1958 Libya's national income was scarcely half that figure. The oil boom attracted many other foreign companies who have been much better placed than Libyan concerns, handicapped by insufficient local capital and trained personnel, to seize the new opportunities. Though Libyans have been playing a more prominent role recently, the foreign sector of the economy is still of great importance.

Some Libyans have made fortunes and people are definitely better off than five years ago, but large shantytowns still exist around Tripoli; the poverty of rural areas and provincial towns contrasts sharply with the opulent new suburbs of Tripoli and Benghazi. Rural workers, farmers and even Bedouin are pouring into the main towns in search of high wages. They often find that high prices offset the better wages, and, as they leave the countryside, land is abandoned and agricultural production falls.

Most foreign experts agree that oil revenues must be invested in agriculture to provide work and a decent standard of living for the majority of Libyans. They also agree that Libya's agricultural potential is rich enough to provide the food and fiber needs of the 1.25 million population, leaving a big margin for export, and that this potential can only be realized by a revolution in land management. Oil will provide the capital, but it will not supply work for more than 5 per cent of the labor force. Industrial opportunities are mainly confined to agricultural processing, and apart from oil there are few known major sources of industrial raw materials. Industries based on imported products are handicapped by the relatively high labor costs and the small local market.

Formidable problems must be overcome before agriculture can be developed: land ownership is confused, soil erosion is advanced and water conservation methods primitive, and farmers lack the money and education needed to modernize agricultural techniques.

The government's principal critics are themselves mainly civil servants. Influenced by the Arab revolutions, they demand a more energetic and dynamic attitude to reform. They blame the government's casual and unhurried attitude to development on its structure. Power has been concentrated in the hands of King Idris and though his role in building Libya into a nation is acknowledged, he is . . . [over seventy-five] and becoming more remote from everyday affairs. This permits strong outside interests to interfere in government. Cabinets are constantly reshuffled and each change brings a new policy. Though able ministers have been appointed (particularly during Dr. Fikini's premiership), the influence of members of the royal family, tribal leaders and business interests often hamper progressive legislation. Corruption is still widespread despite an effort by the king to curb it.

The most telling criticism leveled at the government is that, while the men with real power are playing at politics, ordinary Libyans are becoming increasingly impatient with the slow rate of economic progress. If things do not change soon, they may look to Cairo or pro-Egyptian politicians to initiate reform.

These critics have been among the most vocal opponents of Libya's military treaties with Britain and America. They believe that British troops are pledged to support the present government in the event of external aggression and violent internal opposition. With this support, they claim, the Libyan government feels it can afford its unhurried attitude to reform.

If the foreign bases are withdrawn, the Libyan government will have to defend itself by its own progressive policies. It will have to show its people that it is as capable as any alternative of providing them with a better life and a more dynamic foreign policy. The government's opponents believe that with the bases gone, their own position will be stronger. If the government does not listen to their demands, it will be inviting trouble.

BIBLIOGRAPHY

An asterisk (*) preceding a reference indicates that the article or a part of it has been reprinted in this book.

BOOKS, PAMPHLETS, AND DOCUMENTS

*American Universities Field Staff Reports Service. North Africa series. C. F. Gallagher.

Toward constitutional government in Morocco. v 9, no 1. Ja. '63.
Moroccan constitution: text and comment. v 9, no 2. Ja. '63.
Algerian notebook. v 9, no 3. Ap. '63.
Death of a group: members of the Casablanca Pact fall out. v 9, no 4. My. '63.
Meanings of the Moroccan elections. v 9, no 5. Je. '63.
Algerian year, part I: events and comments. v 9, no 6. Jl. '63.
Algerian year, part II: choices and interpretations. v 9, no 7. Jl. '63.
Algerian year, part III: chronology and biographies. v 9, no 8. Jl. '63.
Discovery of Morocco. v 9, no 9. Ag. '63.
Co-operation: the new French revolution. v 9, no 10. O. '63.
Tunisian way. v 9, no 11. N. '63.
Small saga: the Swedish role in Tunisia. v 9, no 12. N. '63.
Peace corps in the Maghrib. v 10, no 1. F. '64.
North African problems and prospects, part I: rural reform and revolution. v 10, no 2. F. '64.
North African problems and prospects, part II: industrialization and development. v 10, no 3. Mr. '64.
North African problems and prospects, part III: language and identity. v 10, no 5. Je. '64.
Reprinted in this book:
Note on northern Africa. v 10, no 4. Je. '64.

Anthony, John. Tunisia. Scribner. New York. '62.

Ashford, D. E. Morocco—Tunisia: politics and planning. Syracuse University Press. Syracuse, N.Y. '65.

Ashford, D. E. Political change in Morocco. Princeton University Press. Princeton, N.J. '61.

Barbour, Nevill. Morocco. Walker. New York. '65.

Barbour, Nevill, ed. Survey of North West Africa (the Maghrib). 2d ed. Oxford University Press. New York. '62.

Behr, Edward. Algerian problem. Norton. New York. '62.

Beling, W. A. Modernization and African labor: a Tunisian case study. Praeger. New York. '66.

Berger, Morroe. Arab world today. Doubleday. New York. '62.

Brace, R. M. Morocco, Algeria, Tunisia. Prentice-Hall. Englewood Cliffs, N.J. '64.

Brace, R. M. and Brace, Joan. Algerian voices. Van Nostrand. Princeton N.J. '65.

Brace, R. M. and Brace, Joan. Ordeal in Algeria. Van Nostrand. Princeton, N.J. '60.

Briggs, L. C. Tribes of the Sahara. Harvard University Press. Cambridge, Mass. '60.

Cooley, J. K. Baal, Christ, and Mohammed; religion and revolution in North Africa. Holt. New York. '65.

Cooley, J. K. East wind over Africa: Red China's African offensive. Walker. New York. '65.

Coon, C. S. Caravan: the story of the Middle East. rev. ed. Holt. New York. '58.

Cremeans, C. D. Arabs and the world; Nasser's Arab nationalist policy. Praeger. New York. '63.

Fanon, Frantz. Wretched of the earth. Grove. New York. '65.

Foreign Policy Association. Great decisions 1963. The Association. 345 E. 46th St. New York 10017. '63.

Fact sheet no 3. Algeria—what future? p 2-12.

*Foreign Policy Association. Great decisions 1964. The Association. 345 E. 46th St. New York 10017. '64.

Reprinted in this book: 3, Egypt and the Middle East: what prospects for stability? p 27-37.

Gabrieli, Francesco. Arab revival. Random House. New York. '61.

Gallagher, C. F. United States and North Africa; Morocco, Algeria, and Tunisia. Harvard University Press. Cambridge, Mass. '63.

Gidal, Sonia. My village in Morocco. Pantheon Books. New York. '64.

Gillespie, Joan. Algeria: rebellion and revolution. Praeger. New York. '61.

Gordon, D. C. North Africa's French legacy, 1954-1962. Harvard University Press. Cambridge, Mass. '62.

Gordon, D. C. Passing of French Algeria. Oxford University Press. New York. '66.

Halpern, Manfred. Politics of social change in the Middle East and North Africa. Princeton University Press. Princeton, N.J. '63.

Hatch, J. C. History of postwar Africa. Praeger. New York. '65.

Hoffman, P. G. World without want. Harper. New York. '62.

Libya: a microcosm. p 98-110.

Hottinger, Arnold. Arabs; their history, culture and place in the modern world. University of California Press. Berkeley. '63.

Kerr, M. H. Arab cold war, 1958-1964: a study of ideology in politics. Oxford University Press. New York. '65.

Kerr, M. H. Egypt under Nasser. (Headline Series no 161) Foreign Policy Association. 345 E. 46th St. New York 10017. S.-O. '63.

Khadduri, Majid. Modern Libya: a study in political development. Johns Hopkins Press. Baltimore. '63.

Kirk, G. E. Contemporary Arab politics: a concise history. Praeger. New York. '61.

Kraft, Joseph. Struggle for Algeria. Doubleday. New York. '61.

Lewis, W. H. ed. French-speaking Africa: the search for identity. Walker. New York. '65.

Macdonald, R. W. League of Arab states: a study in the dynamics of regional organization. Princeton University Press. Princeton, N.J. '65.

Micaud, C. A. and others. Tunisia: the politics of modernization. Praeger. New York. '64.

Mikesell, M. W. Northern Morocco: a cultural geography. University of California Press. Berkeley. '61.

Moore, C. H. Tunisia since independence; the dynamics of one-party government. University of California Press. Berkeley. '65.

Murdock, G. P. Africa; its peoples and their cultural history. McGraw-Hill. New York. '59.

Nickerson, J. S. Short history of North Africa: Libya, Tunisia, Algeria, Morocco; from pre-Roman times to the present. Devin-Adair. New York. '61.

Nutting, Anthony. Arabs; a narrative history from Mohammed to the present. Potter. New York. '64.

Pickles, D. M. Algeria and France; from colonialism to cooperation. Praeger. New York. '63.

Polk, W. R. ed. Developmental revolution: North Africa, Middle East, South Asia. Middle East Institute. 1761 N St., N.W. Washington, D.C. 20036. '63.

Polk, W. R. United States and the Arab world. Harvard University Press. Cambridge, Mass. '65.

Remba, Oded. Economic development in the Near East and North Africa. Near East Report. 1737 S St., N.W. Washington, D.C. 20006. Mr. '65.

Rivlin, Benjamin, and Szyliowicz, J. S. eds. Contemporary Middle East; tradition and innovation. Random House. New York. '65.

Rosenthal, E. I. J. Islam in the modern national state. Cambridge University Press. New York. '66.

Roy, Claude, and Sebag, Paul. Tunisia. Orion. New York. '62.

Servan-Schreiber, Jean-Jacques. Lieutenant in Algeria. Knopf. New York. '57.

Sharabi, H. B. Nationalism and revolution in the Arab world (the Middle East and North Africa). Van Nostrand. Princeton, N.J. '66.

Stewart, C. F. Economy of Morocco, 1912-1962. Harvard University Press. Cambridge, Mass. '64.

Sulzberger, C. L. The test: De Gaulle and Algeria. Harcourt. New York. '62.

Tillion, Germaine. France and Algeria; complementary enemies. Knopf. New York. '61.

Toynbee, A. J. Between Niger and Nile. Oxford University Press. New York. '65.

Tütsch, H. E. Facets of Arab nationalism. Wayne State University Press. Detroit. '65.

Zartman, I. W. Destiny of a dynasty: the search for institutions in Morocco's developing society. University of South Carolina Press. Columbia. '64.

Zartman, I. W. Government and politics in northern Africa. Praeger. New York. '63.

PERIODICALS

Africa Report. 10:6-14. Jl. '65. Hassan's Morocco. Stuart Schaar.
*Africa Report. 10:8-16. N. '65. Algeria changes course. W. H. Lewis.
African Affairs (London). 64:25-31. Ja. '65. Independent Africa and its links with Europe. Tom Soper.
*Afro-Mideast Economic Bulletin. Spring 1965 supplement: Modern Libya. p 8-9. Historical highlights over three millennia. Philip Hitti.
America. 108:362-5. Mr. 16, '63. Algeria: year I of independence. Robert Bosc.
Annals of the American Academy of Political and Social Science. 362: 36-43. N. '65. Nonalignment in the Arab world. Don Peretz.
Annals of the American Academy of Political and Social Science. 362: 52-61. N. '65. Nonalignment in Africa. T. P. Melady.
Atlantic. 212:28+. D. '63. Atlantic report: Morocco.
Atlantic. 213:14+. Ap. '64. Atlantic report: Algeria.
Atlantic. 215:112-13+. Ja. '65. Marrakesh. Keith Williams.
*Atlantic. 216:14+. S. '65. Atlantic report: Algeria.
*Atlantic. 216:24+. N. '65. Atlantic report: Tunisia.
*British Survey (London). 198:1-19. S. '65. North Africa.
      Reprinted in this book: Libya. p 10-19.
*British Survey (London). Popular Series 222:1-16. F. '63. Morocco today.
Business Week. p 102. Ja. 26, '63. Oil alone can't solve Libya's economic woes.
Commentary. 34:198-203. S. '62. Jewish future in Algeria. Jean Daniel.
Commonweal. 79:217-20. N. 15, '63. Arab world in ferment: the scorpion and the frog. Gabriel Gersh.
Contemporary Review (London). 202:86-90+. Ag. '62. President Bourguiba. George Bilainkan.
Contemporary Review (London). 205:129-33. Mr. '64. Libya and oil. Issam Azzam.
Contemporary Review (London). 205:174-8. Ap. '64. Report from Morocco. Anthony Sylvester.
Contemporary Review (London). 205:239-43. My. '64. Report from Algeria. Anthony Sylvester.
Contemporary Review (London). 205:409-12. Ag. '64. Spain and Morocco: a new phase. R. C. Carr.
Current History. 44:1-50+. Ja. '63. North Africa; symposium.
*Current History. 50:136-41. Mr. '66. Africa's Arab fringe. H. L. Hoskins.
Department of State Bulletin. 53:315-22. Ag. 23, '65. North Africa: active crossroads. D. D. Newsom.
Economist (London). 210:499. F. 8, '64. Spain and Maghreb; narrowing Strait.

*Economist (London). 213:253-4. O. 17, '64. Spanish Sahara; windmills in the desert.

Economist (London). 213:1344. D. 19, '64. Maghreb: wider still and wider.

Economist (London). 214:657. F. 13, '65. Moroccan frost.

Economist (London). 214:1260. Mr. 20, '65. Home truths from abroad [Bourguiba].

Economist (London). 214:1374. Mr. 27, '65. East-west is best [Libya].

Economist (London). 215:170. Ap. 10, '65. King and people [Morocco].

Economist (London). 215:286. Ap. 17, '65. Thrice blessed [Algeria].

Economist (London). 215:894. My. 22, '65. Maghreb: salutes and saboteurs.

*Economist (London). 215:1266+. Je. 12, '65. Morocco: back to autocracy; down to earth.

Economist (London). 215:1323. Je. 12, '65. When will the desert bloom? [Libya].

Economist (London). 215:1380. Je. 19, '65. Ins and outs at Algiers.

Economist (London). 215:1433. Je. 19, '65. Morocco's new staff of life.

Economist (London). 215:1501-2. Je. 26, '65. Algeria without Ben Bella.

Economist (London). 216:26-7. Jl. 3, '65. Warm handshakes, cool glances.

Economist (London). 216:116. Jl. 10, '65. Inner-directed [Algeria].

Economist (London). 216:138-9. Jl. 10, '65. Presidents kick out.

Economist (London). 216:595-6. Ag. 14, '65. Murmur of a summer's day [Algeria].

Economist (London). 216:689. Ag. 21, '65. No time for nonsense [Algeria].

Economist (London). 216:804. Ag. 28, '65. Where Sicilians are welcome [Libya].

Economist (London). 217:833. N. 20, '65. Many go barefoot [Algeria].

*Economist (London). 218:1225-6. Mr. 26, '66. Libya: a sort of freedom.

Economist (London). 219:354. Ap. 23, '66. Algeria: for whom the clock chimes.

Encounter (London). Ag. '62. General and the tragedy [Algeria]. Raymond Aron.

Encounter (London). Ja. '64. Letter from Tangier. James Morris.

*Financial Times (London). D. 12, '63. Will Bourguiba's ideal come to life?

*Financial Times (London). Jl. 31, '64. Libyan scene: a growing demand for reform.

*Financial Times (London). Mr. 12, '65. Libyan scene: too few people, too much money. M. H. Fisher.

Foreign Affairs. 39:591-600. Jl. '61. Settler politics in Algeria. Joseph Kraft.

Foreign Affairs. 43:501-12. Ap. '65. Arab world's heavy legacy. Charles Issawi.

Foreign Affairs. 43:519-27. Ap. '65. Spain's discreet decolonization. René Pélissier.

Foreign Affairs. 44:100-10. O. '65. Nature of modernization: the Middle East and North Africa. W. R. Polk.

Foreign Affairs. 44:111-26. O. '65. Lost goals in Africa. Arnold Rivkin.

Foreign Affairs. 44:480-8. Ap. '66. Tunisian way. Habib ben Ali Bourguiba.

*Guardian (London). Mr. 14, '66. Who are the Arabs? Michael Adams.

Harper's Magazine. 227:24-9. Ag. '63. Fly-by-night trip to Morocco. Russell Lynes.

Holiday. 33:42-53+. F. '63. Journey through Morocco. Paul Bowles.

Holiday. 37:60-1+. Je. '65. Algerian woman. Gabrielle Estivals.

*International Conciliation. 541:3-62. Ja. '63. Sahara: bridge or barrier? I. W. Zartman.

Journal of International Affairs. 19 no 1:1-122. Winter '65. Arab world: paths to modernization.

Journal of Modern African Studies (London). 3:103-14. My. '65. New perspectives in the study of North Africa. Manfred Halpern.

Journal of Modern African Studies (London). 3:155-73. Ag. '65. Politics of boundaries in North and West Africa. I. W. Zartman.

Listener (London). p 141-3. Ja. 23, '64. Arab nationalism and the West. Erskine Childers.

*Listener (London). p 792-4. N. 19, '64. Arts in Tunisia. John Ardagh.

Maghreb Digest.
     Monthly review.

Middle East Journal. 18:27-40. Winter '64. Moroccan-American base negotiations. I. W. Zartman.

Middle East Journal. 18:163-79. Spring '64. Some implications of the new constitutional monarchy in Morocco. W. A. Beling.

Middle East Journal. 19:20-34. Winter '65. Determinants of Libyan foreign policy. C. O. Cecil.

Middle East Journal. 19:45-53. Winter '65. Islamic republic of Mauritania. William Eagleton, Jr.

Middle East Journal. 19:273-83. Summer '65. Peace corps in Morocco. F. C. Thomas, Jr.

Nation. 202:116-18. Ja. 31, '66. Algeria: brakes on revolution. Schofield Coryell.

National Review. 15:442. N. 19, '63. Reflections on the Barbary Coast. Russell Kirk.

New Leader. 47:18-20. Ag. 31, '64. Algeria: an uneasy coalition; a crisis in authority. Immanuel Wallerstein.

New Leader. 47:8-9. S. 28, '64. North Africa's great migration. Edouard Roditi.

New Leader. 48:6-9. Ag. 30, '65. Tunisia & Algeria. L. H. Hahn.

*New Leader. 48:9-11. Ag. 30, '65. Morocco's reluctant autocrat. Ronald Steel.

New Leader. 48:18-21. O. 11, '65. Middle East mystery. Hal Lehrman.

New Leader. 49:12-14. Ap. 11, '66. "Red menace" in Algeria: the Russians remain. Peter Braestrup.

New Leader. 49:12-15. My. 23, '66. Ben Barka fester: Gaullist techniques of terror. Ray Alan.

New Republic. 152:10-11. Je. 19, '65. Ahmed ben Bella, would-be leader of the third world. R. W. Howe.

New Republic. 153:11-12. Jl. 3, '65. Who and what is the real Boumedienne? R. W. Howe.

*New Society (London). p 10-12. S. 23, '65. Islam as a world force. P. J. Vatikiotis.

*New York Herald Tribune (Paris edition). D. 25, '63. Tunisians found better off. Nora Beloff.

New York Herald Tribune (Paris edition). Ja. 21, '66. Middle East: coming to a boil. J. A. Morris, Jr.

New York Times. p 2. F. 9, '64. Town in Sahara hot high and dry.

*New York Times. p 30. Ap. 27, '64. Price of peace runs high [Morocco]. C. L. Sulzberger.

*New York Times. p 40. Ap. 29, '64. Middle-of-the-road in Africa [Morocco]. C. L. Sulzberger.

*New York Times. p 8. Ja. 23, '65. Tripoli strikes it rich. Hedrick Smith.

New York Times. p 9. Ja. 25, '65. Workers on farm in Algeria say nationalization has brought few gains.

New York Times. p 47. Ja. 25, '65. Wealth in Libya flowing like oil. Hedrick Smith.

New York Times. p 74. Ja. 25, '65. Algerian road to socialism is no path of roses. Peter Braestrup.

New York Times. p 20. My. 31, '65. Economy of Tunis under strain. Peter Braestrup.

*New York Times. p 5. Je. 20, '65. Algeria finding freedom costly.

New York Times. p 28. Jl. 17, '65. Sahara oil accord. Peter Braestrup.

New York Times. p E3. O. 17, '65. On the Nile a pause. Hedrick Smith.

*New York Times. p 16. Ja. 23, '66. Ben Barka case: why the abduction? Peter Braestrup.

New York Times. F. 7, '66. Morocco: nation pays a high price for water. Stephen Hughes.

New York Times. F. 8, '66. Algerian hopes turn to a wealthy desert. David Ottaway.

New York Times. F. 8, '66. Tunisia: tourists and oil offset an unfavorable turn in trade.

New York Times. p 5. O. 26, '66. Moroccan secret police chief surrenders in Paris. Henry Tanner.

New York Times Magazine. p 28+. My. 26, '63. New dilemmas for the *pieds noirs.* Peter Braestrup.

*New York Times Magazine. p 26-7+. Je. 6, '65. Bourguiba: portrait of a nonconformist. Jean Lacouture.

*New York Times Magazine. p 76-7+. N. 7, '65. Cruel desert is Algeria's wealth. Peter Braestrup.

*New York Times Magazine. p 36-7+. F. 13, '66. In Algeria it's not 'Yah, yah Boumediene!' but 'wait and see.' Peter Braestrup and David Ottaway.

New Yorker. 41:38-40+. Jl. 17, '65. Letter from Algiers. Robert Shaplen.

*New Yorker. 41:147-8+. O. 30, '65. Letter from Algeria. Robert Shaplen.

Newsweek. 66:32. Jl. 19, '65. Reluctant strong man [Algeria].

Newsweek. 66:39. N. 29, '65. Shaking the throne; French press points to Gen. M. Oufkir as instigator of Ben Barka plot.

Political Science Quarterly. 79:335-59. S. '64. Algeria, the army and the Fifth republic (1959-1961): a scenario of civil-military conflict. G. A. Kelly.

*Reporter. 32:21-5. Je. 17, '65. Morocco's troubled young king. Claire Sterling.

Reporter. 34:22-8. Mr. 10, '66. Ben Barka affair. Claire Sterling.

Senior Scholastic. 86:14-16+. My. 6, '65. Arab world in ferment.

*Sunday Times (London). N. 21, '65. Algeria catches up on Ben Bella. Peter Mansfield.

Time. 85:31B. Je. 18, '65. Royal premier [Morocco].

Time. 86:54. N. 19, '65. J'accuse! chill into Franco-Moroccan relations following Barka kidnaping.

*Times (London). Je. 11, '64. Libya's new wealth and old problems.

*Times (London). Ag. 1, '64. Morocco's struggle towards modernity.

*Times (London). p 13. Mr. 31, '66. New Algeria loses momentum. J. H. Huizinga.

Wall Street Journal. 164:1+. N. 13, '64. Libyan oil production soars as nation gives firms wide latitude. Igor Oganesoff.

Wall Street Journal. 164:8. D. 22, '64. Socialism in Algeria: former French colony gradually ending private enterprise. Igor Oganesoff.

Wall Street Journal. 165:16. My. 6, '65. Arab disunity: enmities in Mideast mock Nasser goal of an empire there. Ray Vicker.